# CHEKHOV'S SAKHALIN JOURNEY

# CHEKHOV'S SAKHALIN JOURNEY

## DOCTOR, HUMANITARIAN, WRITER

*Jonathan Cole*

BLOOMSBURY ACADEMIC
LONDON • NEW YORK • OXFORD • NEW DELHI • SYDNEY

BLOOMSBURY ACADEMIC
Bloomsbury Publishing Plc
50 Bedford Square, London, WC1B 3DP, UK
1385 Broadway, New York, NY 10018, USA
29 Earlsfort Terrace, Dublin 2, Ireland

BLOOMSBURY, BLOOMSBURY ACADEMIC and the Diana logo are trademarks of
Bloomsbury Publishing Plc

First published in Great Britain 2024

Cover design by Rebecca Heselton
Cover image: Anton Chekhov, photographed by Yalta in 1900 © Chronicle / Alamy Stock Photo

A catalogue record for this book is available from the British Library.

Library of Congress Cataloging-in-Publication Data
Names: Cole, Jonathan, 1951- author.
Title: Chekhov's Sakhalin journey : doctor, humanitarian, author / Jonathan Cole.
Description: London ; New York : Bloomsbury Academic, 2023. | Includes
bibliographical references.
Identifiers: LCCN 2023030478 (print) | LCCN 2023030479 (ebook) | ISBN 9781350367500
(hardback) | ISBN 9781350367517 (paperback) | ISBN 9781350367470 (pdf) |
ISBN 9781350367487 (ebook)
Subjects: LCSH: Chekhov, Anton Pavlovich, 1860-1904–Knowledge and learning. | Chekhov,
Anton Pavlovich, 1860-1904–Travel–Russia (Federation)–Sakhalin (Sakhalinskai͡a oblast') |
Chekhov, Anton Pavlovich, 1860-1904. Ostrov Sakhalin. | Authors, Russian–19th century–
Biography. | Physicians–Russia–Biography. | Medicine–Russia–History–19th century. |
Sakhalin (Sakhalinskai͡a oblast', Russia)–History–19th century.
Classification: LCC PG3458.Z9 M4336 2023 (print) | LCC PG3458.Z9 (ebook) |
DDC 891.72/3–dc23/eng/20230718
LC record available at https://lccn.loc.gov/2023030478
LC ebook record available at https://lccn.loc.gov/2023030479

ISBN: HB: 978-1-3503-6750-0
PB: 978-1-3503-6751-7
ePDF: 978-1-3503-6747-0
eBook: 978-1-3503-6748-7

Typeset by Deanta Global Publishing Services, Chennai, India
Printed and bound in Great Britain

To find out more about our authors and books visit www.bloomsbury.com and sign up
for our newsletters.

*First and foremost, I am a doctor, not a writer.*

*Chekhov*

# CONTENTS

# ILLUSTRATIONS

## Maps

## Figures

# ACKNOWLEDGEMENTS

My interest in Chekhov's medical and humanitarian work was triggered by reading *Sakhalin Island*, so my first thanks are to Brian Reeve for his translation. This interest deepened during a collaboration with Andrew Dawson on his theatrical piece *The Russian Doctor/Chasm of Sorrow*. It is a pleasure to thank him for his company during our two trips to Sakhalin for research, as well as for sharing a carriage on the Trans-Siberian Railway, from Siberia to Moscow, during which we dissected the book in detail. Our visits were facilitated by the staff of the two museums to Chekhov's Sakhalin project; thanks to them for their interest, support and generosity of spirit.

These visits were facilitated by two Wellcome Trust Science/Art Awards; this book is, in part, my repayment for the Trust's faith in our project. The award also enabled us to commission Alexander Iosad to translate Chekhov's census cards for what may be the first time.

Thanks to Berry Stone for the maps, done purely out of interest and as a favour. Always prompt and efficient, the library staff at University Hospitals Dorset were also unquestioning of obscure loan requests far removed from their usual clinical fare.

As I researched what was for me a new area and new discipline, I approached Donald Rayfield for occasional advice. He may not have known how important this was. He was also influential in our second Wellcome Award, and would send me nuggets of Chekhov material, including a copy of Chekhov's hand-written pre-nuptial medical report which he had chanced upon.

A number of people have read earlier drafts. Thanks to George Lloyd-Roberts and my wife, Sue, for their encouragement and to several anonymous reviewers for their constructive criticism.

I was fortunate to find Ben Doyle of Bloomsbury, who has supported publication. Thanks to him, and to his colleagues Laura Cope, Ellie Jardine, and Mohammed Raffi for such seamless support.

Last, as ever, thanks to Sue for putting up with me, and Chekhov, uncomplainingly, for years.

# PROLOGUE

Thirty years ago, I read Brian Reeve's new translation of *Sakhalin Island* and never forgot it. I enjoyed Chekhov's work, especially his short stories, and became interested in the man himself and so turned to his biographies. They mentioned his extraordinary trip to Sakhalin Island, the penal colony off the far East coast of Siberia, in 1890. Here was Chekhov, the clinical – even detached – observer, plunging himself into risk to report on the barbaric conditions in the penal colony there. It seemed so out of character to someone acquainted with him through his other writings.

Years passed and I was approached by Andrew Dawson, a choreographer, playwright, performer and hand double.[1] He had seen a BBC *Horizon* programme I had helped make about Ian Waterman, who lives without any sense of touch or movement/position sense below the neck.[2] Like others interested in movement for performance, Andy was fascinated to see Ian's ability to move by substituting mental effort for peripheral feedback. Andy and I found that we were both interested in taking neuroscience and the experience of impairment to wider audiences and so decided to collaborate. Our first effort, *The Process of Portrayal*,[3] was a series of narratives of those with chronic neurological conditions, and the second, *The Articulate Hand*,[4] about the hand and the effects of impairment in its use, whether from fracture or paralysis after stroke. The latter played to the Wellcome Trust in London and in India, as well as taking Andy to a TEDMED lecture. We even performed it at the World Science Festival in New York.[5]

Andy asked what we could do next and I suggested Chekhov and Sakhalin. I explained to Andy that Chekhov, in 1890, aged thirty, had travelled five or six thousand miles across Russia and Siberia to the penal island of Sakhalin to expose its conditions. Though long and at times dense, through it Chekhov assembled narratives and, where possible, harder data on the impossibility of making Sakhalin, barren and frozen for much of the year, into a sustainable colony, like Australia or French Guyana. It also showed the near complete breakdown in humanity there, particularly in its treatment of the most vulnerable – women and children.

Andy looked into it, liked the topic and so we began work. We sought the advice of Chekhov's biographer, Donald Rayfield, who invited us to lunch at his home, deep in the Weald of Kent. Slowly a plan formed, which Wellcome Trust liked enough to support with two grants, for research and then for a full theatrical piece. These allowed us to visit Sakhalin, twice, to research and to visit the museums[6] on the island where the staff were amazingly generous towards two Englishmen wandering round looking for Chekhov's ghost. Wellcome also guided us towards another academic, Marius Turda, who in turn arranged for the first translation, by Alexander Iosad, into English of Chekhov's near 8,000 census cards from Sakhalin. Andy and I had loved their look when we saw them at the Sakhalin museums, and we were excited to have them in English, over a century after Chekhov had written them, largely in his own hand.

Despite working closely for a year or so, we had not really agreed on what form the piece might take. My Sakhalin play would have a big cast, or at least lots of parts, and be full of action and noise, with Chekhov the innocent through whose eyes the hell on Sakhalin unfolded. During our visit to Sakhalin we had toured one museum, located in a house Chekhov had visited for lunch, which retained the furniture and feel of his time. Like Stoppard's *Arcadia*, or at the end of Philip Pullman's *Dark Materials*, I imagined a single theatrical set used for two different times; for Chekhov eating borsch while fed lies about the prison from the governor, and our being shown round now by our Russian guide, in a twin set, shawl and tortoiseshell glasses, who told of how his visit had been preserved through artefacts and photographs. In contrast, Andy's preferred method was far more muted and, since he was the performer, I withdrew. *The Russian Doctor/Chams of Sorrow*,[7] a mosaic of mime, music and pre-recorded recited passages from the book, had a refined arthouse beauty (see 'Sakhalin Now' for more detail), and was previewed at Winchester New Theatre, and then premiered at Birmingham Rep, where there were three performances in all.

My interest in Chekhov's obsession with Sakhalin was reawakened by Andy. Our original purpose had been to dramatize the book to make people aware of Chekhov's journey, and I felt guilty that the play had not done this to my satisfaction. As I went into the subject more, however, other themes emerged. In addition to exploring the book and journey, I saw how his approach originated from his teaching at medical school, and how his visit, like his other humanitarian projects, revealed another side to Chekhov's life and work.

# Prologue

## Notes

1. His work includes choreography at the New York Met and English National Opera, writing and starring in the stage plays, *Thunderbirds FAB* and *Wallace and Gromit the Panto*, as well as a one man show, *Absence and Presence*, on his estrangement from his father.

2. *The Man Who Lost His Body*. Director Chris Rawlence, a Rosetta Production for BBC2 *Horizon*, 1997. It is available on YouTube.

3. We asked Chris Rawlence, who had directed the *Horizon* documentary, and Lucia Walker, a mutual friend who was a modern dancer, and Alexander Teacher to join us. Perhaps the most fascinating study was with Michael, whose motor neuron disease had left him, for a year or so, paralysed in the body and limbs, though still able to swallow, talk and breathe unaided. Michael had been a cello teacher and was unable to listen to music when he became paralysed, so painful was it to listen to without also making it. Then, later,

   > Towards the end of his life, he began to listen to music again . . . at first it had been unbearable, but now he had reached a peace and could joke about the pleasures of no longer having practice. [Extraordinarily] when he heard music he saw the musical notation, as though hovering in front of him. Listening to the cello he also felt his hands and fingers were moving. The sounds awakened his brain to fill the perceptual and motor losses imposed by his disease.

4. http://thearticulatehand.com/

5. In New York it was put on in a night club in Queens with the audience sat at tables set on islands in an indoor pond.

   > Andy acted as MC, explaining the several pre-recorded scientific pieces and interviews, as well as performing and finding humour where appropriate; his enthusiasm and presence making it sparkle and live. The most moving piece was from an afternoon we had spent at a tea club for those with chronic stroke. I had noticed before that patients paralysed down one side. often caressed their still hands with their other, as though trying to reconnect and awaken them. As these men sat, having tea and being social, we filmed this close-up and then reduced the frame rate. Something in this slow intimacy, as one hand explored its inert other revealed the sense of loss in a way no clever words could.

6. One to his book and the other to his visit.

7. Chekhov's name for a deep valley, between the sea and the hills, in which the worst prison on Sakhalin was built.

# MAPS

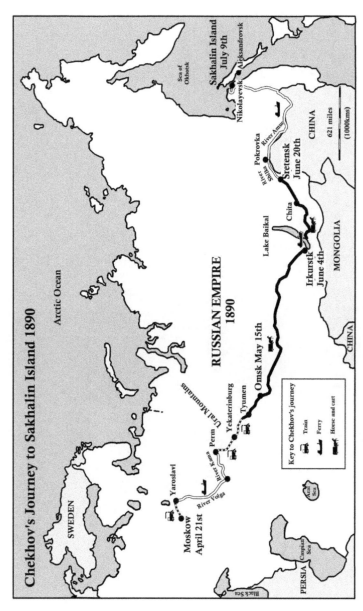

**Map 1** Journey from Moscow to Sakhalin. (By Berry Stone, with thanks for the use of NASA images in the preparation of the maps. Courtesy NASA/JPL-Caltech.)

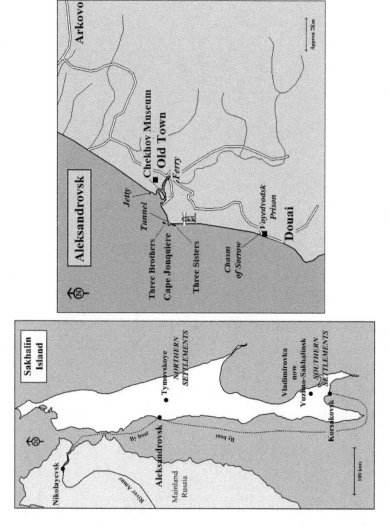

**Map 2** Travels around Sakhalin. (By Berry Stone, with thanks for the use of NASA images in the preparation of the maps. Courtesy NASA/JPL-Caltech.)

# PART I
## BEGINNINGS

# INTRODUCTION

In 1900, towards the end of winter, the whole ensemble of the Moscow Arts Theatre, actors, wives and children, tutors, nannies and nurses, set and costume designers and hairdressers, boarded a train for the warm spring in the Crimea. As they went they changed winter clothes for summer dresses and light suits. All were excited.

They went to visit Chekhov. He was marooned on doctors' orders in Yalta by the TB which was to kill him four years later.[1] The Theatre's boss, Stanislavsky had said, 'Anton Pavlovich cannot visit us because he is sick, we shall go and see him'. They arrived in Sevastopol on 7 April, but Chekhov was too ill to visit for some days. When the weather warmed up he arrived, just as one of the actors was sick. Chekhov insisted on treating him. 'Listen, I am the doctor of this theatre company'. Stanislavsky was used to this; Chekhov would often tell them, 'I am a doctor by trade and sometimes I do literary work in my free time'. 'He was sincerely proud of being a doctor, and considered his medical work more important that his literary work'. Later during their visit, praising another's play, Chekhov repeated, 'I am not a playwright. Listen, I am doctor by trade' (Stanislavsky, quoted in Sekirin, 2011: 135ff).

We see Chekhov now as a pre-eminent figure in literature, but his own perspective may well have been more modest. His plays had not always been well received but he had found a company, and an audience, with the Arts Theatre. He had also written over seven hundred short stories, one collection of which had been awarded a Pushkin Prize. How could he have placed medicine above all this?

He practised medicine most of his life, and also engaged in educational and humanitarian work which took him away from writing for months. But there was one such episode which he placed above all others. Donald Rayfield, Chekhov's biographer, told me that,

> Chekhov's most important achievement in his own eyes was not a body of plays or stories: it was his self-sacrificing journey across Siberia to the penal island of Sakhalin, the painstaking enquiry he

undertook into conditions there, and the extensive exposé he wrote on his return. (Rayfield, D. personal communication)

Further, the critic and academic Juras Ryfa suggests that Chekhov's written account, *Sakhalin Island*, was the 'apotheosis of his entire social and writing career and reflected his basic moral principles' (Ryfa, 1990).

What was this medicine he so revered? How could his visit to Sakhalin be so elevated? As I began working on the present volume, I wanted people to see what an astonishing feat by Chekhov this was, an early attempt at social change in the most unlikely and difficult of places by a writer often thought detached and cool. As I spent longer with the book, and with Chekhov's other work, I also began to see how Sakhalin influenced his approach to his literary work during his remaining fourteen years of life. It became apparent, too, that far from being a singular, idiosyncratic act – a footnote to his literary career – it was an important episode in his life and work. His approach to Sakhalin could also be traced back to his own medical training. Placing this experience within his medical life seemed to make sense in a manner not always apparent from the predominant literary biographies.

Another thought began to emerge. Chekhov qualified as a doctor and never stopped working in clinical and other areas. Medicine then, before antibiotics and modern medication, could do very little in the way of effective treatment and so was as much about what is now public health and preventative medicine as about diagnosis and drugs. During Chekhov's lifetime, medicine became a movement for social change. As we will see he was part of that – for him medicine and humanitarian work were inseparable. He would almost certainly have practised medicine more, to the detriment of his writing, had his health allowed. Medicine was no sideshow for Chekhov and, as will be seen, for him, medicine and literature did not stand apart, isolated and separate, but were strands of the same idea – how might mankind be improved.

To understand his trip to Sakhalin, one needs to consider not just the visit but also his view of his work and three frictions within it. The first is that between the writing upon which his reputation depends, and the medicine which he never fully gave up, and which for long periods took him entirely away from literature. The second concerns his conviction that writing was not proper 'doing', and that he felt compelled to do practical and lasting projects as well, thinking that his writing would outlive him by a few years at most. The last concerns his aversion to telling people what to think; rather he tried to show people their lives in his literature, and allow them to reach their own conclusions. This led to difficulties with critics during his lifetime and to misunderstandings beyond it. These three facets of Chekhov's thinking were not independent, rather they entwined around each other, nourishing and sustaining Chekhov throughout his life. He *will* write, and practise medicine; he *will* think and do. And though he would not tell people how to live, behind the scenes his own work outside literature showed something of how he thought a good life might be lived. This is why his trip to Sakhalin is as relevant now as it was to him then.

One place to start to understand these, perhaps surprisingly, is in his relations with Tolstoy. He was over thirty years older than Chekhov, a nobleman, the Great Man of Russian literature. and a philosopher and seer. Chekhov, more modest and from lowlier stock, was intimidated in his presence and said that he could 'not put two words together in a sentence when first around Tolstoy' (Maklakov, in Sekirin, 2001: 85). He even worried which trousers to wear in the great man's presence. Nevertheless, Tolstoy recognized Chekhov's ability and would read his prose out aloud to visitors, for Chekhov – alone among his peers – could 'create music with words' (Semenov, S. in Sekirin, 2011: 82–3). Tolstoy admired Chekhov, though he could never completely understand how he wrote. 'He is a strange writer; he throws words about as if at random, and yet everything is alive. And what understanding! He never has any superfluous details; every one of them is either necessary or beautiful' (Tolstoy on Chekhov, from Goldenveizer, A.R. *Talks with Tolstoi*. Taken from Frontispiece, Narayan, K. 2012).

Gorky wrote that Tolstoy loved Chekhov as a father loves his son, and thought that future literary historians would say that the Russian language was created by Pushkin, Turgenev and Chekhov (Gorky, quoted in Sekirin, 2001: 78). Tolstoy was particularly fond of Chekhov's prose poetry and descriptive powers, 'like fine lace, the embroidery of words' (Tolstoy, quoted by Gorky, in Sekirin, 2001: 79).

Their respect and affection, however, though mutual, were not uncritical. Tolstoy had two problems with Chekhov and his work. The first was Chekhov's insistence on continuing to practise medicine – Tolstoy thought that medicine stood in his way and that he would have been a much finer writer if he hadn't been a doctor. Chekhov would have none of it; one of his most famous lines is 'Medicine is my lawful wife and literature my mistress; when I get tired of one, I spend the night with the other' (Chekhov, in Garnett, C., 1920: 99). This is usually treated as a joke, as though he knew his worth was in writing and that medicine was therefore a sideshow, abandoned or at least neglected as his literary output increased and the money came in. But for Chekhov jokes and the serious often coexisted. The full quote begins 'I feel more alert and more satisfied with myself when I think of myself as having two occupations instead of one . . .' and then continues, 'This may be somewhat disorganised, but then again it's not as boring, and anyway, neither one loses anything by my duplicity. If I didn't have medicine, I'd never devote my spare time and thoughts to literature. I lack discipline' (Chekhov, in Garnett, C., 1920: 99). Medicine was never abandoned and actually often preferred to his literary mistress. Moreover, through his public mistress he tried to show us our lives as he saw them, while through his far more private medical wife, he came as close as he ever did to showing us how he thought we might live.

Five years in medical school could not be airbrushed away. He also needed medicine and patients to balance his life. A friend, Ivan Bunin, who later went on to win the Novel Prize for Literature, wrote that Chekhov would never have reduced the amount of medicine he practiced had his health allowed (Bunin, 2007: 5). As will be seen, throughout his life, Chekhov ranked his medicine above his writing in importance. It was his first and his enduring love.

Tolstoy's other concern reflected Chekhov's morality, or rather the apparent lack of it, in his writing. Once, when Chekhov was exiled to southern Crimea by tuberculosis he made the pilgrimage to Tolstoy's bedside. In one of his most celebrated and reproduced anecdotes, he related how, as he was about to leave, Tolstoy said,

'Kiss me goodbye.'

While I bent over him and he was kissing me, he whispered in my ear in a still energetic, old man's voice,

'You know, I hate your plays. Shakespeare was a bad writer, and I consider your plays even worse than his.' (Chekhov, A. Recollection by Ivan Bunin, in Sekirin, 2011: 81–2)[2]

In common with most critics of the time, Tolstoy thought that a playwright, like any writer, should lead the audience with clear moral purpose. Chekhov's plays like his stories, he thought, did not even try. This mystified Tolstoy – where was morality and guidance in Chekhov's work? Chekhov, at times with some courage, refused to instruct and just wanted, as best he could to his readers and audience, to reflect life as he saw it. This has led to much misunderstanding of his work. He wrote, with a hint of exasperation, that,

> it is not the writer's job to solve such problems as God, pessimism etc.; his job is merely record who, under what conditions, said or thought what . . . . The artist is not meant to be a judge of his characters and what they say; his only job is to be an impartial witness . . . . Drawing conclusions is up to the jury, that is the readers. My only job is to be talented, that is to know how to distinguish important testimony from unimportant. (Chekhov, in Heim and Karlinsky, 1973: 104)

Just as a doctor treats without judgement, so he wrote, observing and leaving others to moralize. In contrast Tolstoy had no such problems moralizing. Coope devotes a chapter to this, and their differing views of science and progress, mentioning particularly Tolstoy's *Kreutzer Sonata* (Coope, 1997).[3] What Tolstoy did not realize was that for Chekhov progress through an increasingly scientific form of medicine was moral. In his recent 'literary masterclass' on stories and how to write them, derived from his own teaching courses, the author George Saunders reviews and celebrates several Russian short stories from the nineteenth century, perhaps elevating Chekhov above others. He, too, focuses on how Chekhov's lack of moralising, did not mean a lack of morals:

> What I admire most about Chekhov is how free of agenda he seems on the page – interested in everything but not wedded to any fixed system of belief . . . . He was a doctor and his approach to fiction feels lovingly diagnostic. Walking into the examination room, finding Life sitting there, he seems to say, 'Wonderful, let's see what's going on.'
>
> As we watch Chekhov continually, ritually, doubt all conclusions, we're comforted. It's all right to reconsider. It's noble – holy even. (Saunders, 2021: 335)

His refusal to impose his views on others, directly or crudely in his writing, led others as well as Tolstoy to think Chekhov amoral. Rather than in his writing, it was in his other life, as a doctor, an educationalist and an environmentalist, in his practical and unfashionable work championing science and medical progress, that one can see his ideas and morality in deed and action. Thus, do the three strands above come together, in medicine and literature, by acting in the world practically and by recognizing that one's morality is revealed by what you do rather than what you say. I contend that to a neglected extent, his whole, vast, extraordinary Sakhalin project shows in action what he would not write in words.

This book focuses on Chekhov's medical and other humanitarian work, showing how important it remained for him throughout his life. If we are to look for morality in Chekhov's work, how he thought one should live, then a good place to start is in his non-literary work. Moreover, looking at his life and work allows us to interpret his literary approach as he himself did, and to see how original it was.

One might argue that an artist's work stands alone and does not need any biographical background – interesting and often juicy though these may be. In Chekhov's case, however, his literary and other work only complemented each other in his eyes. He was self-effacing and private about this, and chose to work in areas deliberately unfashionable and un-newsworthy. Few people knew that Tzar Nicholas II granted him, the grandson of a serf, 'hereditary nobility' for 'exemplary zeal and exertions directed towards the education of the people'. He never spoke or wrote of it (Laffitte, 1974: 175). Only in one work, *Sakhalin Island*, his only biographical writing and by far his largest and longest gestating piece – does he speak to us directly of his other work, and his other life.

He was born in a small, declining town on the Black Sea, Taganrog, in 1860, one of five brothers and two sisters. His father, a storekeeper, beat them regularly – his grandfather had bought his freedom from serfdom. When the store failed his father fled with his family to Moscow and further squalor. Chekhov, by then in his teens, stayed behind for three years to finish his studies at the local grammar school before rejoining his family in Moscow, to study medicine. 'In 1879, I enrolled in the medical school of Moscow University. I had a very dim idea of the university at the time, and I do not remember exactly what prompted me to choose medical school, but I have had no reason to regret the choice' (Chekhov, from Heim and Karlinsky, 1973: 365–6). Finke suggests it was his parents who may first have pointed him towards medicine (Finke, 2021: 25). While at medical school, like one of his brothers, he began writing short stories for popular magazines, initially for money, it is said, to buy his mother a birthday cake (Suvorin, quoted from Laffitte, 1974: 78).[4] He spent five years studying, living in rented accommodation with his family and with two students as paying guests. It was during this period that Chekhov started to write, to support his family. 'During my first year, [as a medical student] I began publishing sketches in weekly magazines and newspapers, and by the early '80s, these literary activities had taken on a permanent, professional character' (Chekhov, in Heim and Karlinsky, 1973: 365–6). Once qualified, his first medical fees were for treatment of toothache in a young woman, a monk with dysentery and for settling the stomach of a Moscow actress – his first minor surgery was to relieve a tight foreskin (Coope, 1997: 27). He spent the money wisely, on vodka and beer.

His literary career was from 1880, aged twenty, to his death in 1904. He published over seven hundred works before 1888, highly readable short stories and melodramas for popular magazines,[5] and boasted he never spent more than a day on a story. Then, in 1886, he received a letter praising his work and noting his talent from the eminent author Grigorovich. Surprised and delighted, Chekhov began to take more care of his writing and after that his output fell, from sixty stories in 1886 and forty-nine the year after, to eight in 1888 and six the next. Thereafter, he published half a dozen or less per year, as he concentrated on the plays and on editing his previous, hastily written, stories. His mature period of genius lasted sixteen years or so, from 1888 onwards, and towards its end he was slowed by the TB which killed him, and by the demands of an ill-advised publisher's contract to revise his collected works. Yet for five of those precious years his focus was on the single most extraordinary episode in his life – Sakhalin. There were other shorter periods when his medical wife banished his literary mistress, but none for quite as long.

Chekhov's medical skills were in diagnosis and prognosis, in telling people how long they had left – essential skills before antibiotics neutered most infectious diseases (for the time being at least). Despite this, he denied he had TB to most people until quite late, after he had first coughed blood in his mid-twenties.

'I had my first haemorrhage three years ago. It last three or four days and put my mind in a whirl . . . since then I have had at least two every year . . . . It alarms me when I see blood; there is something menacing in blood pouring from my mouth, as there is in flames from a fire' (to Suvorin, from Laffitte, *Chekhov*: p. 116). In his beautiful literary account of Chekhov, Michael Finke cites instances of Chekhov denying or avoiding talking about these episodes. When a brother saw him coughing up blood, Chekhov ordered him not to talk about it to his sister or mother. Chekhov knew the impotence of medicine and how, instead, it often simply lied to patients 'standard protocol in cancer and TB'. But he knew – as a doctor he must have known. Finke discussed with a physician friend, Dr Robert Coles,

Look, he was a doctor and had an illness that is not silent and secret
. . . . You know when you have tuberculosis. You cough up blood. You
feel chest pain . . . a tangible, physical, concrete, palpable phenomenon
of the body. Chekhov knew, as a physician. Of course he knew. He
knew he was dying . . . . (Coles and Finke, in Finke and De Sherbini,
2021: 133)

In 1897, he nearly died from a haemorrhage while dining with his friend
Suvorin. Recovering in Suvorin's suite, he said that 'to calm patients
we tell them when they're coughing that its gastric and when they're
haemorrhaging that its haemorrhoidal. But there's no such thing as a
gastric cough, and the haemorrhage is always from the lungs' (Finke, 2005:
197–8). He must have known then that going to Sakhalin would worsen
his illness. The atrocious journey – and to a lesser extent his other medical
and humanitarian work – undoubtedly shortened his life. None, therefore,
were trivial.

He spent around a year researching the trip, and nearly three months
travelling the 5,000 miles or so over land, bog and river, across Siberia, and
nearly starving and coughing blood along the way, to the penal island, across
the Tatar Straights above Japan. The only person to go there voluntarily, he
was on the island for three months and three days, working up to seventeen
hours per day, before sailing back via Hong Kong and Sri Lanka. On his
return, he was too ill to leave the house for weeks and his TB worsened
permanently. He returned, with a trunk full of notes, a mongoose and a
civet cat from Sri Lanka, and spent three years or so writing up his account.

Though his visit is detailed in his many biographies, the book itself has
been somewhat side-lined, considered long, 'dense' or just plain boring.
Biographers have cited his letters on the way to Sakhalin and then during
his return, with less analysis of what happened on the island itself or
mention of the book itself, as though put off by its 500-plus pages, and with
the implication that this was something he had to get out of his system,
before he went back to being 'our' proper Chekhov. He wrote no letters
home from Sakhalin either, further limiting a biographer's heft. Some add,
rather disappointedly, that he did not write *Sakhalin Island* like Chekhov at
all, and that, if social commentary was his aim, then his stories are far more
effective, eloquent and, above all, brief. One suggested that the work is 'as
exhaustive as it is exhausting' (Popkin, 1992).

The book, therefore, remains daunting and difficult to approach, a
visit to one of the most poorly understood parts of his life, and both can

sometimes be considered outside the trajectory of the rest of his work. Part of the present purpose is to question such views.

One reason people are surprised by Chekhov's going to Sakhalin, and by the book, is that he is seen today, almost exclusively, as a literary figure, so his approach in *Sakhalin Island* stands apart. Yet this can be traced in large part to his time at Moscow University as a medical student, where his teachers inspired him, and his generation of fellow students, with the possibilities of environmental and social medicine. So, in Chapter 1, 'Medical School', we follow him through his medical student days, showing how the approaches he learned there informed his humanitarian work on Sakhalin and indeed throughout his life.

Chapter 2, 'Why', considers his reasons for going to Sakhalin. Over his Sakhalin period his short story output fell further to two per year. The perverse island project slashed his income and that of his family (and his appalled publisher). His career had taken off – he had won a prestigious Pushkin Prize for a collection of stories and published several masterpieces, including *The Steppe*. What mystified his friends has continued to puzzle since – why did he go, and then devote a large part of the next few years writing it up, to the detriment of his more lucrative 'creative' writing? People thought him mad.

One of the few ways he could earn money from the trip was to promise his publisher and friend Suvorin a travel commentary. Aleksey Suvorin had been born in 1834, the son of a peasant, and risen to become editor of the right-wing *New Times* newspaper. Wealthy and influential, his friendship with Chekhov was unlikely, but Suvorin had written short stories and plays for liberal journals in his younger days, so he may have been more sympathetic to Chekhov. He also recognized his genius. Chekhov's letters to him are among his most revealing and they went on European and other holidays together. Later, though, Chekhov distanced himself from Suvorin in the 1890s, unable to tolerate Suvorin's increasing anti-Semitic and other pronouncements any longer. The commentary, *From Siberia*, was of his impressions while travelling across Russia and Siberia. This forms the basis of the third chapter, 'Going to war', detailing his journey, over 5,000 miles or more and taking eleven weeks, by train, ferry, open cart and steamer. He nearly starved and could have drowned, and died in a road traffic accident with a postal wagon. The account shows how Siberian people lived, with his detailing hardship aplenty, but tenderness too.

He landed in Aleksandrovsk, the main post on Sakhalin Island, and settled in for a few weeks, meeting officials, convicts and settlers. Chapter 4,

'Everything Is Chained' draws on *Sakhalin Island* to reveal the differences between what he sees and what he is told by the governors. To meet people, he also started a census, the record cards from which still exist today. The population of convicts and settlers was around 10,000 at the time and he filled in around 8,000 cards, most in his own hand, as he met people. He also described the prison and its conditions in detail, since a major aim was to show the conditions under which the convict exiles lived.

A few weeks later, once he had the relevant papers, he travelled through the rest of the island. Chapter 5, 'The Chasm of Sorrow', details his visits to settlements around Aleksandrovsk, to the original settlement at Douai and to the worst prison on the island at Voyevodsk. He describes the desolation and despair, together with corruption in a mining company. In other villages where conditions were officially described as good he discovers degradation beyond his imagination. 'South', Chapter 6, follows Chekhov to the southern tip of the island and the last part of his survey. This was probably the low point of his journey, and of his book, as he is exhausted and dulled by the long days and unrelieved horror.

The remaining parts of his book leave behind a narrative and travelogue to give his more considered views on the position of women and children, on crop yields and the island's fishing potential, on guards and priests, on morality, medical facilities and on escapes. These are given in Chapter 7, 'Thesis Assembled', since this is the beginning of his critique of the official version of the colony and of the system which produced and maintained it. His words, as ever, are measured but their meaning clear. Clinically, and at times drily, he dissects the colony's inadequacies.

In Chapter 8, 'Numbers', we consider how much hard data Chekhov could find on the island and what use he made of his census. We also give an analysis of the remaining census cards using, for the first time, an English translation and contemporary statistical methods. He was apologetic about the census, but it was one of the first large-scale ones in Russia and was not substantially overturned by subsequent analyses.

Chapter 9, 'Monday to Wednesday', details the somewhat tortuous and intermittent way he wrote *Sakhalin Island*, weaving notes, impressions and census into some sort of order. On his return, he was so ill he could not leave his house for weeks. Once well enough there were parties to attend, and then a trip around Europe, followed by a major move by the family to their first country estate. After these upheavals, Chekhov signed on as a physician as typhoid threatened. All delayed the project. But perhaps his main concern was to present at least some of Sakhalin's horror dispassionately and allow the reader to make up his or her own mind. During this period he parcelled his working week between Sakhalin, on Monday to Wednesday and his short stories during the rest of the week making this a unique outburst of creativity

Chapters 7 to 9 are grouped under a broader heading, 'Writing Up'. Though friends presumed his obsession with Sakhalin would be short lived, he took several years to assimilate and encompass what he had seen in a way that he could present to others. Finding a way to write about such unimagined depravity without his own perspective, as he itemized the colonies failings and loss of humanity, preoccupied him.

The last three chapters differ in approach. Having given an account of his motivations, journey and findings, in the part 'Interpretations', a more personal approach is taken. In Chapter 10, 'Busy Years', the short stories he wrote as he was writing up *Sakhalin Island* are analysed, to see if they cast light on his thinking and state of mind at the time. After so long away, he and his family were desperate for money, so he needed to write new short stories. Some were trivial and fun, welcome diversions from Sakhalin one imagines, though two were related to his journey. Other more substantial stories may reveal his thinking during the writing-up period. One shows his concerns over the two cultures, art and science, and the difficulties the latter has in reaching a general audience. The second part reveals how Sakhalin altered his perspective on respected figures while the last story, the descent of a doctor to incarceration and madness, may reflect his fears for the way his 'Mania Sachalinosa' might be seen by others.

The reception of the chapters serialized in the periodical *Russian Thought*, and then of the book itself, is considered in Chapter 11, 'Conscience, Irony and Understatement'. In the last chapter, 'Holy of Holies', the ways in which Sakhalin influenced his subsequent literary development are considered both directly together with an assessment of his deeper view of the world. After Sakhalin, he continued to perform medical work and engaged in many humanitarian projects, in famine relief and in education, as well as writing, despite, and to the limits of, his declining health. His journey and the book, and his continuing humanitarian work, it is suggested, reveal aspects of Chekhov's character and motivations in a manner not always apparent from his other work. The postscript *Sakhalin Now* gives a short account of two visits to Sakhalin to show how his flame is being kept alive to this day – of the eight museums to Chekhov in Russia, two are on the island.

Donald Rayfield continued his quote at the top of this introduction thus:

It is time that admirers of the writer saw how important and original were the achievements of Chekhov the doctor. Exploring this journey to a modern hell will lead to a revolution in the way we regard Chekhov the writer and the man.

The project led many at the time to question his sanity, something people have continued to do, even in the late twentieth century. The aim of this book is to demystify and explain Sakhalin and to focus on Chekhov's medical, educational and humanitarian work. It was for him not peripheral, but of great importance to his life and a necessary balance to his literary work. He returned from Sakhalin in late 1890 and yet did not publish his book, or its serialized chapters, until several years later. This was in part because of the sheer amount of data and how difficult it was to assemble into a coherent, though ill received, thesis. But perhaps the main problem was that the project threatened Chekhov's approach in general – how could he observe such inhumanity, cruelty and degradation, impassively and without judgement? If he did not condemn would that not be heartless? If he did condemn, had he not taken sides and compromised the neutrality of his gaze? He also had to gauge how much his readership might stomach, for what he saw was so much worse than he expected that he left out the most extreme details. As will be seen, he did judge, but rather than blaming individuals caught up in the madness, he questioned the viability of the whole project and the methods of punishment and exile. If there was blame then it was the system's and the authority's rather than those caught up in it, whether guards or governors, convicts or settlers, since all were exposed to and degraded by such harsh a physical and social environment. As a result, it affected his view of the world.

As a medical doctor by training and not a literary scholar, I am aware that I might be ill-equipped for such a project. Apart from not being trained in literary criticism, I cannot read Russian.[6] This has prevented my reading some key Russian texts, especially that by Mikhail S. Vysokov (2010). In my defence, many people have written on Chekhov without Russian, and indeed, many famous recent playwrights have worked on his plays from the literal translations of others. My other defence is that my focus has been on his medical and other non-literary work, trying to drag this more centre stage, something also at the heart of Jack Coulehan's introduction to his collection of Chekhov's stories about doctors (Coulehan, 2003), and in John

Coope's classic account of his medical life, *Doctor Chekhov* (Coope, 1997). Both are physicians, like Mukherjee who is also an enthusiastic about *Sakhalin Island* as we will see (in Chapter 11), so perhaps there is something about medical practitioners wanting to reclaim Chekhov as their own. Where I do discuss his writing, mainly a small number of his short stories, I have conflated and cited the interpretations of Chekhov scholars, and only then added some of my own tentative suggestions. Where I can, I also have used his own letters to build up the account.

While acknowledging the wonderful literary analysis of Chekhov's work that has and is taking place, my presumption in daring to focus on his medical and humanitarian work comes from some, perhaps tenuous, resonance. In addition to neurological work, I have written a number of works on the subjective experiences of living with neurological conditions, whether proprioceptive loss, facial disfigurement or spinal cord injury (Cole, 1998, 2004, 2016; Cole and Spalding, 2012). Chekhov was drawn to the first-person experience too and towards what now might be called psychology and neuroscience (see Chapter 1). This was encouraged by his teachers at medical school, but arguably was always implicit in his writings and observation, where the larger truths are often revealed by focus on the elements and minutiae of experience. He also developed, in his later life, an interest in the newly emerged discipline of psychiatry.

I have also been torn as to a title. I was first drawn to 'Chekhov's Gap Year', since his Sakhalin project contained both elements of adventure and a chance to withdraw from the treadmill he had been on for ten years or so, combining medicine and writing to support his family. But his humanitarian work extended throughout his life, so 'Gap Year' as the overall title felt too restricting. Next came 'Chekhov's First Love', referring to his famous saying about medicine being his wife and literature his mistress. I was trying to suggest that medicine was his first and principal love. Though I think this is correct, as a title it may be too obscure and might have needed too much emphasis through the text. So, the present title is less literary but more explanatory.

## Notes

1. The warm climate was thought to slow down consumption. In Middle Europe similar patients were sent up to Alpine sanatoria since the clear cold air was thought similarly therapeutic.

2. This probably took place around 1900 after Tolstoy had seen *Uncle Vanya* in Moscow. Finke suggests it is Chekhov's most anthologized anecdote. Finke, M.C. (2021) *Freedom from Violence and Lies. Anton Chekhov's Life and Writings.* London: Reaktion, 170.

3. John Coope was born in the north of England, one of seven children. His parents were primary care physicians and he took over their practice with his wife and brother, and then lived his whole life in their town. Active in medicine, in the arts and in community activities, he died aged seventy-seven on Christmas Day, 1997. It is clear that his labour of love, writing about Chekhov, was a retirement project.

4. Rayfield also mentions this but adds that the story, *Bored Philanthropists*, was rejected and his mother received no cake. Rayfield, D. (1997, 2010), *Anton Chekhov – A Life.* London: HarperCollins, 75, but see also second edition (2021), *Anton Chekhov – A Life.* London: Garnett Press, 75.

5. This is a very conservative estimate, based on the number found in his final published work. He edited and omitted those he did not think worthy late in his life. Thomas Garullo, editor and translator of Chekhov's friend Bunin's memoir, mentions 600 stories before he was twenty-eight. Bunin, I. (2007). *About Chekhov.* Evanston, IL: Northwestern University Press, xxix.

6. See http://chehov-lit.ru/chehov/text/rasskazy.htm for a tantalizing glimpse of resources available online in Russian. In the UK, the Anton Chekhov Foundation coordinates activity about his work and preservation of his museums. It has also initiated an Early Chekhov Translation Project, see www.antonchekhovfoundation.org/index.html.

## References

Bunin, I. (2007). *About Chekhov.* Evanston, IL: Northwestern Press, 5.

Chekhov, A. 'Letter to Suvorin, A. 30 May 1888', in Heim, M.H. and Karlinsky, S. (Eds), *Letters of Anton Chekhov*, 104.

Chekhov, A. To Suvorin, 14 October 1888, quoted from Laffitte, S. Chekhov, 116.

Chekhov, A. 'Recollection by Ivan Bunin'. Bunin, I. (1904). *From the Notebook. Chekhov.* Russkoe slovo, 297. Originally published in *Sbornik Zuanie*, 1905, St. Petersburg: Znaine.

Cole, J. (1998). *About Face.* Boston, MA: MIT Press.

Cole, J. (2004). *Still Lives.* Boston, MA: MIT Press.

Cole, J. (2016). *Losing Touch.* Oxford: Oxford University Press.

Cole, J. with Spalding, H. (2012). *The Invisible Smile.* Oxford: Oxford University Press.

Coles, R. and Finke, M. (2021). 'A Conversation with Dr Robert Coles: Anton Chekhov and William Carlos Williams', in Finke, M. and De Sherbinin (Eds), *Chekhov the Immigrant*: 177–8, but quoted from Finke, *Freedom from Violence and Lies: Anton Chekhov's Life and Writings.* London: Reaktion Books, 133.

Coope, J. (1997). *Doctor Chekhov; A Study in Literature and Medicine*. Chalk: Cross Publishing.

Coulehan, J. (2003). *Chekhov's Doctors*. Kent: Kent State University Press.

Finke, M.C. (2005). *Seeing Chekhov*. Ithaca, IL: Cornell, 197–8.

Finke, M.C. (2021). *Freedom from Violence and Lies: Anton Chekhov's Life and Writings*. London: Reaktion Books, 25.

Garnett, C., trans. (1920). *Letters of Anton Chekhov to his Family and Friends, with a Biographical Sketch*. New York: The Macmillan Company, 99.

Gorky, M. (1923). *AP Chekhov*, Besesda (Conversation), Berlin, 2.

Heim, M.H. and Karlinsky, S. (1973). *Letters of Anton Chekhov*. New York, Evanston, San Francisco and London: Harper Row.

Laffitte, S. (1974). *Chekhov*. London: Readers Union/Angus Robertson, 175.

Maklakov, V.A. (1909). 'Memoires about Chekhov'. *Rannee Utro*, 201.

Popkin, C. (1992). 'Chekhov as Ethnographer; Epistemological Crisis on Sakhalin Island', *Slavic Review*, 51(1), 36–51.

Ryfa, J. (1990). *The problem of genre and the quest for justice in Chekhov's The Island of Sakhalin*. Studies in Slavic Languages, Volume 13. Lewiston, Queenstown and Lampeter: The Edwin Mellon Press.

Saunders, G. (2021). *A Swim in a Pond in the Rain (in Which Four Russians Give a Masterclass on Writing, Reading and Life)*. London: Bloomsbury, 335ff.

Sekirin, P., Ed. and trans. (2011). *Memories of Chekhov*. Jefferson and London: McFarland.

Semenov, S. (1914). 'Chekhov Meets Leo Tolstoy', *Peterburgski kurier*, 159.

Stanislavsky, K. (1958). *Sobranie sochinenii* (Works). Moscow, Volume 5, 229–360.

Tolstoy, L. cited in Gorky, M. *AP Chekhov*.

Tolstoy, L. on Chekhov, from Goldenveizer, A.R. *Talks with Tolstoi*. Taken from Frontispiece, Narayan, K. (2012). *Alive in the Writing. Crafting Ethnography in the Company of Chekhov*. Chicago, IL: University of Chicago Press.

Vysokov, M.K. (2010). *Sakhalin Island*. Vladivostock: Rubezh.

# CHAPTER 1
## MEDICAL SCHOOL

Chekhov's approach to Sakhalin, indeed his self-admitted obsession with it – his so-called Mania Sachalinosa, puzzled many at the time and has continued to perplex ever since. This is because now, as then, we see Chekhov as a literary figure whose works have not only lasted but also increased in their appreciation, and hardly considered his medical career, let alone his training. Yet although he made his living and received his fame from writing, he never abandoned medicine. Seen in this light Sakhalin becomes less of a singular act or uncharacteristic interlude but, rather, as the greatest example of the social and humanitarian actions which Chekhov pursued throughout his life. It then becomes important, at the outset, to understand that his approach to Sakhalin was largely conditioned by, and directly referable to, a medical education which stressed the environmental factors of a disease and, as a result, blurred the lines of social action and medicine. His time in medical school helped expand and form his social and intellectual horizons.

Becoming a doctor was a big thing, then as now, especially for a bankrupt shopkeeper's son from a small town on the Black Sea. While his parents wanted him to become a doctor, as we have learned, in his last year at school he took part in a doctor's club with others who went on to read medicine (Finke, 2021: 25). He received a scholarship to study at Moscow University and had five years' training there, immersed in the teaching and ideas of the leading medical brains of the day, with the best Russian teaching being on a par with Western Europe.[1] The teaching, and his feeling of indebtedness to his professors, was not easily thrown away, even with literary success.

For Chekhov to read medicine would have been impossible only a few years before. His choice reflected a comparatively recent change in education and in the status of medicine. Early in the nineteenth century, medical training was poor, with old textbooks and little academic rigour. The degree took five years but included botany and minerology among other subjects. Medicine was controlled by the state with little independence for universities, while professors passed on chairs to their sons. Arguably this did not matter much, since doctors had little to offer in the way of treatment beyond potions and powders of dubious efficacy. Even by the middle of the century, 'physicians stood in the doorway, not daring to sit down. . . . Paid at holiday time with oats, flour and poultry. Their advice and time were judged lightly and superfluous'. As Mandelker Frieden writes, though they practised the healing arts, 'the wonder was that they actually healed some patients, or at least convinced their patients they did' (Mandelker Frieden, 1981: 7).

But progress was coming, in part as a result of Western medical advances dribbling across Europe, and in part due to changes within Russia itself. One shock was the Crimean War (1853–6), in which 450 physicians died, mainly from infection rather than combat. Following this, efforts were made to attract more students to medicine rather than to the more fashionable and less demanding subjects like archaeology, history and literature. And yet by 1863 little had changed; medicine was simply not attractive. Doctors tended the sick without antibiotics and so were very vulnerable to infection themselves. Most died young, with the average age of forty, and only 16 per cent reached their pension at fifty-five. Something had to be done. Scholarships and better state salaries were introduced, and they began to attract a better standard of student, bright grammar schoolboys like Chekhov. He, the son of a storekeeper and grandson of a serf, almost epitomised the new breed of medical student.

This new cohort was not attracted solely by money. Other forces were altering the effectiveness and status of medicine in the latter half of the nineteenth century. After 1856 and the emancipation of the serfs, medicine benefitted from increasing professionalization and from social and political reform. Between 1856 and 1890 physician numbers doubled. They were less dependent on the state and, more importantly, as they could do more, so their status and calibre improved.

This was not because of radical new drugs, these had to wait nearly a century, but because of developments in bacteriology, antisepsis and social awareness. The big killers were infectious diseases; cholera, diphtheria, typhoid and smallpox. In the big cholera epidemics, the death toll was large among doctors too. But they knew how, in England, public health initiatives to do with clean water had reduced its spread. They also saw how industrialization had crowded people together in appalling conditions, increasing the chances of epidemics. In parallel with this, the advances of Koch's Germ Theory had shown the causes of these diseases; previously most physicians believed in the 'Filth Theory'. Russian physicians now saw how improvements in public health reduced the spread of bacteria, so the obvious medical treatment, before antibiotics, was to improve hygiene and living conditions. For these increasingly radical doctors, social reform became an essential part of medicine.

At the time, rural medicine lagged behind that in towns and cities, with around one doctor for 7,000 people over Russia as a whole, but only one to 33,000 in rural areas. To correct this imbalance a free government rural health programme was set up in the 1870s and 1880s, as part of the wider zemstvo reforms of Tsar Alexander II. These reforms established local representative government and a range of relaxations in social policy. This attracted a new committed group of well-educated doctors to rural areas. The Tsar ceded local government control in two areas – education and medicine – and it is perhaps no accident these were Chekhov's main areas of concern. Chekhov eventually went on to work in one zemstvo hospital and was an enthusiastic supporter. Zemstvo physicians saw the effects industry had on the environment; water pollution, infection and pollution from raw materials – and wanted change. They began to challenge authority with demands going way beyond those of the old, gentler, respectful medicine. Before zemstvo, aspiring, idealistic medical students might have left medicine rather than join the profession, dominated as it were, by aristocrats and conservatives. Now, they were committed to marrying their idealism to practical tasks. Mandelker Frieden states:

> If a physician wished to prevent disease, there was only one way – to cease to be a physician and occupy himself with improvement of economic, material and moral structure of our life . . . . Medicine must prescribe those conditions that will make possible the good health and care of the people . . . . A physician must before all fight for the removal of conditions which make his work fruitless and senseless, he should be a community activist, not only recommending but also fighting and searching for means to bring his recommendations to life. (Mandelker Frieden, 1981: 228ff)

By 1895 doctors had even successfully challenged the authority of Tsar Nicholas II over some hospital reforms. Having let go of science and medicine, the government found it difficult to regain its control.

Chekhov started medical school at Moscow University in 1879, three years after the government act increased the number of medical scholarships. Though, somewhat laconically, he subsequently could not recall why he'd enrolled in medicine, the next five years gave him a lifelong passion for medicine and public health.

He was shy and diligent. His love of writing and extended study was evident early on; he started several academic projects including, 'A History of Authorities on Sex and Women's Diseases' and a 'History of Doctors' Work in Russia'.[2] Though ambitious, and showed his interest in research and academic medicine, neither was completed. A third project, 'A History of Sexual Dominance', was, Finke details, planned to raise the female sex to similar intellectual levels as men. In this he was heavily influenced by Herbert Spencer, Charles Darwin and an English historian, Henry Buckle (1821–62), who thought intellectual development was related to environmental conditions (Finke, 2005: 100ff). This too was unfinished.

Although in his fiction he describes how, 'Gloomy university gates, bored janitor, dilapidated buildings, gloomy corridors, grim walls, play an outstanding part as a conditioning factor in the history of Russian pessimism' (Chekhov, *A Dreary Story*), in reality he was fascinated by several of his professors and their theories.[3]

One of his most influential teachers was Fyodor Erisman. Trained in Switzerland as an ophthalmologist, he married a doctor who became one of Russia's first women physicians. Moving to St Petersburg, he saw the living and working conditions, rates of endemic and epidemic diseases, and infant mortality (double those of Western European countries), and moved into environmental medicine and hygiene. He gathered statistics on living, working and health conditions to show their effects on those diseases. In one project, he assembled a team which surveyed an astonishing 1,080 Moscow factories and conducted interviews with 114,000 factory workers, showing how environmental conditions affected the health of the workers, and of people surrounding those factories too. Such monumental work led to a teaching position at Moscow University, and to Russia's first laboratory. He argued that empirical analysis of environments – soil quality, water sources, rainfall, living conditions (especially heat and lighting), diet and clothing – could contribute to an understanding of diseases and how they spread, and that improvements in health would follow improvements in living conditions.

Chekhov was very receptive to ideas about the importance of such environmental and preventative medicine, especially when medical treatments were so ineffective: 'the more experienced the doctor, the better he knows the power of hygiene and the relative weakness of treatment. Only preventative medicine can hope to conquer disease'. Such ideas, on the interactions between a society's health and that of the individual, flow through some of his short stories and through *Sakhalin Island* especially. His interest in, and enthusiasm for, zemstvo hospitals was kindled in part not only by their free delivery of medicine but also their alignment with promises of environmental and social improvement (Tulloch, 1980: 55).[4] And, as we will see, he worked in zemstvo hospitals when he could.

Chekhov's favourite teacher was Grigorii Zakharin, professor of clinical medicine. He taught from the case histories of patients with various illnesses. He was the first Russian physician to tailor treatments to individual cases, and to establish age- and gender-related clinics. His clinical histories required in-depth verbal exchanges with each patient, including their living conditions, social life, diet and sexual history. Zakharin turned physicians into storytellers. Ivan Merzheevskii, a psychiatrist, also argued for a social and environmental dimension to disorders of the mind. In addition, he considered that to truly understand a patient's experience, expressed through speech, gesture and physical symptoms, doctors should be cognizant of the subjective mental life of a patient.

Such ideas remain astonishingly prescient. That physicians might enter the world of their patients remains at the edges of much of medicine today. Thus, Oliver Sacks, who has done as much as anyone in this regard, wrote in 1996 that

The study of disease, for the physician, demands the study of identity, the inner worlds that patients, under the spur of illness, create. But . . . these worlds cannot be comprehended wholly from the observation of behaviour, from the outside. In addition to the objective approach of the scientist, we must employ an intersubjective approach, to see the world with the eyes of the patient himself. (Sacks, 1995: xiv)

While the phenomenological philosopher Havi Carel paralleled such an approach,

it is necessary to supplement a naturalistic account of disease, (physiological function) with a philosophical study of the experience of illness (how that disease is experienced) itself . . . to study illness without viewing it exclusively as a subject of scientific investigation. It is not enough to see illness as an entity studied with the tools of science. In order to fully understand illness it also has to be studied as a lived experience . . . to explore its existential, ethical and social dimensions. (Carel, 2016: 1)

Entering the experiences of another as a medical discipline may be more relevant in some conditions than others (chronic impairment rather than acute and emergency medicine for instance), but one can only imagine the potency – and appeal – of such ideas to Chekhov as a medical student and writer.

Accounts of Chekhov's medical manner suggest he absorbed these teachers' ideas deeply. He was apparently always sensitive to an individual's feelings and mental condition as well as their physical symptoms (Rossolimo, GI, quoted from Tulloch, 1980: 97). Dr Pavel Archangelsky, a zemstvo physician who supervised Chekhov's first medical practice, noted that his young apprentice 'did everything with attention and a manifest love of what he was doing, especially toward the patients who passed through his hands' and that he was preoccupied with the subjective state of patients:

He always calmly listened to his patient . . . even when the patient spoke about something unrelated to the clarification of the illness . . . the mental state of the patient always drew his particular attention, and along with conventional medicine, he attached great significance to the effects the doctor and the surrounding environment had on the psyche of the patient. (Coope, 1997: 27)

It seems likely that his medical education opened him up to ideas which informed not only his medical practice but also the environmental and social concerns to be found in some of his literary writings. But this is not to say that he ever wrote straightforward medical stories; he was careful to use medicine sparingly and appropriately in his fictions, though in some he did explore mental conditions including paranoia and hallucinations. Neither did his stories and plays laud the medical profession, at times almost the reverse (see Chapter 12). He was also critical of writers, including Tolstoy, who use illness for dramatic effect without adequate knowledge of the facts. To one young writer he replied:

To write about illness or psychosis, the writer has to be scientifically acquainted with them. I keep the following rule; I write about sickness only when it forms part of the characters or adds colour to them. I avoid terrifying my readers with illnesses. (Coope, 1997: 116)

His five years at Moscow University, as a young impressionable man, may have imbued Chekhov with a perspective which never left him. The eminent Russian literary critic Kataev considered that it is:

> Generally accepted that Chekhov owed to medicine such features of his writing as scientifically based materialism, objectivity, and keenness of observation, and that he was better placed than anyone to highlight the symptoms of an illness and its course . . . Zakharin taught his students how to apply the scientific method not only in their medical practice but 'in every field of practical activity in the real world.' . . . 'think medically,' that was significant for Chekhov. Zakharin's ideas assimilated and reinterpreted became one of his main principles of artistic reconstruction . . . for Chekhov human beings are not simply objects acted upon by social and natural forces, they're themselves active cognitive subjects. (Kataev, 2002: 93)

Though he adopted a social model of medicine in his approach to the horrors of Sakhalin, he did not neglect a more personal, subjective dimension. Indeed, Kataev suggests that in his literary work, Chekhov time and again comes back to the theme of false generalizations and stereotyped solutions, learned from Zakharin:

> rigorous individualisation of each case of disease. Do not treat the illness as if it were identical for everyone, treat the patient with all his individual peculiarities . . . . Do not treat an illness, treat the patient with all his individual peculiarities. (Kataev, 2002: 94–5)

This foreshadows Osler's famous aphorism, 'it is much more important to know what sort of patient has a disease than what sort of disease a patient has' (John, M., 'From Osler to the Cone Technique': 57–8). Kataev suggests that Zakharin developed his own scientifically based method of questioning and examining patients to enable the individual peculiarities to be accurately defined in order to allow a diagnosis. Paying attention to how patients perceive their own condition was an important principle. Zakharin aimed to turn this questioning into a highly skilled art. Chekhov sat at his feet and placed him on a level in medicine with that of Tolstoy in literature. Zakharin could not have known that perhaps his most famous medical student would be a literary genius (Kataev, V., 2002: 93).

This emphasis on the individual might be placed in the context of medicine emerging from what Kataev describes as 'ballast built up over centuries of sub-scientific data from imperfect research . . . so that classifications and terminology of diseases frequently do not correspond to actual state of affairs'. He does not mention it, but treatments were even more limited before the intervention of antibiotics and other modern medicines. The first stage, then, was to delineate and differentiate a patient's condition as Zakharin did. Chekhov, of course, though absorbing his teachers' ideas, was not blind to the inadequacies of the medicine he had been taught. In *Three Sisters*, Chebutykin says, 'They think I'm a doctor, that I can treat all kinds of diseases, when really I don't know the first thing about it.'

His literary work is also dotted with insights into medical practice's changing status throughout his life. Among the drunken, unscrupulous and heartless doctors in his stories, he also depicted the elevation of doctors' social standing as their expertise improved in a way few others have in literature. In his early stories the doctors' status is low. In *Late Blooming Flowers* (1882) he contrasts the *hauteur* of a princess and the humble origin of doctor, and in *Enemies* (1887) a nobleman demands to see a doctor as he would any other workman. Even later, in *The Princess* (1889), he wrote, 'I am a doctor of medicine and a gentleman, trained in Moscow; that is I am a worm and non-entity that I can be thrown out on my ear without any explanation' (Hingley, *The Oxford Chekhov, Vol. 5, Stories, 1889–1891*: 26). In contrast, in his later stories, doctors are accorded an improved status, since with the increase of scientific knowledge they became more effective. For instance, by 1896, in his play, *Uncle Vanya*, Dr Astrov can tell Vanya, 'You and I are the only two respectable, intelligent people in the district'. As Mandelker Frieden suggests, this implies a social equality not present in his earlier works. 'The Russia of rank, heritage and caste had given way to a more modern society where physician could gain respect as scientist and social reformer' (Mandelker Frieden, N. 1981: chapter 1).

In parallel with his literary work, he continued to work in medicine throughout his life, especially during cholera epidemics. He was also in contact with medical leaders and was much respected by them. Curiously, he rarely charged for his medical services, as though inverting his quip about wife and mistress. One usually supported one's wife and paid for one's mistress, in contrast he earned from his writing and supported his medicine.[5]

Many have left medicine for writing and expressed some regret and even guilt. Chekhov never left medicine, and strove to repay his debt to medicine throughout his life. But he also knew his worth. His skills as a physician were perhaps not of the first order, though he was good at diagnosis and prognoses; he knew roughly how long a consumptive had left.[6] He thought if he had not been a writer he would have gone into psychiatry, but preferred to be a 'first rate writer than a third-rate psychologist'. This may have been false modesty, since the psychological insights in the stories and plays are far from third rate.

Where Chekhov's medicine and literary interests coincided was in a love of people. Though of course he had many other loves and hobbies: planting trees, gardening, fishing (when he did much of his thinking), and his dogs – he once wrote, 'Dogs are wonderful people', which should be on a T-shirt sold outside Crufts (Sekirin, 2011: 164, attributed to Kuprin A.). It was the idiosyncrasies, motivations, thoughts and feelings of others which really fascinated him. A friend, Merezhkovski, who described visiting Venice with Chekhov, noted how even though surrounded by such wondrous architecture, his interests were in the foibles of people.

> Chekhov walked by my side, tall, stooping a little as usual, with a gentle smile. He too was in, Italy for the first time. For him too, Venice was the first Italian town he had seen, but I noted no enthusiasm about him. It even shocked me a little. His attention was taken up with minor, unexpected details; the guide and his uncommonly bald head, the voice of the violet seller in San Marco. (quoted in Laffitte, 1974: 143)

Suvorin noted that

> he loved everything living, emotionally moving or moved, everything colourful, gay or poetry. Arts, statues, paintings, churches, held little interest for him. (Suvorin in 'Russkoe Slovo', 1904)

And with this love of people came a deep compassion towards them. Taught at medical school to see the conditions in which people lived as being relevant to their well-being primed him for Sakhalin. More widely, his writing is infused with this clinical and environmental knowledge; Chekhov the doctor is never far from Chekhov the writer.

## Notes

1. Coope suggests his scholarship was for 300 roubles a year, and that the first instalment was swallowed up to pay off family debts. Coope, J. *Doctor Chekhov*, p.20.

2. At the time prostitutes were expected, by law, to be inspected once a week or more for infection. This was a good source of income for junior doctors. Some suggest Chekhov may have combined work with pleasure.

3. For details on Chekhov's teachers I am indebted to Matthew Mangold's recent translation and studies. Mangold, Matthew (2021). 'Chekhov's Environmental Psychology: Medicine and the Early Stories', *Slavic Review* 79, no. 4 (Winter 2020): 709–30. Published by Cambridge University Press on behalf of the Association for Slavic, East European, and Eurasian Studies doi: 10.1017/slr.2021.8.

4. Tulloch quotes from a letter to Pleschcheyev, 9 October 1888. This admiration was shown in letters to Suvorin, the first in 1888, 'I do not conceal my respect for the zemstvo, which I love', and then two years later, 'If given a choice between the "ideals" of the famous "sixties" or the most wretched zemstvo hospital, I would choose the latter without hesitation.'

5. Laffitte quotes one example from his patients, MD Teleshev, who met,

> 'an old man, a silk winder'. We sat chatting in a railway carriage. I said I had an acquaintance in Lopasnaya.
>
> 'Who?'
>
> 'Doctor Chekhov.'
>
> 'Ah, Anton Pavlovich,' the old man smiled, clearly pleased about something but then said, 'funny chap', and added more severely with an air of disapproval, 'No sense.'
>
> 'Who has no sense?'
>
> 'Anton Pavlovich. What do you think? My wife when she was old kept going to him for treatment. He cured her. Then I fell ill and he attended to me. I gave him money but he wouldn't take it. So I say, 'Anton Pavlovich, my dear chap, what are you doing? What are you going to live on? You are not stupid . . . where will you go if they dismiss you? You can't take to trade.' So, he laughs and says, 'If they chase me away I'll have to marry a wealthy woman merchant.'
>
> He did not of course marry a merchant but an actress, late in his life and with some controversy. (Laffitte, S. *Chekhov*)

6. In 1895 he said that he would live between five and ten years 'whether he saw a doctor or not'. He died nine years later.

# References

Carel, H. (2016). *The Phenomenology of Illness*. Oxford: Oxford University Press.

Chekhov, A. (2001). *The Steppe and Other Stories, 1887-91*. London: Penguin Books.

Coope, J. (1997). *Doctor Chekhov; A Study in Literature and Medicine*. Chalk: Cross Publishing.

Finke, M. (2005). *Seeing Chekhov*. Ithaca: Cornell.

Finke, Michael, C. (2021). *Freedom from Violence and Lies. Anton Chekhov's Life and Writings*. London: Reaktion.

Hingley, R., Ed. and trans. (1970). *The Oxford Chekhov, Vol. 5, Stories, 1889–1891*. London: Oxford University Press.

Kataev, V. (2002). *If Only We Could Know*. Chicago: Dee.

Laffitte, S. (1974). *Chekhov*. London: Readers Union/Angus Robertson.

Mandelker Frieden, N. (1981). *Russian Physicians in an Era of Reform and Revolution, 1856–1905*. Princeton: Princeton University Press.

Mangold, M. (2021). 'Chekhov's Environmental Psychology: Medicine in the Early Stories', *Slavic Review*, 79(4) (Winter 2020), 709–30. Published by Cambridge University Press on behalf of the Association for Slavic, East European, and Eurasian Studies. doi: 10.1017/slr.2021.8.

Sacks, O. (1995). *An Anthropologist on Mars*. London: Picador.

Shavrova letter, 28 February 1893. Quoted in Coope, J. *Doctor Chekhov*, 116.

Suvorin's memoirs of Chekhov in 'Russkoe Slovo', 1904.

Tulloch, J. (1980). *Chekhov: A Structuralist Study*. London: Palgrave Macmillan.

# PART II
## GAP YEAR, 1889-90

# CHAPTER 2
# WHY

Chekhov qualified in medicine as a general practitioner in June 1894 and by the autumn had opened a practice from home. Though doctors could become wealthy, much depended on the patients they attracted. Chekhov's were poor – or pretended to be, or were friends who paid in kind. He was also wary of mismanaging infectious diseases or that he might become infected himself. By 1889, though he continued to practise throughout his life, he stopped charging.

His short story writing was quite different. Following his elder brother Aleksandr's efforts to earn money in this way, Anton tried too, initially with little success. His first published story was in 1880, but he to wait until summer 1882 to place stories in better journals. Later that year he started contributing to more prestigious and well-paying St Petersburg journals (Rayfield, 1997, 2010: 74ff. Rayfield comments that despite his increasing success, his first collection was banned by the censor). He began with parodies and inconsequential pieces, but began to explore deeper themes. The path to success went through St Petersburg rather than Moscow, and in 1886 he first placed stories St Petersburg's *New Times*, owned and published by the influential press baron, Aleksei Suvorin, who became Chekhov's benefactor, friend and confidante for many years.

His work also attracted increasing critical acclaim too. The writer Dmitri Gregorovich took up his cause, sure that he had found 'a genius to succeed him' (Rayfield, 1997, 2010: 129), and wrote to Chekhov of his talent, '. . . your vocation is to write truly artistic works. You will commit a moral sin if you do not justify these expectations . . . . Stop doing hack work' (Rayfield, 1997, 2010: 130). Uncertain of his worth and anxious to disguise the author of some more questionable descriptions of life around him, Chekhov had used a variety of pseudonyms. Grigorovich urged him to use his proper name. Grateful for the acknowledgement and praise, Chekhov responded fulsomely and started taking his writing seriously, with a subsequent drop in his output. In 1888 he was awarded one half of the Russian Academy's Pushkin Prize for Literature, by a panel run by Grigorovich. He had not only arrived, the 500 rouble prize money helped him escape from debt (Rayfield, 1997, 2010: 180).

Trying to understand why Chekhov ever abandoned his increasingly successful literary career to risk his life journeying to Sakhalin is made no easier by the fact that Chekhov's pronouncements could be somewhat contradictory and misleading. He would sometimes place his feelings in the mouth of a comic, and have his other characters mock any seriousness.[1] In this way, he might reveal himself without becoming too vulnerable.

George Saunders discusses the beautiful, simple and yet profound short story, *Gooseberries*, with its centrepiece, a meditation on, and questioning of, happiness:

> We see the people who go to market, eat by day, sleep by night, who babble nonsense, marry, grow old, good-naturedly drag their dead to the cemetery, but we do not see or hear those who suffer, and what is terrible in life goes on somewhere behind the scenes . . . everything is peaceful and quiet and only mute statistics protest; so many people gone out of their minds, so many millions of gallons of vodka drunk, so many children dead from malnutrition – And such a state of things is evidently necessary obviously the happy man is at ease only because the unhappy one bear their burdens in silence. (Chekhov, quoted by Saunders, 2021, 337)

This made such an impression on me that it forms the frontispiece to my first book on Ian Waterman, published thirty years ago. (Cole, *Pride and a Daily Marathon*, 1991, 1995). Written in 1898, it has obvious resonances to Sakhalin. But within the story, when spoken by Ivan, Saunders writes,

> Ivan's speech is the stuff of an excellent essay: articulate, earnest, precisely expressed, supported by examples, infused with sincere content. That's why we believe it and why we're moved by it. But then Chekhov makes double use of the speech by attributing it to Ivan. When Ivan, speaking through Chekhov, diverges from Chekhov, Chekhov lets this be and allows the story to react to that new Ivan. Chekhov has it both ways; the power of his heartfelt opinion, destabilised by its attribution to Ivan. He does this again and again.

Throughout his work, Chekhov's views do emerge through his characters, but usually leavened with humour or with any pomposity deflated.

His reasons for going to Sakhalin have never been fully explained. It has been put down to a variety of impulses and motivations, from depression, boredom, ennui and stagnation, to frustration, evasion, self-advancement and adventure.

From the age of twenty or so Chekhov had been supporting his family through his writing as he studied and then worked as a doctor in Moscow. Perhaps Chekhov, by his late twenties, dreamed of stepping off the treadmill. He wrote to Suvorin, his friend and publisher,

> I don't love money enough for medicine, and I lack the necessary passion – and therefore talent – for literature. The fire in me burns an even, lethargic flame; it never flares up or roars . . . I never do anything outstandingly stupid or notably intelligent . . . I have very little passion. There is a sort of stagnation in my soul. I explain it by a stagnation in my personal life. It's not that I'm not disappointed, or exhausted or cranky. It's just that everything has somehow grown less interesting. I'll have to light a fire underneath myself. (Letter to Suvorin A. 4 May 1889, from Heim and Karlinsky, 1973: 139–41)

Later, near the end of the year, he approached his thirtieth birthday with dread, feeling he was looking at a lonely old age and useless life. He wanted to 'rouse himself', to step outside himself, to be someone else, someone who took risks and saw new things in new places. He had achieved literary success, but, as Hingley suggests 'wanted a change, having become dissatisfied with literary success and the cultural life of the two capitals with its gossip, backbiting and malice' (Hingley, 1976: 128ff). He had spent a decade studying, and then supporting his family through his writing too. Nearer the time of his departure he wrote to a friend, Shcheglov 'I am going . . . simply for the sake of living for six months differently from how I have lived hitherto' (Heim and Karlinsky, 1973: 162–4. Letter to Ivan Leontyev, (Shcheglov) 22 March 1890). He wanted a Chekhovian gap year.

One of Chekhov's sisters died in infancy, when he was eleven, but the death of his brother, Nickolai or Kolia, aged thirty-one in June 1889 from TB, affected him so deeply that some have suggested it too was a trigger for his journey, out of depression and a need to get away (Finke, 2021: 36; Rayfield, 1997, 2010: 93). While there is evidence that he had periods of depression, and this has been suggested to be an important reason for his trip, Sakhalin took months of energetic research and planning which are surely incompatible with an enduring depression. He was, however, unsettled after Kolia's death, in part because he had been coughing up blood for six years himself. He made light of it, and denied that he had TB for many years, but it still gnawed away.[2] Chekhov was expert at judging prognosis and must have known how long he had left. Time was too precious to waste.

Another possible reason is one never far away in Chekhov's life – women trouble.[3] Tall, slim, intelligent and handsome – one of his statues on Sakhalin looks like George Harrison in his White Album phase – women surrounded and pursued him. But this was a particular girl, Lidia Mizinova (Lika), described by a friend of Chekhov and a writer, Tatiana Shchepkina-Kupernik, herself a connoisseur of female beauty, as:

> A real Swan Princess . . . her ash blonde flowing locks, wonderful grey eyes, her extraordinary softness and elusive charm, combined with total absence of affectation and an almost severe simplicity made her spellbinding. (Rayfield, 1997, 2010: 207)

They met in October 1889 and Chekhov was no more immune to her spell than she to his. When he set off for Sakhalin, Lika was one of those who travelled some of the way with him. But he was not good at commitment and, when they parted, signed a photo to her, 'To the kindly creature I am running away from to Sakhalin . . .'. Despite being infatuated he had said to another confidante, in January 1890 'Actors and artists should never get married. Any loves only their art, in entirely, only absorbed by it' (Rayfield, 1997, 2010: 207, Letter, January 1890).

Chekhov broke many hearts and yet did not set off on journeys over vast distances as a result. Another possible reason was more professional. Despite his Pushkin prize, and the publication of one of his major short stories, *A Dreary Story* in October 1889, his writing was not uniformly well received. He had also begun to write plays, some of which were successful and so had high hopes for *The Wood Demon*. It was, however, rejected by the committee of the Aleksandrinsky Theatre in the same month as being 'unorthodox, undramatic and obscure' (Rayfield, 1997, 2010: 210). The middle one of these might have appeared to be true, remember that in his later successful plays he evolved a more nuanced and subtle form of theatre, but this was no comfort at the time. Others suggested it was 'boring, drawn out and strange', and that he should burn it and stick with stories. Chekhov himself seemed unsure of his playwrighting. Michael Finke quotes a letter from Chekhov to Suvorin from 1895 '[I am] probably not destined to be a dramaturge. But I don't despair, for I have not ceased writing stories – and in that domain I feel at home, whereas when writing a play I experience discomfort, as though someone were pushing at my neck' (Finke, 2005: Letter 13 December 1895). A performance by a lesser troupe the next month was booed. Chekhov was devastated, he had presumed he could live off the royalties for a few months, not least since his previous play, *Ivanov*, had done quite well, and – perhaps more importantly – felt his artistic development had been rejected. Writing to Suvorin in December he did not hold back about those who judged him 'writers . . . help the devil multiply the slugs and woodlice we call intellectuals. Jaded, apathetic, idly philosophising, a cold intelligentsia which . . . is unpatriotic, miserable, colourless, and visits 50 kopeck brothels.' In contrast he defended medicine – Suvorin, trying to stop his star author from going east, knew he was losing. After the failure of *The Wood Demon*, as Rayfield wrote, 'the writer felt humiliated and the doctor-scientist took the lead'. (Rayfield, 1997, 2010: 213. Letter to Suvorin, 27 December 1889).

Thus far the reasons have been negative – reasons to leave or to avoid. Even then he could have spent a few months swanning around Italy or the south of France writing stories of bored ex-Pats and flirting with their even more bored wives. Why a penal colony on the far side of the world?

Chekhov did not equate writing with 'doing', and presumed his name would not last: 'No one will have heard of me in 5 or 10 years.' He wanted to 'do' something – something lasting, something monumental. His imagination had been kindled by tales of famous explorers, Humboldt and Darwin for instance – maybe it was time for an expedition to a far off, godforsaken place.

Since childhood, he had known of Ivan Goncharov's journey from St Petersburg by sea to Ceylon, Japan and the eastern coast of Russia before returning overland across Siberia (Rayfield, 1997, 2010: 215; and see Goncharov, I. (1858), *The Frigate Pallada*. St Petersburg). A greater inspiration was Nikolay Przhevalsky, (1839–88), an explorer and adventurer who, in the words of his biographer, Donald Rayfield, 'thrust through Russia's empire in Asia like a conquistador, exploring an area larger than the black heart of Africa' (Rayfield, 1976, 2013). He explored Russia's eastern and southern extremities, and, in so doing, helped his mother country's claims for territory against those of China in the east and the British moving north from India. Above all, he was an explorer, most at home, most alive, in the thin air of a high pass or when crossing a dry desert surrounded by his faithful men. His life, so well told by Rayfield, might have interested Bruce Chatwin. His combination of derring-do, science and territorially acquisitive nationalism made him a national hero. Chekhov was as captivated as others.

In a series of near fatal expeditions Przhevalsky roamed the barren mountains and deserts of Mongolia, central Asia and northern Tibet, exploring, mapping, hunting and collecting specimens and species, many of which he named after himself. In addition to the famous wild horse, *Equus przewalski*, there were species of Przhevalsky lemming, poplar, rose, rhododendron, carp, gerbil and gecko. He collected thousands of specimens, preserved them and sent them back to be catalogued, a process still incomplete today. Knowing he would meet hostile natives, he always practised his shooting beforehand and took the latest rifles – nothing impressed more than superior firepower.

On his return from each expedition he would be feted as a hero, write a book and then, restless, start raising funds for the next trip, either by lobbying government and Geographical Societies or, if that failed, by gambling at cards. His fame spread far and wide – quite early in his career he was awarded the Imperial Geographical Society's Konstantin Medal and elected to the Berlin Geographical Society.

On his first expedition, camping on snow, his beard froze, dripped down his shirt and then froze again. In one Siberian winter, they had to cut up saddles for fuel and the fat from their meat froze solid on their hands. A camel froze to death, blocking the tent door with its carcass and there was insufficient fuel to melt Przhevalsky's ink. On another expedition, an intense itchy rash covered him, particularly on the scrotum. He washed it twice a day in a tobacco infusion. Becoming more and more unwell, he reached an outpost and spent two months in private quarters anointing his groin with the only things that brought even temporary relief – tar and mutton lard.[4]

During his Great Tibetan Expedition, he was within 125 miles of Lhasa before turning back, facing certain death from Tibetan forces. His camels were so hungry that they tore open their saddles to eat the straw inside. At 17,000 feet snow blinded the sheep and the camels' eyes had to be washed with strong tea and a lead poultice. Mercury in their thermometers froze.

On his return to St Petersburg in 1881, he was celebrated as though he had come back from the dead, met the Tzarina and advised the thirteen-year-old, future Nicholas II.

Yet he was no hero for today in his attitudes. Ruthless and arrogant, he was convinced of the superiority of Europeans, though he loathed its society and was only happy on his country estate, to which women were not invited, and on expedition. Darwinian evolution, he thought, had stopped with man in its perfection (rather than woman, one suspects). In dealing with 'Asiatics', one had to be 'insistent and even insolent to get one's way'. Peking was a place of 'unimaginable foulness, unimaginable filth and stench. A whip the only way of putting sense into the impudent fellows . . . . Only rifles and cannons can do any good here'. Back in Russia, a prominent citizen asked him to tutor his twelve-year-old daughter. Horrified, he gave her a copy of his Geography textbook with an inscription 'Get this into your thick head'. His expeditions, like those of Livingstone and, later, Shackleton and Scott, lasted years. During one he was disappointed to hear that no world war had started, since it would revitalize a stagnant world: 'Diplomacy and governments today have a lack of moral fibre . . . .' In his 1886 'An Outline of the Present Situation in Central Asia', he wrote that the eight million peoples of Tibet, Mongolia and Turkestan were 'laggards in the evolutionary process'. Moreover, it was a waste of time ingratiating with China: 'International law does not apply to savages.'

He died as he would have wanted, high in the mountains of Kyrgyzstan. It was typhoid – justification for his lifelong abhorrence of drinking-water. His obituary in *The [Russian] New Times* suggested that

'One Przhevalsky or one Stanley is worth a dozen polytechnics and a hundred good books. Their loyalty to an idea, their noble ambition . . . their stubbornness, their urge, undaunted by privations, dangers or temptations of personal happiness to reach the goal they have set, their wealth of knowledge and their love of work . . . their fanatical belief in Christian civilisation and science make them in the eyes of the people, heroes who personify a higher moral force . . . .

In sick times, when European societies are in thrall to idleness, apathy and doubt . . . when even the best people . . . lack a definite goal in life, heroes are as vital as the sun.

Reading his biography, none will ask, 'Why?', 'What for?', 'Where's the sense?' But everyone will say; 'He's right.' (Chekhov, A, in *The New Times*, quoted from Rayfield, 1997, 2010: 203)

Perhaps surprisingly, Chekhov wrote this in 1888, anonymously. At the time, he had not read of Przhevalsky's more extreme views and was responding instead to the hero/explorer. He was not the first nor last to be in thrall to such a man of action but, as Rayfield suggests, he was not enthralled for long. In his post-Sakhalin story, *The Duel* (1891), he satirizes a neo-Darwinian social reactionary. Despite this though, eighteen months later Chekhov set off on his own big adventure.

Yet – still – why Sakhalin? This was a revolutionary idea. Others had written of their experiences of having been sentenced to a period of exile, but he was the first person to go voluntarily to a penal colony, a place where the inhabitants had no right of return. Some suggest the idea came from his brother Michael's law lecture notes when he was revising, in the autumn 1889, for his civil service exams in criminal law and prison management. On reading these Chekhov apparently decided to go, there and then. He was not completely unaware of the law before that having reported Court proceedings, and indeed used the subject, in several short stories (*In Trouble, In Court, An Incident at Law*. For discussion see Ryfa, 1999). In *The Bet* (1888) he debates capital punishment and life imprisonment, while in *Daydreams* (1886) a vagabond bound for Siberia, describes a ludicrously rosy picture of life there: "'I am not afraid of Siberia,'" the tramp went on muttering . . . . There is more freedom there and people are better off. Everything is better there. Take the rivers there, for instance; they are far better than those here. There's no end of fish; and all sorts of wild fowl . . .'. Chekhov said that he wrote not from direct experience but from memories sifted through his imagination – here it seems he wrote from imagination alone. More experience came from a chance meeting.

A few months earlier, when invited by the Maly Theatre in Moscow to Odessa, to get over Kolia's death, he had met an actress, Kleopatra Katyrgina, who appears to have been his only 'older' woman. She was forty-one and had been a governess in Mongolia and then spent ten years touring Siberia. She had had a 'lucky marriage; two days of complete happiness and then her husband died'. To make ends meet she toured with the Irkutsk Theatre and, in the end, spent ten years touring including performances on Sakhalin for the prisoners. Not only does it seem possible they had an affair – as he was squiring Lika – she also filled his head with Sakhalin.

He could still have gone, satisfied his Przevalskian lust for adventure, and come back to being Chekhov, writing short stories to keep him and his family, and trying again at the plays. Why did he spend years writing it up, to the detriment of his lucrative fiction? And why did he choose to go not as a writer, but as doctor and humanitarian, and a scientist.

One reason was that he had hopes it might lead to an MD thesis and that this would be a passport to an academic career at the university. He had tried to write long projects before, as a medical student, histories of authorities' attitude to sex, on women's diseases and a history of medicine in Russia, but these had proved too exacting (Coope, 1997: 20–1). Perhaps, he hoped this visit would allow him a return to the university to teach and escape his relative failure in practice.

As we have seen, at the time doctors' ability to change the natural history of disease was limited. Without antibiotics the biggest killer, infection, was difficult to touch. It was, however, becoming known that improvement in people's health followed changes in their living conditions. So, putting down his stethoscope to pick up his pen, his went to explore and expose conditions on Sakhalin under which the exiles lived, and also with an eye on its ecology and climate, to consider how viable it was as a penal colony. He also felt guilt over how his writing predominated over his medicine – the trip was a way to 'repay his debt to medicine' (Rayfield, 1997, 2010: 216, attributed to Burenin). As Hingley suggests he may also have felt 'a young man's recurrent obsession with his "treachery" in not practising regularly as a doctor' (Hingley, 1976: 128ff). It may also have been a way to silence those left-wing critics who found his lack of social instruction puzzling, as we will see.

Still his motives remained suspect in some eyes. His right-wing critics suggested he might be washed up, misunderstanding his reduced output following Grigorovich's letter. He was going to Sakhalin selfishly, for material to resurrect his career, for the Great Russian Novel (that he never wrote), they scoffed.

> The talented writer Chekhov
> To distant Sakhalin trekked off.
> He searched its grim quarries
> For ideas for stories,
> But finding a total lack,
> Took the first steamboat back.
> Inspiration, says the fable,
> Lies beneath the kitchen table. (Rayfield, *Chekhov, a Life*: 250)

Suvorin was also unconvinced by his journey (not least because he would have less to publish) and criticized him in a letter which does not survive (like the rest of his letters to Chekhov).[5] Chekhov's reply has a sense of indignation which may, unusually for Chekhov, come straight from the heart, even with its self-deprecation.

> I am going there absolutely secure in the thought that my journey will not make any valuable contributions to literature or science. I want

to write . . . and so do something, however little, for medical science, which, as you are aware, I have neglected shockingly.

You write that Sakhalin is of no use or interest. Is that really so? Sakhalin could be of no use or interest only to a society that doesn't deport thousands of people there and doesn't spend millions on it. Except for Australia in the past and Cayenne [French Guyana] Sakhalin is the only place where the use of convicts for colonisation can be studied . . . Sakhalin is, a place of the most unendurable suffering . . . . We have let millions of people rot, unthinkingly and barbarously. We have driven people through the cold, in chains, across tens of thousands of versts, we have infected them with syphilis, debauched them and bred criminals. All of us are . . . to blame. (Heim and Karlinsky, 1973: 158–60. Letter to Suvorin, 9 March 1890)

Some have dismissed this as pious or but one justification among many for the trip, but most biographers appear to cite this reason more frequently than others. That it was also the predominant reason for his visit is also surely suggested by the effort and time he subsequently spent preparing the articles and book. On receiving this letter Suvorin argued no more and gave Chekhov money for the journey.

Whether stagnation, a desire to do something while he was still able, the death of his brother, professional disillusionment, a genuine desire to improve social conditions and his career prospects, which reason or reasons for his trip predominated remain unclear. One thing is clear, however. Sakhalin took him from fiction for a whole year or more, and though he wrote some of his greatest stories while also writing up *Sakhalin Island*, it cost him hugely both in lost earnings, reduced literary output, and in deteriorating physical and at times mental health. His desire to repay his debt to medicine was profound. Even then, he could have made notes and lobbied hard on his return without writing his unsuccessful thesis, journal chapters and then book. For him this was a singular, sustained effort.

In her book *Reading Chekhov*, Janet Malcolm contrasts his writing in the stories with that in *Sakhalin Island*.

. . . Even Chekhov, when writing non-fiction, doesn't write like Chekhov. *Sakhalin Island* is a worthy and often interesting work, but rarely a moving one and never a brilliant one.

[It] isn't an artistic failure, since Chekhov has no artistic ambitions for it . . . [he wrote] from cards and scholarly books and reports. His customary artist's fearlessness gave way to a kind of humility, almost servility, before the ideal of objectivity and the protocols of scientific methodology. He drags along the burden of his demographic, geographic, agricultural, ethnographic, zoological and botanical facts. He cannot omit anything; his narrative line constantly being derailed by his data. The conflict between science and art is almost always resolved in sciences favour.

Chekhov tells it like it is, and allows his narrative to go where his mountains of information push it, which is all over the place and ultimately nowhere . . . . [He] could not achieve in three hundred pages what he achieved in a four-page passage at the end of his story *The Murder* (1895) about convicts loading coal onto a steamer on a stormy night. (Malcolm, 2012: 125ff)

What Malcolm saw, so Chekhov must also have been aware of. Therefore, why did he write the three hundred pages (and one hundred or more of notes) on the conditions, the climate, the soil and the statistics (such as they were)? He must surely have considered the ways in which artistic narratives and scientific exposition could be used to show what was happening on Sakhalin. In his literary work, as we will see, he never forgot his medicine or science. Chekhov was an early – and possibly one of the greatest – scientists–artists. He must have considered the question of the relations between the two and their relative strengths and weaknesses. However, as ever and tantalizingly, given his reticence to make statements, especially overt political ones, it's hard to prove. We must presume that he considered the likely effects of different styles of writing on their readerships. *Sakhalin Island* reflects his solution to the necessary balance between art and science for his purpose or purposes.

This makes it sound worthy and perhaps as dull as Malcolm suggests and for the most part she is right. But, though writing as a doctor and with a non-literary purpose in mind, the book is still frequently brilliant and moving. Just as science and medicine informed his creative writing, so his artistic side could not be completely subdued in the book – prosaic scientific description and human, artistic insights lie side by side. He does write like Chekhov – he cannot help but write like Chekhov – infrequently perhaps, but we just need to see it. Malcolm quotes two passages from short stories elsewhere in her book to convey Chekhov's brilliance, and imply its absence in *Sakhalin Island*. In one short story he describes graffiti:

> When a man in a melancholy mood is left tete-a-tete with the seam or any landscape which seems to him grandiose, there is always, for some reason, mixed with melancholy, a conviction that he will live and die in obscurity and he reflectively snatches up a pencil and hastens to write his name on the first thing that come handy. And that, I suppose, is why all convenient solitary nooks like my summerhouse are always scrawled over in pencil or carved with pen knives. (Chekhov, *Lights*, 1888)

Yet this is echoed on Sakhalin, when he walks along the cliff outside Aleksandrovsk,

> I was told that there had been benches standing on the path to the Lighthouse, but that they have been forced take them away because, while out strolling, convicts and settled exiles had written on them and had carved with their knives filthy lampoons and other sorts of obscenities. (Chekhov, 1895: 104)

His artistic insights on Sakhalin were sometimes recycled too in his fiction. In *Sakhalin Island*,

> While on the other far distant imagined shore lies America, to the left the capes of Sakhalin are visible in mist, while all around there is not a single living soul. Not a bird, not a fly, and it is beyond comprehension who the waves are roaring for. Who listens to them at night? What they want and who will they roar for when I am gone? (Chekhov, 1895: 197)

Malcolm quotes from *The Lady with the Dog*, 1899:

> The leaves did not stir on the trees, grasshoppers chirruped, and the monotonous hollow sound of the sea rising up from below, spoke of the peace, of the eternal sleep awaiting us. So, it must have sounded when there was no Yalta, no Oreanda here; so it sounds now, and it will sound as indifferently and monotonously when we are all no more.

Chekhov's writing is often viewed as being filled with melancholy, even hopelessness and depression, with the cool detached gaze of a clinician. 'Chekhovian' the adjective evokes introspection and frustration. Even Nabokov, a great admirer, described a certain greyness in his world.

> The magical part is that Chekhov … managed to convey an impression of artistic beauty far surpassing that of many writers who thought they knew what rich beautiful prose was. He did it by keeping all his words in the same dim light and exact tint of grey, a tint between the colour of an old fence and that of a low cloud.

> The variety of his moods, the flicker of his charming wit, the deeply artistic economy of characterisation, the vivid detail and the fade-out of human life, all the peculiar Chekhovian features are enhanced by being suffused and surrounded by a faintly iridescent verbal haziness. (Nabokov, 1981)

This needs to be challenged not only by looking at his writing but by considering all he did outside literature. One might indeed wonder whether he kept his undoubted melancholia at bay by reaching out and throwing himself into action, whether in medicine, famine relief or in educational projects.

Interestingly, in his Sakhalin book, despite the autobiographical elements, with him as observer, there is little or no discussion of his own feelings. His focus is usually outwards and towards the measurable and, where possible, the empirical as might befit a doctor's writing. Without knowing about the period from 1889–94, when he focussed on Sakhalin, we miss something of his development which affected his subsequent literary output. Not because he churned out prison camp potboilers, horror stories or heroic escapes by wrongly convicted heroes, but because Sakhalin permeated his world view in complex and unexpected ways. As Rayfield suggests 'Although the artist took precedence over the scientist in his make-up, the central body of his work, (roughly between 1888 and 1895) forces us to reconcile the two' (Rayfield, 1999, 2010: ix). His literary career took place over twenty-four years; five of those years he was a medical student, dashing off stories for cash and one-sixth of this time – the period between promise and greatness – was dominated by Sakhalin and his work on famine and cholera relief (though even then he wrote some masterpieces in an incredible period of creativity). Medicine and his visit to the penal colony were interludes from more creative writing, but interludes essential to the making of the mature Chekhov.

## Notes

1. He also loved to tease, though only people he liked. See Shchepkina-Kupernik, T. in Sekerin, *Memories of Chekhov*: 67.

2. He also had undiagnosed peritonitis as a teenager.

3. The degrees of physical intimacy involved in Chekhov's various flirtations remains controversial.

4. Rayfield suggests he was homosexual and that the scabies were 'what you get from sleeping with a Cossack' (personal communication).

5. There are 333 of Chekhov's letters to Suvorin and these contain some of his most heartfelt and open of thoughts. But after Chekhov's death Suvorin asked for all his letters to him to be returned and then destroyed them.

## References

Chekhov, A. (1895). *Sakhalin Island*, translated by Reeve, Brian (1993). Throughout translations are from the London: One World Edition, 2007 (updated 2014).

Cole, J. (1991, 1995). *Pride and a Daily Marathon*. London: Duckworth, Cambridge, MA: MIT Press.

Coope, J. (1997). *Doctor Chekhov: A Study in Literature and Medicine*. Chalk: Cross Publishing.

Finke, M. (2005). *Seeing Chekhov*. Ithaca, IL: Cornell.

Finke, M. (2021). *Freedom from Violence and Lies. Anton Chekhov's Life and Writings*. London: Reaktion.

Goncharov, I. (1858). *The Frigate Pallada*. St Petersburg.

Heim, M.H. and Karlinsky, S. (1973). *Letters of Anton Chekhov*. New York, Evanston, San Francisco and London: Harper Row.

Hingley, R. (1976). *A New Life of Chekhov*. Oxford: Oxford University Press.

Malcolm, J. (2012). *Reading Chekhov: A Critical Journey*. Cambridge: Granta.

Nabokov, V. (1981). *Lectures on Russian Literature*. New York: Harcourt Brace Jovanovich.

Rayfield, D. (1976, 2013). *The Dream of Lhasa; The Life of Przhevalsky, 1839–1888, Explorer of Central Asia*. London: Faber.

Rayfield, D. (1997, 2010). *Anton Chekhov A Life*. London: HarperCollins, reprinted by Garnett Press 2021. Unless stipulated, quotes are from the 2010 edition.

Rayfield, D. (1999, 2010). *Understanding Chekhov*. London: Bristol Classical Press/Bloomsbury.

Ryfa, J.T. (1999). *The Problem of Genre and the Quest for Justice in Chekhov's The Island of Sakhalin*. Studies in Slavic Languages and Literature, Volume 13. Lewiston, Queenstown and Lampeter: The Edwin Mellon Press.

Saunders, G. (2021). *A Swim in a Pond in the Rain*. London: Bloomsbury.

# CHAPTER 3
## GOING TO WAR

Having decided to go, Chekhov researched for months beforehand, not just of the penal colony's history but all aspects of the island including its climatology, botany and geology.[1] He consumed books and articles – he read the last forty years of the *Marine Journal*, the memoirs of Admiral Voin Rimsky-Korsakov, first commander, Siberian Fleet, and George Kennan's banned book exposing conditions in Siberia (Kennan, 1958). He corralled Maria and her friends in the Rumyantsev Library in Moscow (now the Russian State Library), to copy hundreds of articles from journals and books, while Alexander did the same in St Petersburg from newspapers. Their research was substantial and Chekhov used it not only for planning before his visit but also on his return during writing up. Despite his misgivings, Suvorin sent many references and articles. Chekhov alternated between fascination and fatigue, joking that he was suffering from 'Mania Sachalinosa', and pronouncing he was as much a geographer, geologist, meteorologist and ethnologist as a writer.

Kleopatra Katyrgina obtained letters of recommendation for him, while Suvorin put him up in St Petersburg and arranged for him to meet government officials. Galkin-Vrasky, director of the National Prison Administration, listened inscrutably to his plans when Chekhov was, finally, given an interview. Immediately after he had gone, Galkin-Vrasky wrote to the Director of Prisons on Sakhalin to prevent Chekhov from seeing any political prisoners.

Chekhov wrote to his friend Shcheglov, giving him the itinerary and half-heartedly suggested he come too:

> If I escape being eaten by bears and convicts . . . I shall return in December. Would you like to come with me? We shall devour sturgeon on the Amur and swallow oysters at de Kastri, fat enormous oysters, on Sakhalin we shall buy bearskins and in Japan we will get a dose of Japanese clap . . .'. (Chekhov letter to Shcheglov, 16 March 1890, in Chekhov, 1895: 480)

He was not able to concentrate entirely on the journey, however. Just before he was to leave, his most recent collection of stories was met with significant criticism of the familiar type – that he did not take a sufficiently clear moral position. Even Suvorin suggested, gently, that he had not been critical enough of those stealing horses in his story *The Thieves*. Chekhov replied with a letter outlining, with some candour, his artistic approach:

> You scold me for my objectivity, calling it indifference to good and evil, the absence of ideals and ideas . . . . You want me to state that stealing horses is evil. But nobody needs me to tell them that. Let juries judge horse thieves; my job is simply to show what they are like . . . I rely on the reader, assuming he will supply the subjective elements missing in the story. (Chekhov letter to Suvorin, 1 April 1890. Quoted from Troyat, 1987: 118)

This was written on 1 April, a few weeks before his departure. Just after this, there appeared an article in the left-wing literary journal, *Russian Thought*, by its editor, Lavrov, going far further, accusing him of being a 'high priest of unprincipled writing'. Authors were expected to edify and moralize, not simply describe. Stung, Chekhov felt, for once, that he had to reply:

> I might have let even libel go by, except that in a few days I will be leaving Russia . . . perhaps never to return.
>
> . . . I have never been unprincipled, nor – what amounts to the same thing – a scoundrel.
>
> True, my literary career has consisted of an uninterrupted series of errors, but that can be explained by the dimensions of my talent, not by whether I am a good or bad person. I have never gone in for blackmail . . . I have never toadied, nor lied, nor insulted . . . . If we assume that what you mean by a lack of principles is the sad situation that I have done nothing for those I love and that my writing career has left no trace on, say, the zemstvo, the new law courts, the freedom of the press, freedom in general and so on, then in this respect think of me as a comrade. (Heim and Karlinsky, 1973: 165. Chekhov letter to Lavrov, 10 April 1890)

In that, Chekhov suggests, he is like the rest of the left-wing press and goes on, ironically, to suggest that Lavrov's piece could not have been a 'careless lapse since your editorial office consists of unimpeachably decent and civilised people, who do not simply write articles but take responsibility for what they write. After your accusation, professional collaboration and even social acquaintance are impossible'.

The spat, no doubt, confirmed in his mind that he was tired with the literary set, though it happened too late to influence his journey. He had written to Suvorin, in late 1889, of how he was no lover of woolly-minded liberals. While he respected intelligence he mistrusted the intelligentsia 'Our sluggish, apathetic, cold-blooded intellectuals are full of idle philosophising . . . gloomy, colourless, get drunk, go to fifty copeck brothels, grouse all the time, renounce everything, because a lazy brain finds it easier to reject than confirm, refuse to marry . . . Sluggish souls, sluggish muscles, inertia . . .' (Rayfield, 1997, 2010: 213. Chekhov letter to Suvorin, 27 December 1889). Going away was probably no bad thing. In any case, though not the farewell from colleagues he might have wanted, it was too late to brood – his preparations were complete. He had bought various essentials for the journey – a large rigid trunk, a fur coat, a water-resistant greatcoat, high boots, a coffee maker, and a knife for 'salami and tigers'.

He told family and friends where to send mail. Suvorin gave him 1,500 roubles advance for articles during his journey. In a letter to him a week before he left, he wrote,

I'm feeling rather as if I am going to war, though I don't anticipate any dangers except toothache . . . .[2] The only document I am taking is a passport, so I may well have some awkward encounters with the powers that be. If I should drown, please note that everything I have and may have in the future belongs to my sister; she will settle all my debts. (Troyat, 1986: 120. Chekhov letter to Suvorin, 15 April 1890)

At 8.00 pm of 21 April, fortified by Santurini wine and surrounded by tearful family and friends, one of whom gave him brandy to be drunk on the shores of the Pacific, he left Moscow by train.[3] At the last minute, his brother Vania and some friends accompanied him for the first thirty miles, while Olga Kundasov, an astronomer and past 'close friend', stayed with him on the train and then steamer down the Volga to Kineshma. Then – at last – he was on his own.

His letters begin simply, especially to his family, describing life on the steamer. Mischief was never far away, though, here directed at any woman trying to get too close.

There are beautiful tugs on the river; each tows four or five barges. It's rather like watching an elegant young intellectual straining to run ahead but all the time being hampered by clumsy women dragging importunately at his coattails – a wife, a mother in law, a sister in law, a grandmother. (Bartlett, 2004: 213–16. Chekhov letter to Chekhov Family, 23 April 1890)

He took the ferry to Perm, to the west of the Urals, arriving at 2.00 am in driving rain. At 6.00 pm, he left for the 200 mile all night train journey through the Urals to Ekaterinburg, where some years later the Tzar and his family were murdered.[4] He stayed three days, planning and, as ever, appreciative of the local people. From Ekaterinburg, on 29 April 1890, he wrote to a friend:

Instead of delightful people like yourself I see only people with the high cheekbones and bulbous foreheads of Asiatics who, one would think, have resulted from the coupling of Urals pig-iron with a beluga whale ... (From Bartlett, 2004: 216–17. Letter to Obolonsky, 29 April 1890)

He had to lay up there for a few days to recover from a further episode of coughing up blood (Laffitte, 1976: 117. Letter to Maria Chekhov).

Two-hundred-miles further due east the railway ended. After that he had a choice – either a 1000-mile trip overland to Tomsk or to join steamers along rivers which, unfortunately, flowed south to north when he was going west to east. From Tiumen, the Tobol and then Irtysh rivers went north and then joined the Ob which had travelled north-west from Tomsk. So, by going down the first two and up the Ob to reach Tomsk, along two sides of a triangle, he could have avoided the long overland trip over bog, snow and mud and several expected dangerous river crossings.

The problem was that he was told in Ekaterinburg, on 28 April, that no passenger ships could leave Tiumen till 18 May – the Tobol was still too icy, and the Irtysh flooded. Knowing how short time was if he was to reach Sakhalin, work for two months and get a steamer home before winter, he could not wait. He went by train to Tiumen and then hired a cart, or *tarantas*, a driver and his two horses, and set off. He started well, with his observations lyrical and deeply appreciative of the countryside, even though untouched by spring,

It's May now, and by this time in European Russia, the woods are turning green and the nightingales are pouring out their songs, while in the south acacia and lilac have been in blossom for ages . . . yet here along the road from Tyumen to Tomsk, the earth is brown, the forests are bare, there is dull ice on the lakes, and snow is still lying on the shores and in the gullies.

But to make up for this, never in my life have I seen such a vast number of wildfowl. I catch sight of wild ducks walking on the ground, swimming in the pools and flying lazily off into the birch woods. Amidst the silence a familiar melodious sound rings out, you glance up and see high above a pair of cranes, and for some reason you are overcome by melancholy. Two wild geese have flown across, a row of beautiful swans, white as snow sweep over . . . woodcock wail all around . . . (*From Siberia*, p.3. In Chekhov,1895: 3)

It could not last. The cart had no cover, no springs and no seats. He sat or lay flat on straw as the rutted and frozen track battered him and his haemorrhoids mercilessly. If that was not enough, his ill-advised wooden trunk bounced around in the cart and at times threatened to kill him, broken rib by broken rib. No clothing kept out the cold and it took him three weeks to learn how to use his coffee stove. At least the wayside roadhouses were surprisingly clean, though the food was not to his liking, with the signature dish being a salty soup of half-cooked duck innards. Though he loved the bread it was not often available, so for much of the time he starved.

After four days and 450 miles they reached a large, flooded river.[5] The ferryman would not row across during the gale that was blowing, and the tracks back were, by now, flooded.

In the evening, the ground begins to freeze, and the mud turns to hummocks. We come to a river. We shall have to cross by ferry. On the bank, there is not a soul.

'They've gone rowing off to the other side, a pox on their souls,' says the driver, 'Come on Yer Honour, let's roar.'

To cry out with pain, to weep, to call for help are all know as 'roaring' here, and so in Siberia not only beasts but sparrows and mice roar as well. We begin to roar. The river is broad and, in the darkness, the other bank cannot be seen. Your feet freeze, then your legs and then your entire body . . . we carry on roaring for half an hour. Out of boredom I talk with my driver. He has been married sixteen years and has had eighteen children . . .

At last some rhythmic splashing; something dark and clumsy appears; the ferry . . . it has five oarsmen . . . On pulling into the bank, the first thing they do is abuse each other. They swear with malevolence for no reason, half asleep. Listening you might think that not only my driver, the horses and themselves but even the water, the ferry and the oars have no mother. The gentlest abuse is, 'Pox pustules in yer gob.'

We drive onto the ferry. They are not local but exiles sent here by society. In the village they have been assigned to, they simply cannot exist; it's tedious, they don't know how to till the soil and so they come here to work the ferry. Their faces are haggard, exhausted and battered. Numbed to their marrow, they have lost for ever what warmth they did once have, and only one thing remains in life for them – vodka, sluts, more sluts, more vodka. No longer human beings but wild beasts. In the view of my driver, the next world will be worse – they will go to hell. (*From Siberia*, in Chekhov, 1895: 5–6)[6]

Eventually they crossed, soon to meet another flooded river and another wait. As they pressed on, sharing the track with carts and convicts, he overheard one group talking,

'It won't get any worse!' he would say and smile with his upper lips alone. In response you would remain silent . . . a minute late he would repeat: 'It won't get any worse!' 'It will get worse!' A nasty ginger lout would reply. I think, 'To cut loose from a life which seems to be going badly and to sacrifice one's own locality can only be done by an exceptional human being, a hero . . . '

Then, a little later, we overtake a party of convicts walking to Siberia. Shackles jangling, a group of thirty to forty prisoners is going along the road, soldiers with rifles at their side, and behind, two carts. One looks pallid, emaciated with a grave face, like a monk on a long fast.

The prisoners and guards are exhausted, the road is bad, they have no strength to carry on . . . there are still 7 miles to the village.

'Walking to Siberia', Chekhov does not elaborate; he knew that, initially, many convicts walked, taking between two and three years, though later the Voluntary Fleet took the bulk of them. He had read George Kennan's account and his lack of comment may suggest he presumed many of his readers would have known that too.

Kennan was an American who, with an artist, George Frost, travelled through Siberia in 1885, covering 8,000 miles over one summer and winter. He had been to Siberia twice before, in 1865–7 as a telegrapher. In those trips he had not seen the penal system and his accounts of the Russian government's control were very favourable. His 1885 trip was specifically to look at the exile system and the banished revolutionary movement. That he obtained permission reflected his previous pronouncements that the Russian government had been misrepresented by discontents and that Siberia was not so bad.

He explained how exiles had been sent to Siberia from 1648. Those not impaled, hanged or beheaded, but merely flogged, branded, mutilated and with bits amputated were sent east. Later the government had the bright idea of developing Siberia by populating it with criminals. Crimes securing one's passage were initially murder, or desertion, but later trivial offences, including prize fighting, fortune telling and snuff taking (though part of that punishment was to have one's nasal septum ripped out). With abolition of the death penalty in 1753 all criminals who would have been put to death were exiled to hard labour in Siberia.[7] They served their time and could then return.

The punishment system was deeply flawed and random. Kennan heard of many banished by the courts in error with little evidence. It was also possible for villages to banish people without recourse to the law. There were four classes of exile – hard labour convicts, penal colonists, banished and accompanying women and children. The first two lost all civil rights and property and, unless his wife went with him, she could marry again as though he was dead. Convicts walked fettered and with their heads half-shaven.

Kennan liked numbers and writes that between 1823 and 1887 there were 772,979 exiles. Of the more recent, 5,536 out of 15,766 were women and children. Of the 10,230 criminals, only 4,392 had a trial in court, with 3,751 sent by village communes. Up to the close of the eighteenth century, prisoners were herded east like cattle, sometimes starving on the way. Then in 1811 regular guards were established. In 1817 waystations or *Étapes* were established. Convicts reached Tiumen by barge or train and then marching parties 300–400 strong left Tomsk for Irkutsk weekly through the whole year and took three months to cover the 1,040 miles. *Étapes* were at intervals of 25–40 miles, with 'half-étapes' for nights between stations. Prisoners had two days of walking and one of rest. Each had 5 cents per day to buy food from peasants by the roadside and wore shirt and trousers of coarse grey linen, low shoes or slippers, kati, leather ankle guards to stop the fetters chaffing, a visor-less hat and a long grey overcoat. Women wore a petticoat rather than trousers – volunteers their own clothing.

Kennan watched as in the morning an officer read a roll call and the blacksmith checked the rivets of the fetters. Hard labour convicts had to remove their caps to make sure they were half shaved (and that they had not changed identity). Each had a grey bag with possessions – many had copper kettles hanging from a belt. One man was carrying a small brown dog. Off they went – first, marching convicts, then a cart with the infirm, another with their grey bags for possessions and then the guards. They moved at two miles per hour. Dust was the biggest misery during the summer, and mud and ice during winter. Convicts' shoes were entirely inadequate, and some went barefoot. Each night they fought for the best sleeping place.

If they went through a village or town they were sometimes allowed to ask for food, through 'The Begging Song'.

> I shall never forget the emotions roused in me by the song . . . a peculiar, low pitched, quavering sound . . . not singing, nor chanting, nor wailing but a strange blending of all three . . . the confused sobs and moans of human beings subjected to torture whose sufferings were not acute enough for shrieks and high pitched cries . . . No attempt to pitch their voices in harmony or pronounce words in unison and no marked rhythm . . . the singers broke in upon each other with variations of the same slow melancholy air, a rude fugue or funereal chant arranged in a round of a hundred voices, each independent of the others in time and melody . . . accompanied by jingling and clashing of chains. Rude, artless and inharmonious, I had never heard anything so mournful or depressing, the half articulate expression of all the grief, misery and despair felt by generations in the étapes, prisons and mines. (Kennan, 1958: 135–6)

Each exile party organized itself with its own leader and its own standards of honour and duty. Two crimes, disobedience and disloyalty, were punishable by death. A convict could lie, murder, and rob, as long as it did not threaten the union or *artél*. If he betrayed its secrets, even under torture, he could count himself dead already. Sometimes the chief of the *artél* and the guard the commander would agree to remove the fetters. The *artél* would agree that its members would not try to escape – if they did they would be killed by fellow convicts.

Kennan concludes that 'The suffering involved in transporting criminals is not paralleled by anything in the civilised world outside the Russian Empire'. He had expected to find the banished political prisoners 'wild social theorists and wrong-headed fanatics . . . long haired, wild eyed beings with an incoherent recital of wrongs . . .'. In fact, they were 'quiet orderly, reasonable human beings'. One example was 'a blond man, aged 30, an artist, with an aquiline nose, erect and cultivated, giving a pleasant and favourable impression. A quiet, modest and frank well-bred and self-possessed gentleman'.

The book was published in English in 1888–9 for an American audience and was immediately banned in Russia, as was Kennan himself. Illicit Russian translations soon appeared, one of which Chekhov read. He presumed his readership would have been aware of the book too, which is one reason he does not go into conditions for exiles on the journey.

Chekhov was wary not just of drowning or food poisoning – travelling the convicts' road itself was dangerous. Worse than the convicts seemed to be the mailmen.

On the night of the 5th May I am being driven out of a sizeable town, 300 miles from Tyumen . . . Straight towards us, at full tilt, thundering over the hummocks, is a mail troika. The old man, my driver, swings to the right. But, suddenly, a new din; . . . another main troika at top speed. To my huge perplexity and terror, the troika swings straight at us. A crashing sound and our horses and the mail troika are mixed together. The tarantas rears up on end and I am plunging to the ground, with my cases and bundles on top of me. While I am lying thoroughly shaken up, on the ground, a third troika makes towards us. I bellow at the top of my voice, 'Stop.'

From the bottom of the empty post cart a figure rises and grasps the reins and the troika comes to a halt almost on top of my belongings.

A couple of minutes pass in silence. A kind of dull bewilderment, as if none can understand what has happened. The shafts are smashed, the harness snapped, the old man sighing and groaning gets up . . . the first two troikas are coming back and a fourth is approaching, and a fifth.

Then commences the most ferocious abuse.

Five troikas were heading back to the village, with the mail; though by law they had to go at walking pace, the leading coachman, wanting to get into the warmth quicker, had driven his horses at full lick, while the remaining the four drivers had fallen asleep, and their horses had raced off after the first.

How much wit, malice and mental impurity is expended in concocting these vile words and phrases! Only Siberian coachmen and ferrymen know how to curse this way . . . In the night, just before daybreak, in the middle of this wild cursing, beside these restive and agitated horses, I feel an isolation and loneliness difficult to describe. (*From Siberia*, in Chekhov, 1895: 7–10)

They struggle to the village for repairs. Chekhov lays his head on some sacking and falls asleep. Two or three minutes later, it seems, he is woken with banter over his laziness and aversion to the cold:

We are off again . . . light already and the sky glows golden just before sunrise. The road, the grass and the forlorn young birch trees are covered in hoar frost, as though sprinkled with sugar. Somewhere woodcocks are calling . . .

On the 9 May he writes of drinking tea in the room of a free driver, which is bright, clean, spacious and furnished well. In one corner, there is a bed piled with a 'whole mountain of mattresses and pillows in pretty cases; to clamber up you need a chair and the instant you lie down you sink. They love to sleep in a soft bed'.

He describes their icons and artwork – sweet papers and labels from vodka bottles and cigarette packets stuck on the wall. 'There is a high demand for artistry, but God has not supplied the artists . . . But they do not take off their gloves and flex their fingers for nine months of the year. The whole year is a brutal struggle with nature, when is there time to paint?'

Across the hall is another room, the landlord's – 'seething with exertion'. The women are kneading dough, cooking blinis and pouring boiling water over a recently killed piglet. The landlord presses wool into felt to make boots. Only the old are idle – grandmother sits on the stove, legs dangling, while grandfather lies in bed, coughing. Chekhov hears a child cry and notices a small cot between stove and bed. The baby, Sasha, was left with them by a woman travelling through, who'd become ill after her confinement and stayed with them for a few days. She asked them to look after the baby till she got back from Omsk 'in a week's time'. The landlord and lady who 'punished by God, had no children of their own', took him in with joy. Two months later the mother had not returned – the landlady told of her fear 'the evil moment when she comes back to take him; her eyes redden and fill with tears. The landlord,' Chekhov writes 'has grown accustomed to the boy too, but he is a man and to acknowledge this is awkward for him.' In a few economical pages Chekhov has shown how people live, how a desperate mother deserted her unwanted baby, and a couple as Siberian Silas Marner.

He sees someone at a window, and this triggers a consideration of Sakhalin's and – indirectly – his own purpose too:

> I do not like it when an educated and cultured exile stands at a window and gazes in silence at the roof of the neighbouring house. What does he think about . . . ? I do not like it, because all this time I felt infinite pity for him. (*From Siberia*, in Chekhov, 1895: 11–13)

Russia had suspended the death penalty in the late eighteenth century except for treason and mutiny – murderers were, instead, sentenced to ten to fifteen years' hard labour. Though convicts were isolated, and worked on forestry, mining and road building, their sentences were finite and return home was the rule. The successes of Britain and France in Australia and Guyana, building colonies with convicts sent without return, led Russia to consider the same. Sakhalin was originally set up as a colony in the middle of the nineteenth century. People were encouraged to settle there by grants – when that did not work, they tried promises of exemption from military service. When that failed too, it became a penal settlement with men, and some women, being sent there for life.

> The frequently employed expression, that the death penalty is utilized today only in exceptional cases is not entirely correct; all the measures which have replaced [it] continue to bear a more significant and material aspect, namely that they are for life, for eternity, and have objectives inherited directly from the death penalty – to remove

an offender from the normal human milieu for ever . . . . The person is considered dead just as much . . .

None of the 'higher measures' of punishment yields the offender rest in the grave . . . The lifelong aspect of punishment, the consciousness that hope for anything better is impossible . . . permit me to feel that the death penalty has not been repealed but merely clothed in another form less repugnant . . .

. . . we have absolutely no idea what prison is, or exile is . . . . Just take a glance at our literature on prison and exile; what utter poverty. Two or three short articles . . . . The extraordinary want of education of our lawyers and legal experts. They sit university exams to judge a person. They do nothing but pass judgement and sentence and where the offender goes, and Siberia consists of, they have no idea. (Chekhov, 1895: 24)

Despite everything, he reached Tomsk in a week, on 15 May, averaging 100 miles per day. Exhausted, deprived of sleep, hungry, with a sore back from the cart and bad haemorrhoids, he also had a further haemorrhage from the lung. He recovered soon enough to write, though was as careful as ever in tailoring his words to his reader. To his sister, Maria, he wrote, how the 'Little Russians',

bake the most delicious bread; the first few days I made a pig of myself. Delicious also are the pies and pancakes. (Hellman, L., trans. Lederer, S. 1955: 108–10. Chekhov, Letter to Maria Chekhov, 14–17 May 1890)

He continued, introducing some criticism of the food and drink. The soup was dirty, the corned beef vile and the tea an infusion of sage and cockroaches. In a letter to Suvorin, he was more forthcoming,

I starved like a dog all along the way. I crammed my belly with bread in order not to think of turbot, asparagus and the like. I even dreamt of buckwheat kasha. (Hellman and Lederer, 1955: 119–20. Chekhov letter to Suvorin, 20 May 1890)

His boots were too tight, so he wore felted ones which soon turned to jelly in the wet. A sausage he bought, smelt 'as if you had entered a stable at the moment the coachmen was unwinding his puttees; when you started chewing the stuff you experienced a sensation like sinking your teeth in to a tar smeared dog's tail'.

He spent a week in Tomsk and wrote six chapters for Suvorin, suggesting as a title '*From Siberia*'. It seems fair to say he enjoyed the writing more than Tomsk.

Tomsk is a boring, drunken town; no beautiful women at all. The only notable thing is that governors die. (Rayfield, 1997, 2010: 224)

People came to his hotel to pay their respects, but he found them all uninteresting and gave instructions that he was not receiving anyone. One man got through – the local police chief, with literary aspirations and a long moustache – who brought some of his own stories for Chekhov to read. Vodka was ordered and Chekhov, for once, was diplomatic, even writing a letter of commendation to Suvorin. Then they went on a tour of the local brothels. He finished his letter to Suvorin on his return, repulsed though apparently none too exhausted, at 2.00 am (Chekhov, 1895: 486. Chekhov letter to Suvorin, 20 May 1890).

He decided to buy his own cart and hire a driver, replace the by now wrecked trunk with a far more practical large leather bag, and left on 21 May on the longest and worst part of his journey, to Irkutsk, 1,000 miles away. He had met some army officers and so travelled with them to keep expenses down. They were company and reassurance, though also rough, talkative and at times abusive. Interestingly, when one suggested he find himself a woman, Chekhov replied that 'I can't, I have a bride in Moscow. Only I doubt if I'll be happy with her – she's too beautiful' (Rayfield, 1997, 2010: 224. Recollection of one of the officers). He wrote to Lika frequently, though she not to him.

After 400 miles, the bog and peat of the central plain was replaced by taiga or birch forest. The track, if anything, worsened. Siberia seemed endless: 'The power and enchantment of the taiga lie not in titanic trees or the silence of the graveyard, but in the fact that only birds of passage know where it ends' (Chekhov, 1895: 35). But end it did – they reached Irkutsk, capital of Siberia, on 4 June. By then his companions were spending his as well as their own money on drink. At least in town he had a bath and a bed, and some clean clothes. Irkutsk had a theatre, a museum and a tree-lined park with music playing – he wrote that it was splendid. After his last few weeks it is not surprising that he was impressed. He sold his cart – at a loss since it was damaged –

and joined his army friends in theirs as they went to Lake Baikal, the largest inland freshwater lake in the world. He was impressed by its scenery and the clarity of the water. They waited three days for a ferry, sleeping on the floor of a shed of a room with 'fleas and cockroaches, bad food and vodka'.

Once across Baikal they made good progress and were in Sretensk on 20 June, just in time to catch a steamer on the Shilka River, a branch of the Amur, which formed the border between Russia and China, flowing north and then south to Khabarovka (now Khabarovsk). To avoid the officers, he took a first-class cabin, hoping to write letters and an article or two, but the steamer shook so much that writing proved all but impossible. Despite this he managed a few letters from the comparative luxury and safety of the boat. To his family, as usual, he skated over any difficulties, and gave a bland, optimistic account:

> And so ended my mounted journey . . . It has taken me two months, and if you don't count time by rail and ship, the three days in Ekaterinburg, the week in Tomsk, day at Krasnoyarsk, week in Irkutsk, two days at Baikal and the days waiting for floods to subside, you get an idea of the rapidity of my progress. I have had as good a journey as any traveller could wish for. Not a day's illness and have lost only a penknife, strap from my trunk and a tub of carbolic ointment.

> I got so used to travelling by road that sitting on a steamer I feel ill at ease . . . (Chekhov, 1895: 495. Chekhov letter to Maria Chekhov, 25 June 1890)

Despite this he was enchanted by the river, by the area and by the freedom:

> The Amur is extraordinary and unusual region and seethes with life . . . the banks of the river so wild and luxuriant one wants to stay forever. I have travelled over six hundred miles and seen a million magnificent landscapes; my head is spinning with excitement and delight. I stare at the banks and see masses of ducks, geese, divers, herons and all manner of long billed creatures.

> The air on board gets hot from the talking. No one worries about saying what he thinks. There's no one to arrest you.

He was even amused when the boat ran aground and was holed. It took some time to repair and a ship coming the other way could not get through.

Fortunately, there was a military band on it, so they had a party. 'The female passengers – particularly the college girls – were having a ball: music, officers, sailors . . .'

In a letter to Suvorin he described the beauties of the Amur, and of the women in Blagoveshchensk's brothel:

It is quite beyond my powers to describe the beauties of the banks of the Amur; crags cliffs, forests, thousands of ducks . . . I've seen such riches and experienced such rapture that death holds no terror. It is beautiful with vast open spaces and freedom.

The Japanese women in Blagoveshchensk are diminutive brunettes with big, weird hair dos. They have rather beautiful figures and are rather short in the haunch.

The Japanese girl has her own concept of modesty. She doesn't put out the light . . . and does not put on airs or go all coy, like Russian women. And all the time she is laughing . . . She is amazingly skilled at her job, so that you feel you are not having intercourse but taking part in top level equitation class. When you come, The Japanese girl pulls with her teeth a sheet of cotton wool from her sleeve, catches you by the 'boy', gives you a massage, and the cotton wool tickles your belly. And all this is done with coquetry, laughing singing and saying 'tsu'. (Rayfield, 1997, 2010: 227–8)

In contrast, to his family 'I've been bathing in the Amur and dining with gold smugglers – is that not an interesting life?' Not quite as interesting as Suvorin could have told them. Later, near Habarovsk, he seemed almost intoxicated by the steamer, the area and the people.

There are meteors flying round my cabin – fireflies, just like electric sparks. Wild goats were swimming across the Amur this afternoon. I am sharing my cabin with a Chinaman who was smoking opium yesterday, which made him rave all night . . . Little by little I am entering a fantastic world. (http://www.gutenberg.org/files/6408 /6408-h/6408-h.htm#link2H_4_0073. Chekhov, letter to Maria Chekhov, 29 June 1890)

I am in love with the Amur; I should be glad to spend a couple of years on it. There is beauty, space, freedom and warmth. Switzerland and France have never known such freedom. The lowest convict breathes more freely on the Amur than the highest general in Russia. (http://www.gutenberg.org/files/6408/6408-h/6408-h.htm#link2H_4 _0073. Chekhov letter to Suvorin, 27 June 1890)

His period of idyll, of refuge and recovery was welcome but short-lived. Beyond the mouth of the Amur lay Sakhalin. When the first explorers pointed to it and asked the local tribe its name they replied 'Sakhalin' thinking these odd people were pointing not to the island but, rather, to the stones lining the river mouth. Nickolayevsk had no hotel, so he stayed on the next steamer for two days waiting for its departure. The town did not impress, its inhabitants living a 'sleepy, drunken life, semi-starved' and subsisting by delivering fish to Sakhalin, embezzlement and by selling stag's antlers to the Chinese for 'stimulant pills'. When his boat, *The Baikal*, weighed anchor on 8 July 8 there were 300 prisoners on board one of whom had his five-year-old daughter with him, who held onto his shackles as he climbed up the ship's ladder. Her face haunted Chekhov for days. As they set out into the Tartar Straits, going south, he could see Siberia to his right. The woods were on fire:

> The solid green mass was throwing up a purple flame. Clouds of smoke merged into a long black static strip hanging above the forest. The blaze was gigantic but all around was peace and calm. It was nobody's business that the forest was perishing. Clearly the green wealth here belongs to God alone. (Chekhov, 1895: 45)

The boat called in at one further port on the Russian mainland before steaming over the Tartar Straits towards Sakhalin. They dropped anchor outside the Aleksandrovsk Post at 9.00 pm. Once more large fires were blazing on shore.

> Through the darkness and smoke spreading over the sea I could not see the landing stages and building and could make out only the dim lights of the post, two of which were red. This fearful picture, crudely cut out of the darkness silhouettes of mountain smoke, flames and sparks from the fires presented a fantastical appearance. On the left side were burning monstrous bonfires, above them mountains and from behind the mountains a crimson glow rising high into the sky from distant conflagrations. It looked as if the whole of Sakhalin was ablaze. Everything is covered in smoke, as if we were in hell. (Chekhov, 1895: 53)

Someone replied,

> 'You haven't seen anything yet. Wait till you see Douai. The coastline
> there is completely vertical with dark ravines and layers of coal. It's so
> depressing we used to bring 2–3 convicts at a time to Douai and I saw
> a lot of them in tears at a sight of the coast.' 'It's not them that do hard
> labour,' said the captain, 'it's us.' (Chekhov, 1895: 53)

That evening it was too late to land. Aleksandrovsk was on small river
with an estuary, but there was no harbour, just a jetty. The next morning at
around 5.00 am Chekhov was woken as the cutter was going ashore for the
last time.

> A minute later I was sitting in the cutter . . . we set off for the shore,
> towing behind us two barges of convicts worn out by the night's work
> and lack of sleep. Prisoners were sluggish and morose and were silent
> the whole time their faces covered with dew.
>
> . . . by the jetty, evidently with nothing to do, 50 or so convicts were
> wandering about; upon my appearance, all 50 took off their caps.
> Very likely no such honour has ever been accorded a single other
> literary figure to this day.[8]

After two and a half months, five or six thousand miles of near death,
haemorrhage and starvation, including 4,000 versts or 2,667 miles in an
open cart,[9] he set foot in hell.

## Notes

1. For instance, he knew the price of coal from 1863 onwards.

2. Omitting to mention the piles which plagued him.

3. He left two months before Joseph Conrad steamed up the Congo, a trip which
   resulted, eight years later, in *Heart of Darkness*.

4. Its name was changed to honour their executioner, the suitably grim
   Sverdlovsk; recently it has been changed back.

5. The rivers of Siberia may be half a mile or more across.

6. In a footnote he details the numbers who came by ship. 'The Voluntary
   Fleet carried 8430 convict men and women and 1146 family members'.

1879–89, p.394. By the middle of the 1880s, all came in ships (Chekhov, 1895: 343).

7. One is allowed some scepticism here. As Donald Rayfield wrote:

> In no country has capital punishment been so often and so briefly abolished as in Russia; twice in the eighteenth century by the Empresses Elizabeth and Catherine, once, unofficially by Tsar Alexander I, once by the provisional government in February 1917 and once in the 1920s (for three years)' (Rayfield, D. (2004). *Stalin and His Hangmen*. London: Viking).

8. Chekhov was being playful. Convicts were required to raise their hats to gentlemen.

9. Figures from Finke, M.C. *Freedom from Violence and Lies*: 80.

# References

Bartlett, R., Ed. (2004). *Anton Chekhov. A Life in Letters*, translated by Bartlett, R. and Phillips, A. London: Penguin Classics.

Chekhov, A. (1895). *Sakhalin Island*, translated by Brian Reeve, from 14/15 of Chekhov's Works from his Complete Collection of Works and Letters Moscow 1978. Nauka (Science) Publishing House.

Finke, M.C. (2021). *Freedom from Violence and Lies. Anton Chekhov's Life and Writings*. London: Reaktion.

Heim, M.H. and Karlinsky, S. (1973). *Letters of Anton Chekhov*. New York, Evanston, San Francisco and London.

Hellman, L., Ed. (1955). *Selected Letters of Anton Chekhov*, translated by Lederer, S. London: Hamish Hamilton; London: Picador.

Kennan, G. (1958). *Siberia and the Exile System*. Abridged from the First Edition, 1891 (New York: Century). Chicago and London: Chicago University Press.

Laffitte, S. (1974). *Chekhov*. London: Readers Union/Angus Robertson.

Rayfield, D. *Anton Chekhov – A Life*. London: HarperCollins. 1997, 2010. Second Edition, London: Garnett Press. 2021.

Rayfield, D. (2004). *Stalin and his Hangmen*. London: Viking.

Troyat, H. (1987). *Anton Chekhov – A Life*. London: HarperCollins. 1997, 2010. Second Edition, London: Garnett Press. 2021.

# CHAPTER 4
## EVERYTHING IS CHAINED

The long west coast of Sakhalin, facing the Tartar Straits and Siberia, has no natural harbour. Sailors first landed, in 1851, at Douai, a few miles to the south, after they saw coal seams in the cliffs and rowed ashore to the beach. Though mining began there, its valley was small and its sides too steep for a major outpost, so they settled on Aleksandrovsk a few miles to the north, where the River Dukya winds to the sea. South of the river the land rises quickly but to the north there is some lower, flatter land upon which to build. It also has a beach, but no shelter and boats landed at a jetty. Chekhov described it thus, tongue firmly in cheek:

> The decision to select Aleksandrovsk, of all places, was prompted, as Mitzul wrote, by the luxuriant water meadows, good building wood, navigable river and fertile land. 'To all appearances,' writes this fanatic, 'it is impossible to have doubts about the successful outcome of colonisation.'[1]

Today, Aleksandrovsk still squats on this elevated, flattish land, with the old town close to the river; wooden houses, battered fences, dirt roads, where apparently feral dogs and children wander. Most buildings are single-storey log cabins, but there are a few beautiful, run-down wooden mansions, reminders of times past. On higher ground are more modern brick and concrete buildings built around the main open space. 'The Square of Shackles' is on the site of – and in the same dimensions as – the old prison. At one end are the town hall and large statue of Lenin, arm outstretched as usual in exhortation, while at the other a small bust of Chekhov, who just watches.

When Chekhov landed, convicts loaded his luggage on a horse drawn wagon and the owner, a man 'with his shirt not tucked into his trousers', drove him into town. On the hills to the right Chekhov saw the barrenness – 'charred tree stumps, sticking out like porcupine quills' – while the estuary was 'burnt out marsh soil and poor black earth. Nothing but pathetic, emaciated larches.' Through the main square, with prison and the governor's house they went to a lodging, five bare rooms and no furniture. The landlady was a young peasant who had come with her mother and convict father and was now married off to a morose old man.[2] She exclaimed 'So, you've come to this Godforsaken hole.' After a while she brought in a samovar. Chekhov was not impressed by him,

> he had served his hard labour, owned two houses, horses and cows and employed many workmen, while he did nothing, was married to a young woman and had the right to settle on the mainland, and he still complained.

Chekhov found a shop belonging to an ex-Guards' Officer and murderer from St Petersburg. The assistant invited him to lunch and he found himself in a room with four other guests, including a junior doctor. The four argued about crop yields on Sakhalin. An official suggested a forty-fold yield one year for wheat – the doctor disagreed. After dinner, Chekhov left his lodging – the peasant girl's unwitting brush with genius over – and moved in with the doctor, who only then told him that he had fallen out with the governor during a medical inspection of cattle.

Next day he called on the governor, V.O. Kononovich. Well-read and humane, he warned him how gloomy and tedious Sakhalin was, and that most of the governmental people wanted to leave. He promised Chekhov full cooperation but said that introductions would have to wait – everyone was busy preparing for the visit of the Governor General from Amur River Territory on the mainland.

Chekhov spent a few days finding his bearings. Waking, he was reminded where he was 'by the most diverse sounds, clanking of prisoners in irons, soldier instrumentalists rehearsing their marches for the visit of the Gov. General, with the flute playing a part from one piece, the trombone apart from another and the bassoon a third; indescribable chaos'. On the streets convicts and exiles walked around the streets unhindered, while other convicts working on a building had axes and hammers. He expected to be threatened or worse. At 4.00 am one morning he heard rustling in his room and expected to be murdered. It was a convict wanting to clean his boots. People mixed without threats or violence, but this could not disguise the misery.

A week or so later the governor general of the larger eastern side of Siberia, Baron Korf, arrived. Chekhov noted that the waiting crowd comprised men, women and young children but no youths 'as though those from 13 to 20 did not exist'. The Baron toured the district listening to petitions and requests. Chekhov relates the 'vexing dimness' of the peasants, who asked 'not for schools or justice, but for trifles which local authorities should have dealt with'.

Korf sent for Chekhov and asked two questions – did he have any authorization from a learned society or from a newspaper. Chekhov had neither. Though he did have a press card in his pocket, he was not planning to publish anything on Sakhalin in newspapers and wanted people to talk with complete confidence. He had come as a doctor/scientist not a journalist. Korf replied,

> I grant you permission to visit wherever and whoever you wish. We've nothing to hide. You'll inspect everything, a free pass to all the prisons and settlements, you'll be able to use all documents, doors will be open. There is just one thing I cannot allow; you may have no contact with any sort of political prisoners. (Chekhov, 1895: 63)

That evening Chekhov attended a ceremonial dinner.

> I became acquainted with almost the whole of the Sakhalin administration. Music was played and speeches delivered. The Baron,
>
> 'On Sakhalin, I am convinced that the "unfortunates" live better than anywhere else in Russia or even Europe. In this respect much still remains to be done, for the path of good is never ending.'

He went on to say that he had been to Sakhalin five years earlier and found that progress since then surpassed all expectations. Even after such a short time on the island, Chekhov was not taken in and describes how,

> his words could not be reconciled with one's consciousness of the starvation, prostitution, brutal corporal punishments . . .
>
> In the evening there were illuminations; lamions, Bengal flares, groups of soldiers, exiles and convicts wandered till late. The prison was opened up. The river Dukya, wretched and muddy, had now been decorated with multi-coloured lanterns; the flares reflected on its surface and on this occasion it was beautiful, even majestic – and comical too, like a cook's daughter trying on the clothes of a lady. They

even fired a cannon which blew up. Yet, despite such gaiety the streets were dismal. No songs, no accordion, not a single drunk; people roamed like ghosts and as silent as ghosts. A penal colony illuminated by Bengal flares is still a penal colony, and music, when heard from a distance by a man who will never return to his homeland, brings only a deadly yearning. (Chekhov, 1895: 63)

The next day Chekhov presented himself to the governor general once more. He suggested Chekhov entitle everything he wrote, 'Description of the life of poor unfortunates'. With some understatement, Chekhov writes 'I thought him a generous and noble-hearted, but not as familiar with the life of the poor unfortunates as he thought'. Korf mentioned that 'No one is deprived of the hope of achieving full rights; there are no lifelong punishments. A life sentence is limited to 20 years. Penal labour is not onerous. There are no chains, no sentries, and no shaven heads'.

Chekhov does not comment. Instead, throughout his book, he documents the lifers, the penal labour, the chains, the beatings, the sentries and the shaved heads, the prostitution, and the impossibility of leaving, undermining Korf's view from paper reports and fawning officials. Korf either knew little of what was going on, or chose not to know. But he does not directly criticize Korf. Presumably, he had to steer a course to avoid both difficulties at the time and with the censor later. Since he knew that medicine was impotent for most conditions, any improvement in people's situation required improvement in their living conditions. As Chekhov tours Sakhalin, he documents all that he can, as a scientist, as an ecologist, agronomist, and climatologist and hence as a doctor and a humanitarian, since the last two were, for him, inseparable. His letter to Suvorin, 'we are all to blame', revealed his view before he travelled. Once there, he had to subvert his own perspective, gather the facts and then, by assembling them, hope the resulting work would persuade others.

Chekhov had been on the island a week or so, met people in authority, the dissident doctor and seen many exiles. But he needed to chat to people. In order to meet them, he decided on a census:

In order as far as possible to visit all the inhabitable spots and to become someone closer acquainted with the life of the exiles, I resorted to a device which in my position seemed the only way. I carried out a census. In the settlements that I visited I went round all the cabins and noted down the heads of the households, members of their families, tenants and workmen . . . my main aim was not its results but the impressions received during the making of it.

This piece of work, carried out in 3 months by one person, cannot in actual fact be called a census; its results could not be said to be distinguished for their accuracy and completeness, but, in the absence of more reliable data, either in the literature in the subject or in the Sakhalin offices, my figures will perhaps be of some use. (Chekhov, 1895: 65)

In fact, Sophie Laffitte suggests that his census was the first carried out in Russia on a scientific basis (Laffitte, *Chekhov*: 136). It accords with one of his aims, the desire to empirically document everything which could be known.

I used small cards produced for me in the printing shop of the police department. The method of conducting the census was as follows;

1.  Name of post.

2.  Number of house.

3.  Status of entrant; convict settled exile peasant in exile and free.

4.  First name surname . . . 'Many curious; Limper, Stomach, Godless and Bone-idle. Ivan Don't remember. Tramps' nicknames included; Mustapha Don't remember, Vasili Countryless, Frans Don't Remember, and Ivan Don't Remember Twenty-Year-Old. Jacob without a Nickname, Vagabond Ivan 35 years' old and Man whose Title No One Knows.'

5.  Age. 'Many did not remember this, "Could be 20, 30 or 50 by now." He was aware of inaccuracies. Youths would reduce their age to below 15 since poorer families received food rations for those under that age.

6.  Religion.

7.  Where born; 'they gave the answers without difficulty; only the vagabonds prevaricated.'

8.  The year they came to Sakhalin. 'Rare did they reply without any effort. A moment of dreadful misfortune and yet their either did not know or could not remember [in some cases].'

9.  Occupation and trade.

10. Literacy.

11. Family status; married, widowed, bachelor. If married where?
    Marital status did not define their family status, since married
    people could be doomed to a lonely celibate life with their spouses
    at home and yet not granting them a divorce.

12. Did they receive a state allowance? The aim of this was to
    determine how many were unable to manage themselves on the
    island.

He marked each female card lengthways with a pencil. He used the census
not for the prisons, they had some information on their numbers and he did
not have the time to fill in cards as he went around, but when going from
cabin to cabin among the settlers and exiles once released from prison. He
would try to go alone, but sometimes, a short way behind, 'there followed,
like a shadow, an overseer with a revolver. He had been sent in case I needed
"some sort of elucidation or anything . . ."' This was likely to be a minder, to
make sure he did not talk to any political prisoners, and so the authorities
could keep tabs on him. Chekhov of course does not say this.

But he did mention the 'sluggish' dogs.

> They only bark at the Gilliaks, [one of the two indigenous peoples],
> very likely because they wear boots made of dog skin. For some
> reason these gentle and inoffensive dogs are on leashes. If there is a
> pig it has a halter round its neck, a cockerel is bound by its foot.
>
> 'Why are they tied up?'
>
> 'Here, on Sakhalin everything is chained,' he replied. 'It's that's sort of
> place.' (Chekhov, 1895: 71)

He described a typical room, with table, stools, bedding on floor or bed. He
saw 'no grandparents, no icons, no old furniture, no domesticity; in other
words, no tradition'. He met a landlord – lonely, bored, frozen with idleness
– who spoke of his life with cold contempt, and the mistress of the house
'The Whore of Babylon, with ugly and dull eyes and a wasted apathetic face
telling of her experiences across Siberia.'

In one of the first hamlets he visited, across the river from Aleksandrovsk,
he notices the relative prosperity without any external source of income.

> Nobody works at a trade . . . official data which would account for
> why the inhabitants are wealthy do not exist either. For a solution to

the riddle one must reluctantly turn to the sole source of information in this case – ill repute. The hamlet had a clandestine trade in alcohol. The import and sale of alcohol was forbidden on Sakhalin and so this encouraged special forms of contraband. More recently they had turned to second-hand clothing and loans. (Chekhov, 1895: 77)

The ferry across the River Dukya was neither a boat nor a raft, but a large square box with the ferryman a penal convict, dressed in rags and bare footed, called, 'Good looking can't remember my relations'.[3] He was seventy, hunchbacked, with shoulder blades that stuck out, a broken rib, one thumb missing, and covered with wheals from past lashings. Despite this he had clear light blue eyes and was good natured, lively and talkative. He was a deserter, caught and sent to Siberia for twenty years' hard labour. He escaped, but only as far as Sakhalin and had been there for twenty-two years.

> I started to head across the river in the box. Good Looking leant continually on his long pole, all the while straining his emaciated bony body. It was heavy work.
>
> 'It must be hard for you.'
>
> 'Not at all, your excellency, no one's breathing down my neck.' (Chekhov, 1895: 79)

In his time on the island he had never been beaten. 'Because when they send me to saw wood, I do it, when they order me to stoke the stoves, I stoke 'em, you've got to obey . . . Life's good.' In the summer, he lived in a yurt by the river and in the winter he gathered wood and lived in an office on the jetty. Later Chekhov saw him, trousers rolled up, dragging a net flashing silver with humpbacked salmon alongside a Chinese man. 'I called across to Good Looking, and he responded joyfully'.

Chekhov details 1,499 inhabitants in 298 households in Aleksandrovsk, not counting soldiers, officials and convicts in prison, which doubles that number. Convicts with families were allowed to live in cabins, as were those who were probationers and had less punishment compared with the 'reformees'. He notes how little land was cultivated, or cultivatable, and was mystified as to how they managed, even considering the illegal gambling, alcohol trade, loan sharks and prostitution.

People have commented how dry *Sakhalin Island* is, and they have a point.[4] It was, after all, written as a medical thesis and few of those are memorable reads. And yet, part of the dryness reflects Chekhov's reason for going – to document conditions dispassionately and accurately, as part of his extended medical approach. By documenting them his medicine was social, and from the government's perspective subversive. Writing in detail about Aleksandrovsk's hard labour prison is such a case – describing how convicts lived was at the heart of his purpose of questioning the conditions. If the aim of a medical doctor is to improve the conditions under which people live, then he or she has to go beyond health (conventional medicine to treat people when they are sick), to social, educational, dietary, industrial and where relevant penal levels, to try to avoid or reduce sickness in the first place. Even today healthcare inequalities have major social determinants (Marmot, 2005: 1099–104).

The prison was the centre of the town. He was surprised that the gates were always open and that despite sentry boxes and sentries, convicts walked in and out. But then he realized that these were the least dangerous prisoners and that, anyway, there was nowhere to escape too; the whole island – their whole world for the rest of their lives – was a prison.

One cell had a central bed board for up to 170 prisoners who slept in two rows, heads together. The walls and floors were unpainted and there was no bedding, with them sleeping on 'rags, torn sacks or rotting rubbish'. The place was littered with bits of bread, empty milk bottles, boots, caps, bundles of tools and old clothing. Around the boards sauntered a well-fed cat. Each cell 'the same dreadful destitution, as impossible to conceal as a fly under a magnifying glass, that same herd-like life, nihilist in the fullest sense, which denies property, solitude, comforts and sound sleep'. Chekhov gazed at the criminals in silence, 'as though he had come to buy them'. Prisoners who had tried to escape were in the fetter block, unwashed, emaciated and with half of their heads shaved clean. Surprisingly, despite this, they seemed cheerful. In solitary were 'some interesting people' including the infamous 'Golden Hand', a murderess and thief who – horror – had used her feminine charms to escape on at least one occasion. He describes her simply, as 'small, thin, already greying, with a crumpled, aging face', humanizing an ordinary, elderly person who had lived an extraordinary life. In her small cell, she sniffed the air like a mouse in a trap, and her expression was like a mouse as well.

Chekhov details the kitchens, the appalling latrines and the poor ventilation. Accommodation was 970 cubic sazhens (each sazhen was around two metres) for an average of 1,785 prisoners, so that each person had a cubic metre of space – and air. In the summer working parties were out, so the population fell, but in autumn they returned and large numbers of new convicts arrived, just as temperatures fell and the weather worsened. The conditions were appalling.

> When a prisoner returns from working, his clothes are soaking and there is nowhere to dry them. He hangs some by the bed board and lays the remainder under him in place of a mattress. His underwear, saturated with secretions, not dry or washed for ages . . . his feet wrapped in a decaying cast of clothes, with a suffocating stench of sweat, he himself covered in lice, smoking cheap tobacco and his poor food make the air fetid, dank and sour, with hydrogen sulphide and ammonia smells adding to the mix.

> it is hardly possible to say anything in favour of communal cells. The people are not a society but a gang, with no solitude possible. A violent card game, foul language, idle chatter, banging of doors, often all night make sleep difficult. The cattle-like disordered life and with the inevitable influence of bad on good is most corrupting. Little by little it weans him from domesticity which is the very quality which must be protected in a penal colony above all, since on leaving prison he will become an independent member of the colony. (Chekhov, 1895: 86)

He details their work. 'The most onerous is the carpenters', dragging logs from the forest. In winter some get frostbite, others die pulling. Hours were unlimited and the supervisors 'incompetent, incapable and clumsy'. Though not officially allowed to use prisoners as servants, this was widely ignored. Convicts became unpaid servants. Chekhov, grandson of a serf, was especially sensitive, describing it as 'vexing and sad'.

After ten days in Aleksandrovsk the dissident doctor left, and Chekhov stayed with Bulgarevich, treasurer of island administration and inspector of schools. We hear little of Bulgarevich but much of his servant, Yegor, who seemed to work non-stop and sleep rarely. Kleopatra had advised Chekhov not to ask exiles of their crimes and, on the whole, he did not. But uniquely, he did ask Yegor to tell him everything 'from the very beginning'. This narrative, unusually, occupies a single chapter to itself and as Yegor gives his whole narrative, Chekhov interrupts, asking him to 'Be a bit briefer . . .' Yegor ignores him, telling Chekhov to stop butting in. The story involves half a gallon of vodka, a fight and a murder. He details his time in prison in

Russia, waiting to be sent east, his outwards journey on a ship and his time on the island. But what appears to be a linear story from a simple convict is not what it seems, as we will see later.

Then, after nearly a month in Aleksandrovsk, during which time he filled in 1,432 census cards from those outside the prison, as well as detailing prison conditions, he finally received a permit to travel around the island, so he left the self-styled 'Paris of Sakhalin' to explore further afield.

## Notes

1. In *Sakhalin Island*, before relating his landing at Aleksandrovsk, Chekhov offers a brief geography of Sakhalin,

   > lies in the Sea of Okhotsk, its elongated form stretches from north to south and is in the opinion of one writer, in outline reminiscent of a sterlet [a small Siberian salmon]. The northern part is traversed by a strip of permanently frozen soil. The island is 900 versts in length; at its widest 125 versts and narrowest twenty-five. It is twice the size of Greece.

   > The former division of the island into north, central and south is inconvenient, and now it is only divided into north and south. By reason of its climate and soil, the topmost third is totally unfit for settlement; the central is called northern and the lower third southern . . .

2. Though Chekhov does not name them, they can be traced from the census cards. He was aged forty-six and from St Petersburg, she twenty-six from Tambov – Aleksandr Platonov Pomerantsev and his wife Tatiana Sevostianova Pomerantseva (Chekhov, 1895: 56).

3. Chekhov does not labour the point about people's lost names since Kennan had described it. 'Every convict sentenced to hard labour wants to avoid it by changing identify with someone just exiled. Each marching party has 400 convicts and guards cannot know them all; the parties also change constantly. Names and identities were exchanged "without the least difficulty" . . . in each party there are feckless, improvident, hard drinking peasants, who have lost all their money by gambling who will sell their soul for 5 or 10 roubles. The hard labour convict, who is generally a bold, enterprising and experienced recidivist, approaches a hungry, thirsty, half naked peasant and offers him money and a coat, and say he can explain the mistake at the mines. The artél notes and sanctions each transaction. The more dangerous criminal is turned loose in some east Siberian village while the petty thief ends up in the mines' (Kennan, 1958: 130).

4. For example Malcolm, J. (2012). *Reading Chekhov: A Critical Journey.* Cambridge: Granta.

## References

Chekhov, A. (1895). *Sakhalin Island*, translated by Brian Reeve. London; One World Edition. 1993, 2007, 2014. (Throughout translations are from the 2007 edition).

Kennan, G. (1958). *Siberia and the Exile System*. Abridged from the first edition, 1891 (New York: Century). Chicago and London: Chicago University Press.

Laffitte, S. (1974). *Chekhov*. London: Readers Union/Angus Robertson.

Marmot, M. (2005). 'Social Determinants of Health Inequalities', *Lancet*, 365, 1099–104.

# CHAPTER 5
## THE CHASM OF SORROW

To the south of Aleksandrovsk, the long beach is interrupted by a headland, Cap Jonquière. Beyond, the beach and cliffs carry on as far as one can see to Douai and beyond. Just over the headland is a lighthouse. In Chekhov's time, it was high on the hill – lost in cloud for much of the time it has since been moved down the headland. Chekhov walked there, three or four miles and a decent climb for a man in his health – he needed to get away.

> The higher one rises the more free one breathes . . . it is only up here that one becomes aware how wearing and hard life is below. Day in, day out the hard-labourers undergo their punishment and those at liberty talk about who has been flogged. At one time, there had been benches on the path to the lighthouse, but they had taken way because convicts and settled exiles had carved filthy lampoons and obscenities in 'cabman's' language.' There are free lovers of this 'wall literature,' but in penal servitude the love letters are revolting. It is remarkable that a man will write on a bench even when feeling lost, abandoned and profoundly unhappy. (Chekhov, 1895: 104)

Standing in the lighthouse he looked out at the sea towards Siberia and way beyond to Russia: 'If I were a convict I would try to escape no matter what'.

One of Chekhov's aims was to see whether Sakhalin was viable as a colony, and his interests went beyond the prisons to all aspects of the island including, for instance, its climate and soil. At a house in Korsakovsk, just inland from Aleksandrovsk, was a meteorological station, owned by the Head of the Medical Department. He had gone one spring to represent Sakhalin at the Prison Exhibition in St Petersburg and never returned. The observations were taken on by a trusted convict.

Chekhov compared Sakhalin's weather with that of Cherepovetsk in Russia, where the climate was 'severe, damp and unfavourable to health'. The average temperature there through the year was +2.7, and in Sakhalin, +0.1. 'Winter [on Sakhalin] was more severe than in Archangel, and there was eternal frost in the Dukya Valley. Snow had fallen in July. There had been frost 181 days per year, 189 days of precipitation, with 107 of snow and 82 with rain. Over four summers from mid-May to September there had been 8 clear days'. With little subtlety Chekhov was suggesting that Sakhalin was not ideal for growing crops.

In Korsakovsk he heard that a small infirmary with fourteen syphilitics and three lunatics had just been closed by a young doctor. The place was so far behind civilization that he would not have been surprised 'if they had burned the lunatics on a bonfire by order of the prison doctors'. In one cabin, he saw a clean-shaven man in a jacket, an unstarched shirt and something resembling a tie – to all appearances a member of the privileged classes. 'Are you an officer?' 'No. your Excellency, I am a priest'. Another man, who had murdered his wife with a hammer on St Nikolai's Street in St Petersburg, asked Chekhov to have him assessed as a lunatic, so he could be shut up in a monastery. In the next settlement, where poverty was acute, was a well-worn path to the prisons at Voyevodsk and Douai used by women to sell themselves.

North of Aleksandrovsk, in Arkovo, where officially the soil was 'highly favourable to agriculture and where labour is rewarded with abundance', Chekhov found that the topsoil was only two inches of humus with subsoil of shingle on clay. In summer the roots fried, and in winter drowned. Some root crops were possible, though flash floods frequently washed them away. He saw squalor and hunger, despite the official tales of plenty,

> stunted sickly trees look down from up high on the bank, here out in the open each fights in isolation as cruel battle with the frost and cold winds and during the autumn and winter through long and dreadful nights each of them sways relentlessly from side to side, bends to the ground and creaks in lamentation, and this lamentation is heard by nobody. (Chekhov, 1895: 118)

He visited Douai, to the south and protected by cliffs two to three hundred feet high. There were two ways to Douai, along the beach or over the mountains. The first necessitated a tunnel through the headland which was dug 'without an engineer, with no forethought and as a result it has come out dark, crooked and dirty'. Chekhov was not impressed. The tunnel was costly and unnecessary, since the beach road was impassable every high tide.

> A wonderful expression of the Russian's tendency to waste his last resources on caprices, buffoonery and extravagances. They dug the

tunnel while the convicts were living in filthy damp yurts or dugouts because there were not enough people to build barracks.

The cliffs between Cap Jonquière and Douai are steep, with fossils, and occasionally a waterfall.

> screes can be seen on the steep sheer coastline. The strata of coal are squeezed between layers of sandstone, slaty clay, clayey slate, clayey sand which have been lifted, bent, moved or pushed down by seams of basalt, diorites and porphyry. It must be considered beautiful after its own fashion.

Chekhov hated Douai, 'a dreadful, hideous place, wretched in every respect, in which only saints or profoundly perverse people could live of their own free will. What inspired the administration to settle them here, in the cleft, is impossible to comprehend' (Chekhov, 1895: 123). Not counting the command, free population and prison there were 291 people, mostly convicts, and only forty-six householders, with six people per dwelling on average. In a single-roomed cabin, he found a family, a soldier's family, two or three convict tenants, as well as juveniles and babies. 'In the evening a convict returns, hungry and wants to sleep, but his wife starts to cry, "You've ruined us, damn you." "Give over howling," a soldier mutters. When most are sleeping, the woman listens to the roaring of the sea, tormented by melancholy. It was monotonously dismal and filthy . . .'

Some families lived in an old, long condemned building in 'cells' made of bed boards. He itemises the arrangements in one cell: a convict, his wife and two children; a convict, his wife and daughter; a convict; his wife and seven children; two convicts plus wives and two sons and a convict, his wife and four children; six families with sixteen children in one space. There was little for the women and children to do, so despite choosing to follow their husbands and fathers into penal servitude, they were neither valued nor respected.

Douai prison was smaller, older and dirtier than Aleksandrovsk, reeking of slops even in summer. It housed hardened criminals, for the most part 'their crimes no more cunning than their faces, dull and commonplace'.

> Terekhov, a grey-haired old man who gives off the impression of being a real villain, is kept in solitary confinement. It is said that he has murdered as many as sixty people. He would spy out new

arrivals, enticing the prisoners who were better off into escaping with him into the taiga, where he killed them and robbed them, cut them into pieces and threw them into the river to cover up his crime.

It is always quiet in Douai. The ear soon grows accustomed to the slow measured jangling of fetters, the thunder of the breakers on the sea and the humming of Telegraph wires, and because of these sounds the impression of dead silence grows still stronger. If somebody should unexpectedly burst out into loud laughter in the street it would sound harsh and unnatural. Right from its very foundation life here has taken a form which can be communicated only through hopeless and implacably cruel sounds, and the ferocious cold wind which on winter nights blows into the cleft from the sea is the only thing here which sings precisely the right note.

Because of this it always sounds weird when amidst the silence, there suddenly rings out the singing of the Douai idiot Shkandyb. He is a convict, an old man who from the very first day on his arrival on Sakhalin refused to work, and all measures of compulsion came to nothing in the face of his unconquerable, sheer wild animal obstinacy; they planted him in a dark punishment cell, and flogged him several times, but he would stoically endure the punishment, and after every flogging would cry out, 'And I'm still not going to work in spite of all that.' They spent a lot of effort and finally gave up. (Chekhov, 1895: 128ff)

Chekhov arrived at Douai's mine at 5.00 am. He realized that though conditions were appalling, they were no worse than in the Donetsk region of Ukraine. What was worse, though, was the petty officialdom, lack of organization and general insolence, injustice and arbitrariness, the squabbles, scandals, and obtuseness met every day by the convicts. 'They knew of nothing but the mine, the prison and the road between them'.

A mile or so to the north along the beach was a large fissure in the coast and here was the notorious Voyevodsk prison, the worst he saw, which even he seemed unable to describe in detail, except to christen it 'the Chasm of Sorrow'. Here were the wheelbarrow men, chained to heavy, wooden wheelbarrows night and day, for years on end, by hand, foot and waist, punishment reserved for the worst repeat offenders.

They live in common cells, with the other prisoners, in complete idleness. Each is shackled in hand and foot irons; from the middle of the hand irons stretches a long chain three or four arshins (1 arshin = 70 cm) long in length which is fastened to the bottom of the small wheelbarrow. The chains and the barrow hamper the prisoner; he tries to make as few movements as possible, and this undoubtedly has an effect on his musculature. The hands become so highly accustomed to every movement, even the slightest, being accompanied by the heaviness, that even after the prisoner has been separated from the barrow and hand irons, he still feels awkwardness in his arms for a long time and makes strong abrupt movements; when, for instance, he grabs a cup, he slops the tea all over the place. At night, whilst asleep, the prisoner keeps the barrow underneath the bed-board. (Chekhov, 1895: 135)

Each morning they got up from their bench and moved outside a few feet, to sit all day, before moving back to the bench. This went on back and forth, for day after day and year after year, a punishment which, extraordinarily, all but abolished movement itself. Though notorious, there were only ever around eight of them at any one time. Chekhov mentions one humane gesture even here in Voyevodsk – one of the wheelbarrow men was obviously dying of consumption, so had been moved closer to the fire.

The convicts at Douai and Voyevodsk all worked in the mine. He says that he knows little of this work, before documenting the organized corruption and poor conditions. A private company used convict labour free of charge and took the profits, while the costs of keeping convicts and guards were paid by the government. With faux naivety, he added that working all day underground prevented any of 'the corrective aspect of punishment'. The average productivity of each man was '10.8 poods per day; 4.2 poods less than the norm'. Given the conditions, their diet and general health, let alone morale and motivation, the output seems not too bad. Settled exiles also worked in the mines, at more difficult seams but with greater productivity. Hired workers were more profitable and some convicts even paid exiles or other convicts to work in their stead. This begs the question of how the mines should be organized. Though often reluctant to opine, here he was clear. If the mines on Sakhalin had a future it was with paid workers not convicts.

Inland of Aleksandrovsk, going northeast is a range of mountains and beyond these a plain, drained by the Tym River many times larger and more interesting than the one at Aleksandrovsk. The abundance of water, grass which grows higher than a human, the fabulous wealth of fish and coalfields would lead one to suppose a well fed and satisfied existence for a million people. But the cold currents and ice floes which drift by the east coast even in June testify with merciless clarity that when Nature created Sakhalin, the last thing she had in mind was mankind.

Here settlers lived, people who had spent five to ten years or more on Sakhalin, who after their hard labour in prison were now released as settled exiles, to build their homes and tend some land. The people lived as miserably as elsewhere. The climate was terrible, with nearly 300 days of precipitation per year and hoar frosts in August. When he was there in summer, the air was thick with mosquitoes. The settlements had few women – they kept the best in Aleksandrovsk and sent them only 'the leftovers'. He found despair to the point of paralysis, with an almost complete loss of initiative, action and hope. Though now exiled settlers, the householders were broken; able to do nothing, bored 'failures' who had tried everything to earn a crust, exhausted what strength they had, and given up. 'Enforced idleness and impotence had become habit and all they were able to do was play cards.' In one settlement, there were seventy-six men and twenty-five women, with no-one between the ages of fifteen and twenty. Despite living in poverty, he could find no workmen.

Further along was Derbinskoye, named in 'honour' of the prison governor.

> Derbin who was murdered by a prisoner for his cruelty was still young, but a harsh, stern and implacable man. According to the reminiscences of people acquainted with him he always walked around the prison and streets with a cane which he took with him for the sole purpose of striking people. He was murdered in the bakery. He struggled, fell into the kneading trough and stained the dough with blood. His death roused general rejoicing amongst the prisoners and they collected 60 roubles in small change for his murderer. (Chekhov, 1895: 143)

The town had around 1,000 people including guards and was one of the few places that looked like a settled, acceptable village. But Chekhov found that the earliest settlers and those with some money had taken the best land, while the rest who arrived later, around 50 per cent, were hungry, in rags and 'created the impression of being unnecessary, superfluous, not living and getting in the way'. One morning he saw a group of twenty convicts, in tatters, soaked through with rain, spattered in mud and shivering, frozen with cold. They were trying to show by acting that they were ill. It was one of only two times, the other being in the barracks for miners, that Chekhov thought that,

> the word 'pariah' came to mind, meaning the state of a human being below whom it is no longer possible to fall. During the entire period I was on Sakhalin, only in the settled exiles barracks by the mines, and here, were there moments when it seemed that I was seeing the extreme and utmost degree of human degradation, lower than which it is simply impossible to go. (Chekhov, 1895: 146)

Sakhalin had not been uninhabited before the Russian's arrived. Stone Age axes had been found as well as objects made of flint which itself is not found on the island. He met one of two tribes, the Gilyaks, nomads who lived in the north of the island, though he noted in diminishing numbers.

> round, flat moon shaped faces, yellowish in colour, unwashed, with high cheekbones, slanting eyes . . . a Gilyak's facial expression does not betray the savage in him; it is always intelligent, gentle and naively attentive. (Chekhov, 1895: 146)

They were lean and wiry, with powerful muscles. They were hunters, with a diet rich in fat, from seal, salmon, whale, meat and blood. They considered working the soil a great sin and thought that anyone who did would die.

He found them cheerful and not stand-offish and mentions, one suspects with enthusiasm, that they have no word for or even concept of 'senior' or 'junior'. In contrast their treatment of women was not so praiseworthy – they would fondle their dogs but never their womenfolk. Marriage was a 'mere trifle, of less importance than a drinking spree'.

General Kononovich told Chekhov that he wished to Russify the Gilyaks. Chekhov could not understand:

> Why I do not know. Proximity to a prison will only corrupt. There is hardly any possibility of making them understand that convicts are

hunted, deprived of freedom, wounded and sometimes killed not for a whim but in the interests of justice. (Chekhov, 1895: 170)

Elsewhere he found childless settlements, forty men living without a single woman, settlers from towns and cities expected to grow crops without any practical experience of farming, and people from vastly different ethnic and religious backgrounds – and different languages – thrown together with no thought of their cohesion. In some places, nothing was safe from thieves – cattle, potatoes and even window frames were ripped out. 'All this drains the households and hardly less important keeps them in a constant state of fear . . . The conditions of life speak of nothing but poverty'.

Despite the despair, Chekhov was even-handed enough to praise where he could. At Rykovo, on the eastern side, was the best prison on the island. The clerks, cooks and bakers were well trained, the place spotless and even the overseers were not so 'overfed, sublimely stupid and coarse as those as Aleksandrovsk or Douai'. The latrines worked, the prison was warm and without the usual smell. It was a shame therefore that the prison governor had a 'rapturous delight in corporal punishment' and 'a constant thoughtfulness for people and birch rods'. Rykovo as a settlement might sustain 200 people, but there were over 500, and every year, with little planning, more hordes arrived.

Punishment and hard labour and its opposite, the broken, hopeless impotence of settlers, were equally shocking. Chekhov knew the relation between these two and expected his readers to as well. Convicts endured years of hard labour, their whole lives controlled and regimented as they were flogged and crowded together day and night. After that, ten years on or so, exhausted and broken, they were set free to fend largely for themselves, to build a house, clear land, grow crops, scrape by, with little support or instruction and for the most part without a partner. As the governor general had told him, 'hard labour does not begin in "hard labour," but in settled exile afterwards'.

## Reference

Chekhov, A. (1895). *Sakhalin Island*, translated by Brian Reeve. London; One World Edition. 1993, 2007, 2014. (Throughout translations are from the 2007 edition).

# CHAPTER 6
## SOUTH

On 10 September, Chekhov boarded the Baikal steamer again and sailed to the south of the island. He had bumped, starved and frozen his way across Siberia and then spent two months researching the prisons and settlements in and around Aleksandrovsk. He was exhausted and jaded. 'I was leaving with great pleasure and felt I needed fresh impressions' (Chekhov, 1895: 171). Note Chekhov's use of the first person and, arguably, the understatement. Though the eyes behind all in the book, he only rarely identifies himself. Here he relates a brief episode on the boat where he can relax, and where he feels able to use the first-person pronoun.

The ship sailed at 10.00 pm. He went past The Three Brothers, which looked in the darkness like 'monks in black habits' and past Cap Jonquière, the roaring waves 'in which could be heard an impotent and malicious boredom' (Chekhov, 1895: 171). Then he passed the lights of Voyevodsk and Douai for the last time. There remained only the dusk and 'a sinister sensation as if after an ominous bad dream'. He went below to a sound he had probably not heard for months, laughter.

There was a group in the wardroom including the wife of a naval officer with 'an enviable disposition. . . who would go off into fits of the most unaffected, bubbling and joyous laughter'. It was infectious, and Chekhov details how he and everyone else joined in. 'Most probably never at any other time in the Tatar Straight, usually so angry and threatening, have people laughed so much'. It carried on the next morning on deck. How he needed that laughter and to forget, even for a few minutes, Sakhalin.[1]

He loved to chat, concealing his genius with a love of gossip and of teasing, jokiness and, of course, flirting. Bunin recollects,

He was very humorous and loved laughter, but he only laughed his charming infectious laugh when somebody else had made a joke: he himself would say the most amusing things without the slightest smile. He delighted in jokes, in absurd nicknames, and in mystifying people. . . . His letters too, though their form is perfect, are full of delightful humour. (Bunin, 2007: 58)

How difficult it must have been on Sakhalin without jokes or wit or irreverence. This brief interlude on board ship, of gossip, fun and laughter, was a much-needed escape, even though he soon found the irrepressibly garrulous woman a trial. This episode was irrelevant to his aim of reporting conditions on the island, but Chekhov could not prevent himself from writing about human life, and this short period of relative normality, for him as for the reader, acts as an interval from the penal colony and its deprivations. Though such interludes are not often to be found in strictly medical theses, he was unable to completely repress his first-person perspective and narrative.

As he sailed down the west coast of Sakhalin he looked across with renewed perspective. The weather was calm and, without settlements, there was space – it even seemed easier to breathe. Lower Sakhalin was level with France, he wrote, and but for the cold currents and weather would be delightful. As he continued his journey he saw no sign of wheat having been sown, even though the warmer climate might support it, in contrast to the 'arctic wastes' of the north where the crops were sown and then failed regularly. The grass was bright green and looked juicy and succulent, and yet there were no settlements. They passed a small village where he learned that some Japanese workers, under a Scottish manager, made a good living from selling seakale to the Chinese for the business's Russian owner. He does not need to make the obvious comparison with the misery he has just left to the north. Nor does he comment further on the foreign workers.

The steamer went past the tip of the island and then turned north into a large bay – Sakhalin being shaped like a fish, they were heading for the base of its two tail fins. Chekhov notes a beautiful water meadow, velvety grass and a red lighthouse 'like an aristocrat's dacha'. He disembarked at Korsakovsk, coming ashore on a whaleboat when, unlike Aleksandrovsk 'joyous voices were heard'.

The town had 'glossy new wooden buildings gleaming in the sunshine and a shining white church in beautiful, old simple style'. That night he dined with the district governor. Afterwards he walked down the main street to the police secretary's, where he stayed the night. As he approached he heard loud laughter and joined his host, together with the inspector of agriculture and the prison governor, in a few drinks. The atmosphere was far more relaxed than up north. Things were looking up.

The next day, despite a storm, he explored. On the jetty lay the skeleton of a young whale 'once merry, frisky and sporting over the northern seas, but now the white bones of this Hercules lay in the mud, and the rain gnawed away at them'. He writes of streetlamps, laid-out trees and pavements swept by an elderly man with 'an identifying tattoo'. Reeve explains, in a footnote, that up to the eighteenth century convicts had been branded and then from 1845 tattooed. This was abolished in 1863, but Chekhov is drawing attention to the fact that men carried the mark of punishment from thirty to forty years previously – they had spent most of their lives in hard labour and exile (Chekhov, 1895: 178). Life in the south appeared more settled and peaceful, though he also found it more conservative, with more floggings. Money and work were more easily found too, though the women still sold themselves.

He met some 'interesting personalities'. A clerk in the police department was tall, lean, handsome with a big beard, hard-working and very polite though withdrawn. He had flayed his wife to death with a whip while she was pregnant for a premarital affair with a Turk. The Giacommini family had all been exiled. The elder had walked across with his daughter who died on the way. His young son had gone by sea and arrived three years earlier. As ever, Chekhov has an eye for human stories, and for the telling points that lie behind them.

He surveyed the prison and surrounding settlements, itemizing the numbers and genders of inhabitants. Whereas in Aleksandrovsk prison workshops and living quarters were found throughout the post, in Korsakovsk the prison was separate from the town. It had 450 inmates when he was there, with most convicts, 1,205 in all, working outside, mostly on the roads. The town was behind the times, with no telegraph or meteorological station to give him records of the weather.

The other settlements were comparatively small and relatively self-sufficient compared with those in the north. He wrote of an exile 'saving his soul in a dugout', spending his entire time in prayer. An old woman in one settlement had killed her baby, burying it alive, thinking for some reason that her sentence might be less. She wept relating this to Chekhov, and then asked if he wanted to buy some pickled cabbage.

There was more prosperity than in the north, which he put down not only to the climate and soil but also to the governance, with the villages less overcrowded 'the fewer households the better and the longer a street the poorer it will be'. One village, Solovyovka, had the best site of all on Sakhalin, beside the sea and near a fishing stream; its people – thirty-four men and thirty-four women – sold cows and milk as well as raising crops.

Despite continuing the survey and his visits to settlements, the book's section in the south is less intense. It is as though he was seeing more of the same, and though important, it was no longer either novel or shocking to him. Chekhov's stamina was ebbing, something he himself admitted:

I had grown either tired or lazy, and in the south, I certainly did not work as hard as in the north. Often, I would spend whole days on walks, outings and picnics [including with Japanese], and no longer felt any desire to go round the cabins; so, when they obligingly offered me assistance I did not turn it down. (Chekhov, 1895: 186)

In four weeks he still filled in around 1,300 census cards, though this is a slower rate than before. One settlement was described as boring to look at, with boring people. He asked a settler if he was married. The man replied, with more boredom 'I was married, but I murdered her'.

On the whole, the men were younger, healthier and more cheerful than up north. They were convicts with shorter sentences who had served their time and were less worn out, and so more able to build their lives as settlers and less likely to try to escape. There was less poverty and better houses, with roofing with boards rather than straw or tree bark. But, as in the Tym area, the number of women was small, and many were old and sick. Officials complained that they kept the younger, healthier ones for themselves in Aleksandrovsk.[2] He discusses one special feature of the settlements of the south – suicide by the poison aconite.[3] Every few pages a wife or penniless gambler seems to have taken it.

In Mitzulka, he met the daughter of settled exile Nikolayev, Tanya, a native of the Pskov Province.

She is 16 years old, blonde, slender and her features are delicate, soft and tender. She has already been promised in marriage to an overseer. Whenever you drove through Mitzulka, she would be sitting at the window thinking. And what a young, beautiful girl who has finished up on Sakhalin can possibly think of, and what she dreams about, God only knows. (Chekhov, 1895: 189)

At a nearby new settlement, with poor soil 'There are fifteen inhabitants. Women; nil'. In another with some agricultural land, there were fifty-five men and thirty-six women. Only one free woman had travelled with her husband 'uncorrupted by prison' and, alas, she had recently been imprisoned for murdering him. The land, though, was worth 'both northern districts put together'. He mentions an ex-forger happily making a living hunting sable. Further along another settlement was on good land, with thirty fit young men. But the authorities in Aleksandrovsk had not given them any tools – in the end the prison gave them some old axes.[4] Even then they did not receive cattle for several years.

In one place he had dinner with officials, served by an old convict. When he was clumsy his host 'Yelled at him, "You blithering idiot." I glanced at this meek old man and the thought came to me that the only thing a Russian intellectual had succeeded in doing with penal servitude had been to reduce it, in the most banal and vulgar manner, to serfdom' (Chekhov, 1895: 196). For Chekhov, grandson of a serf, this was as base as one could go. He reached a post at an estuary on the east shore.

> The roaring sea is cold and colourless, and the tall grey waves pound upon the sand as if wishing to say, 'Oh God, why did you create us.' On this shore convicts can be heard at building work, while on the other far distant imagines shore lies America, to the left the capes of Sakhalin are visible in mist, while all around there is not a single living soul. Not a bird, not a fly and it is beyond comprehension who the waves are roaring for. Who listens to them at night? What do they want and who will they roar for when I am gone? (Chekhov, 1895: 197)

Remember a similar passage from *The Lady with the Dog*, written in 1899, before Sakhalin 'the monotonous hollow sound of the sea rising up from below, spoke of the peace, of the eternal sleep awaiting us . . . it will sound as indifferently and monotonously when we are all no more'. His poetic imagination here summoned on Sakhalin.

In the last chapter of this section, chapter 14 in *Sakhalin Island*, Chekhov considered groups he had not focussed on before. In 1868 a group of 101 voluntary settlers from Ukraine were lured there with a promise of two years' flour and meal, and cattle, equipment and money on credit, together with twenty years' exemption from tax and military service. They arrived in the winter, supplies were late, and the men never recovered. Failed harvests and then a flood in 1875 drove all but three to leave. Chekhov was uncertain whether to blame the soil and conditions, the incompetence of the officials or the lack of stamina of the Ukrainians.

The native population of southern Sakhalin were known as 'Aino', which meant 'a person' in their language. The men were dark and handsome 'like

Gypsies' with large bushy beards; the women in contrast he found hideous and even repulsive, with narrow eyes and coarse features, slovenly clothing and 'an expression of senility'. Despite this, they were gentle, modest, good natured, trusting, communicative and courteous, and some were even considered, by a Dr Rollen, to have been 'cultured and intelligent'. They hated deception and violence – Chekhov described how a group fled when threatened with birching. Despite a lack of war or epidemic their numbers had fallen by half in thirty years or so, though no one knew, or perhaps cared, why.

Last, Chekhov briefly mentions the Japanese occupation of the southern part of Sakhalin. The island is only around 50 kilometres from Hokkaido, the northernmost of Japan's main islands. Sakhalin had only been Russian since 1875 – before that the southern third had been settled by Japan from the beginning of the nineteenth century, having been inhabited by the Aino alone before that. Initially, it seemed the Japanese were no more certain of their right to Sakhalin than the Russians and went only in the summer for fish. This was very profitable, so that when the Russians settled in the north of the island, Japan was concerned it might lose its fisheries. In 1867 a treaty recognized both countries' claim to part of the island though then, in 1875, Sakhalin became Russian with Japan taking the Kuril Islands as compensation.

In truth, this last part of the book is a little dull and lacks the urgency of the north. Fortunately, in the remaining chapters, Chekhov abandons his travelogue to consider 'the particularities, both significant and insignificant, which go up to make the life of the colony at the present time'. This was his chance to demolish the official justifications for the penal settlement, and in his own careful way, point out why Sakhalin could never be a successful colony.

He returned to Russia by boat, missing Japan because of a cholera scare, but stopping off at Hong Kong, where he admired the order established by the British, despite their colonialism. It is not clear that Chekhov was against colonialism per se, or if he thought this was enlightened colonisation. As we will see, apart from the human degradation on Sakhalin, he doubted its suitability in terms of climate, ecology, etc.

He was in Sri Lanka for fifty-eight hours – enough time for a liaison with a local girl and for him and a midshipman to each buy a male mongoose. Chekhov was so enamoured that he went back for another, and was sold a 'female', which was actually a civet or palm cat.[5] He then continued across the Indian Ocean. During this voyage he would drape a line behind the boat, dive into the water and then swim back to catch the line as the ship sailed past (Finke, 2021: 87). The ship then went through the Red Sea and Suez Canal before returning through the Mediterranean and Black Sea. He was moved by Mt Sinai, despite being an unbeliever. From Odessa he took the express train to Moscow, with the animals and somewhat bizarrely, the chief priest from Sakhalin, Father Irakli. The excitement of the journey was over, and he had just about survived. Now was the time to write, once he had recovered. Before that though he needed to return to society and have some fun.

## Notes

1. Though he soon became tired of her 'laughing and jabbering'. Letter to Suvorin, 11 September 1890 in Heim and Karlinsky, 1973: 171).

2. The percentage of women from the census cards is Aleksandrovsk 40 per cent of the total, Tym 32 per cent and Korsakovsk 26 per cent, so there were significant differences. This does not include the prison populations who were exclusively male.

3. Monkshood or wolfsbane, the 'Queen of all Poisons', has been used on arrow tips. Its active ingredient, aconitine, a sodium channel blocker, causes cardiac arrhythmias and is also a nerve toxin. It was apparently used by ancient Romans as a method of execution.

4. Reeve suggests this was to refute the official line that settled exiles were supplied with 'the machines, tools, apparatus and materials necessary . . .' (Chekhov, 1895: 378).

5. Once at home the mongoose was badly behaved, and the palm cat savage. Though initially amused by their anarchy, describing the mongoose as being better than dachshunds 'a mixture of rat and crocodile, tiger and monkey', they became so unruly and destructive that in the end, despite Chekhov's dislike of the place, they had to be given to Moscow Zoo.

## References

Bunin, I. (2007). *About Chekhov*. Evanston, IL: Northwestern University Press.

Chekhov, A. (1895). *Sakhalin Island*, translated by Brian Reeve. London; One World Edition. 1993, 2007, 2014. (Throughout translations are from the 2007 edition).

Finke, M. (2021). *Freedom from Violence and Lies. Anton Chekhov's Life and Writings*. London: Reaktion.

Heim, M. and Karlinsky, S. (1973). *Letters of Anton Chekhov*. New York, and London; Harper and Row.

# PART III
## WRITING UP

# CHAPTER 7
## THESIS ASSEMBLED

In the last nine chapters of *Sakhalin Island* Chekhov moved from travelogue and reportage to more measured observations on the island and its future, which were clearly written with reflection on his return. This part of the book has a series of headings: women and children, hunting, fishing and farming, morality, medicine, diet and soldiers. They may seem unconnected, but he was martialling evidence against Sakhalin as a viable penal colony.

He began this section with a consideration of the aims behind the settling of Sakhalin. In addition to society's revenge, and instilling fear and correction, was the small matter of building a colony, and incarceration – he suggested – was counterproductive to this; prison did not work,

> life in communal cells reduces a prisoner to the condition of a serf, makes him degenerate, stifle[s] the instincts of a permanently settled man and domesticated householder; his health declines, he grows old and weakens morally, and the later he leaves prison the more reasons to fear he will not turn out an active, useful member of the colony. (Chekhov, 1895: 212)

This was why, he said, the Statutes on Exiles mentioned reducing sentence time, especially for harder working convicts, though it was not clear this ever happened. Women convicts lived outside the prison in cabins – Chekhov thought some of the men should too.

He quoted (official) statistics that in January 1890 there were 5,905 convicts on the island, with 36 per cent sentenced to under eight years, 26 per cent eight to twelve, 13 per cent to twelve to fifteen years, 12 per cent to fifteen to twenty years and 7 per cent life. There were 424 convict households living off the land, and 908 people living in the colony as wives and cohabitants. He thought the average age of a criminal was thirty-five, making them well over forty when released, too old to begin colony life.[1] Twenty-three per cent of convicts lived outside the prison without this being a problem. Why were the remaining 77 per cent inside?

the colony would be the gainer if, on his arrival, every convict regardless of sentence, was immediately set to work to build a cabin for himself and his family, and begin his colonising activity as early as possible, while he was relatively young and healthy. (Chekhov, 1895: 214)

He was also very critical of the location of settlements. Sites were chosen by officials with little or no practical experience. In 1888 Governor Kononovich, concerned that Aleksandrovsk and Tymovsk were becoming overcrowded, had ordered parties of convicts and overseers to choose new sites. But they proved no better than the previous officials, with poor locations chosen again and again. The authorities would send 50 to 100 householders to a fresh site, and then add scores more each year, despite no one knowing how many people the land would support.

He calculated that the ratio of men to women was 100 to 53 for those in cabins. If one considered the prisoners and unmarried soldiers 'who have natural requirements to be satisfied', the ratio falls to 100/25. While poor, he accepted it was not low for a penal colony, predisposed as they were towards men. It was also better than Siberia, which at that time was 100/10. More recently, he observed, in addition to female prisoners and prostitutes, free wives and their children were much more common thanks to passage on the Russian Fleet. The problems lay in their uneven distribution through the island.

He was warmly disposed to convict women (who made up 11.5 per cent of the total number of convicts). Since they were, on the whole, young and spirited he seemed to suggest they were very good for the colony. His attitude to their crimes though, at best, has reflected his times. Their sentences were for 'offences of a romantic nature or connected to their families . . . sacrifices to love and family, rather than murderers. Even those sentenced for arson were, in essence, suffering the penalties of love, lured by their lovers into crime'. So, they were either under the control of their hormones or of their men, and arguably not wholly culpable for their actions. His attitude to prostitution was also, at best, of his time. He condemned it in Sakhalin repeatedly, especially of course for children and young girls, though that did not stop him using brothels both on the way out and on the way back.

Chekhov studied how women's status had changed over the lifetime of the colony. Fifteen to twenty years before, convict women entered a brothel, unless 'not worthy of men's favour' in which case they were either 'in the kitchen, or drank themselves silly'. He described how one settlement asked for 'cattle for the supply of milk, and women to set up households with', in that order. 'Local practice has evolved its way of regarding the female prisoner; not exactly a human being, not exactly a creature lower than domestic animals, but somewhere in between'.

> These days when a party of women arrives in Aleksandrovsk they are first of all solemnly conducted from the landing stage to the prison, the women bent under the weight of bundles and knapsacks, plod along the highway, listless and still not having regained their senses from seasickness, while there follows behind them, like after the clowns at a fair, a whole crowd of women and men, children and people attached to the government offices. The picture resembles a herring run, when behind the fish follow hordes of whales, seals, and dolphins wanting to regale themselves on herring full of roe. The countrymen along with several exiles follow the crowd with honest simple thoughts, they need a housewife. (Chekhov, 1895: 227)

Chekhov described courtship:

> At Korsakovsk Post the newly arrived women are lodged in a special barrack hut. The District Governor and Inspector of Prisons decide which settled exiles and peasants deserve a woman, (those of good conduct etc.). They arrive on a certain day, (in their best clothes), and wander around the bed boards, and every so often glance in silence at the women. Each man chooses, wishing to surmise which is a good housewife. She asks if he has a samovar, and what his cabin is roofed with . . . She asks, 'and you won't ill treat me?' (Chekhov, 1895: 228–9)

He quoted a settler: 'There is no point women being sent here in autumn, and not in spring, there is nothing for them to do in winter . . . only an extra mouth'. That is the way people discuss workhorses, Chekhov adds.

Yet it worked both ways. Being in the minority, a woman had some power too and, for some, life was better on Sakhalin that in European Russia. 'There they endured insolence and beatings; in exile the men feel compassion and take care of them. If a woman comes his way, he may hold on tight and honour her'. Though, a general added, 'that does not stop her going about with bruises'. She could also leave a man who mistreated her. There could be tenderness too 'love in its purest and most attractive form is no stranger'. An insane epileptic convict woman was looked after by her cohabitee, another convict, like a conscientious nurse. Chekhov asked if she was a burden. 'No, your excellence, I do it out of humanity'. One settled exile's cohabitant was without the use of her legs and lay in rags in the middle of the room. Chekhov suggested it would be more convenient if she was in hospital. The convict would have none of it, again citing humanity.

Chekhov describes the types of family, with some 'good, middle of the road types', but also cohabitation, with intimacy but without affection – people sharing a cabin and each other mechanically and impersonally as they clung on as best they could, strangers under one roof. 'In such situations, the man may respect his cohabitant's prostitution as a way to earn extra food'.

There were also curious bureaucratic anomalies. Women convicts received a prisoner's rations, even though they lived outside. Once her convict's sentence was served the woman became a settled exile and then received no clothing or food support. The real hard labour began when their prison sentence was over, as we have heard.

Chekhov noted how hard it was for a woman on arrival, whatever her status. 'Free women came out of love, shame, or duty', or because the authorities had lied about conditions on Sakhalin. They were not well received, shocked by conditions into 'total stupefaction', and often hungry until they found their feet. Female convicts escaped prison and cohabited, often against their will, but at least they had prisoners' rations. Free women had no such luxury. They had to share their husband's ration and since he was imprisoned, they had to find somewhere to live as well. As we have heard, he also uncovered wildly differing distributions of women throughout Sakhalin. Chekhov shows, though does not say, that since the aim of the whole project was to build a colony to rival Australia or Guyana, such treatment of its women defied logic as well as humanity.

He was particularly concerned about children and counted them all – 2,122 under fifteen, 644 from European Russia and 1,473 born on Sakhalin or on the way. Of those born there, 203 were under one year old, 45 were aged nine to ten and 11 were aged fifteen to sixteen. Though some settlements had none, overall Sakhalin had a high proportion of children, 25 per cent under the age of fourteen. Though on their arrival a new mouth to feed was not always welcomed, overall children were extraordinarily important:

> Each new human being is not received cordially in the family; they do not sing lullabies over the baby cradle, but only sinister lamentations. The fathers and mothers say that there is nothing to feed the children

with, that they will never learn anything worthwhile on Sakhalin and the best thing would be if the merciful Lord took them as soon as possible. If a child cries or if it is naughty they holler at it venomously: 'Shut up and why didn't you snuff it'.

But whatever people say, however much they wail about it, the most useful, the most necessary, and the most delightful people on Sakhalin are the children, and the exiles themselves understand this well and value them highly.

They inject an element of tenderness, purity, gentleness and joy . . . Sole thing that saves them from despair and terminal decline. In spite of their own purity, they love their depraved mother and robber father more than anything else in the world, and if an exile who has become a stranger to kindness in a prison is moved by the affection of a dog, then what value the love of a small child must have for him! (Chekhov, 1895: 245)

Orphaned children were also adopted by childless couples (Chekhov, 1895: 403). He found that of those living as families, 860 were legal and 782 'free', so that around 'half the population enjoy family life. All the women are taken, so the remainder are all single men'. He is not critical of the free families but rather seeks to explain 'unlawful relations'. When sentenced a convict lost all rights, and ceased to exist for his family, as if dead. Despite this his marital rights remained with his partner, so he needed a divorce before he could remarry. This was not simple, with letters going between Sakhalin and a man's wife back home. And, as Chekhov says, the old wives left by their wayward men would not always agree to him taking another wife. 'Remarry, at his age; the old dog'.

Legalized marriages were a luxury, and 'weddings [usually] frugal and tedious!' though they could be merry and boisterous 'when Ukrainians were involved'. At each wedding the government issued a free bottle of spirits. In Aleksandrovsk, he went to a wedding.

In the church the chandelier was lit, and the choristers were awaiting the bridal pair. Women, convicts and free people glanced impatiently at the door and whispered. Suddenly somebody waved his hand and hissed: 'They're coming!' The choristers cleared their throats. A crowd flooded in through the door, followed by the young couple: a convict typesetter, about 25, in a jacket with a starched collar curled up at the corners and a white tie, and a female convict, three or four years older, in a dark-blue dress with white lace and a flower in her hair. The best men, who were also typesetters, wore white ties, too. A cloth was spread out over the carpet; the groom stepped on it first. Father Yegor entered from the sanctuary and leafed interminably through a small book on the lectern. 'Blessed be our god . . .' he proclaimed, and the wedding commenced. When the priest placed the crowns on the bride and grooms' heads and asked God to crown them with glory and honour, the women wore expressions of deep emotion and joy. They seemed to have forgotten that the ceremony was taking place in a prison church in a penal labour settlement, far, far from home. But soon enough, after the church had emptied, and the candles had been snuffed out, it all grew melancholy again. We went out into the porch. Rain. (Chekhov, 1895: 268–9)

The birth rate was a little higher than the rest of Russia, 49.8 per 100. 'Hunger, captivity, homesickness, none eliminates reproductive capacity'. He put it down to 'idleness, the monotony of life, enforced staying at home when there is no seasonal work and with sexual instincts the only entertainment, and the fact that most women are of reproductive age'.

Though a delight, the children were not healthy:

The children are pale, emaciated and sluggish, dressed in rags and always hungry and die of alimentary tract illnesses . . . a diet of swedes, cold, damp . . . The poorest families had food subsidies till they were 15, and children also had a grant of a few roubles. But this rarely ends up with the family or the child and should have been abolished. It just makes people think the children are well provided for. (Chekhov, 1895: 247)

Despite everything, boys would still be boys, playing at soldiers and convicts. He asked one, 'What's your father's middle name?' 'Dunno'. 'You live with your father . . .?' 'E's not my real one'. 'Is your mother married or widowed?' 'A widow, she came because of him. She murdered 'im.'

Though there were lots of children, he found only 185 between the ages of fifteen and nineteen, 2 per cent of the total, and only twenty-seven of those were born on the island. Nearly all were children of well-off peasants in exile and would leave when they could. He mentions one, Maris, by name, who 'will soon be gone with her husband. Of those born on Sakhalin

20 years ago, not one is left' (Chekhov, 1895: 239). There had been few women in the colony at a time when those children would have been born, but, asking around, he found that the main reason was that later, once their parents had served their sentence and could leave the island for Siberia, they did so, taking their teenaged sons and daughters with them. Teenagers also left without their parents. So grim were conditions on Sakhalin and so pervasive its atmosphere that any young adult who could leave, did so – anywhere else was better. Chekhov shows that the colony was completely failing to keep its next generation.

In a long passage in his footnotes, he makes farsighted suggestions of how to help children on the island. He suggests an abolition of any means test for their benefits, the use of food subsidies for children and pregnant women, and for those suckling. He wanted it given to them directly 'in their hands', to avoid men stealing it. He suggested tearooms for children and mothers, presumably to allow not only nutrition but a kinder social environment. He wanted philanthropists from Russia to have direct information about the Sakhalin children they are supporting. Last, presciently, he did not want the police involved (Chekhov, 1895: 402–3).

Chekhov's sarcasm is scarcely concealed when discussing agriculture. 'This concept has achieved success, [for] the island continues to be called an agricultural one. Ploughing and sowing is carried out each year and the areas of crops expanded as more people come'. 'Some consider it a success', he continues, 'others less so, with the former having no knowledge'. The clear majority of officials were completely unfamiliar with farming, and would not trust those who did know – the exiles (Chekhov, 1895: 249).[2] Presaging Stalinist five-year plans, to oblige the authorities, settlers exaggerated and lied, bringing their best crops to experts who then proclaimed excellent crop yields, with forty-fold yields. But the governor general knew that Sakhalin could never be a sustainable agricultural colony. Oats and wheat had ripened only once in the colony's history and barley twice, with pitiful yields. Vegetables grew better, though that meant people existed on swede all winter. 'Yet exiles continue to plough and sow, the administration continues to hand out grain on credit. The psychology behind such contradictions is totally incomprehensible' (Chekhov, 1895: 250). Sakhalin could never be self-sufficient for crops.

Taking his cue from the Gilyaks he describes hunting, of fox, sable, deer, otter, lynx and even Siberian tiger (though he estimates that there are no more than 200 left) and bears. 'Formerly the bear did not harm people or domestic animals and was considered peaceful. Since the exiles settled in upper reaches of the river and cut down the woods, and so reduced their food, a new cause of death has appeared, "mauled by a bear". There were vast numbers of game – duck, grouse, Capercaillie, curlew, woodcock – as well as other birds such as nightingales, thrushes, tits and siskins. He observed how wolves kept away from settlements – having never seen domesticated animals they were fearful (Chekhov, 1895: 408).

Hunting, though, could not sustain the island. Instead, he thought:

The major future wealth of Sakhalin lies in fish. The salmon run is extraordinary; in summer the river is boiling with fish. They enter the river healthy and strong but then are worn out going upstream and by sexual urge and hunger. The torments of the fish during its period of love are called migration to death . . . irresistible bouts of erotic attraction leading to one's demise.

Not just salmon. The herring run in the sea off Sakhalin was stupendous, with whales, seagulls, albatross and sea lions following in its wake. Fishing, then, could be the future, except that convicts had no idea how to do it. He suggests a good start would be to move towns from their random unsuitable sites closer to rivers and the sea. He mentions that any Russian fishermen would have to compete with Japanese fishermen and whalers, who either pay for permits or do it illegally. Seeing how much better free men were at work he foresees that if fishing is taken up properly, then 'exiles will be seen as a burden and that the state with find it more profitable to use free workers and call a halt to the process of exile. Fish shall constitute the prosperity of Sakhalin, but not of the exile colony'. Even if the island could be made profitable, it would not be as a penal colony.

Food receives short consideration in the main text. Chekhov relates how terrible the bread is, except that baked for the prison authorities. Convicts had meat and fish only in soups, with the fish full of bones and tasteless. They lined up with their bowls and ate sitting on the ground or in cells. Settlers were given an allowance from the state for two to three years (officially at least), with the staple food potatoes, with added swede and turnips. Meat was so infrequent as to be 'not worth mentioning'. Any milk from a house cow was sold rather than drunk. Everyone prized money more than food or health – money might eventually allow them to move to the mainland. They thought they would recover their health once away from Sakhalin.

In a long passage in the footnotes, he goes into details, from a medical report, on the ratios for prisoners in terms of protein, fats and carbohydrates per day (Chekhov, 1895: 414). The Director of Central Prisons had suggested in 1887 that it would be possible to reduce the costs of food 'without detriment to the nourishment of the organism'. An eminent professor reported that this might be awkward without knowing the conditions prisoners lived and worked under, and not knowing how much food they were actually given. But he still thought it possible to reduce the amount of expensive meat. The doctors on Sakhalin, however, 'rose to the height of their calling', and said that given the prisoners' conditions, hard labour and the appalling climate, the present allowances and the eminent professor's recommendation, were both inadequate. Chekhov wrote that the resulting dossier on ration tables contains 'twenty of the most varied reports memoranda and statements and deserves to closely studied by all those interested in prison hygiene'.

He thought prisoners' clothing was adequate. They were issued with a heavy cloth overcoat and a sheepskin jacket each year, which was better than their guards, whose uniform had to last for three. But at least the guards had better sanitary conditions and bedding, and could dry out in bad weather, convicts had to sleep in wet rotting clothes.

Chekhov reminds us that Sakhalin is a 'corrective' colony and that church and schools were some of the main means for this. Though religion is all but absent from the book, Chekhov was generous in his description of the churches' work. He explained that Sakhalin was part of a larger eparchy of the Bishop of Kamchatka, Kuril Islands and Blagoveshchensk, stretching over the whole of the eastern part of Siberia, and that when bishops visited Sakhalin they 'endure[d] the same hardships as priests'. There had been 'stone laying ceremonies, consecrations of buildings, and addresses to exiles with words of comfort and hope. Faith and repentance was to be found in many exiles'. He reminded us that the purpose of prisons, apart from punishment, was the stimulation of moral righteousness so that convicts did not fall into total despair. It is clear that Chekhov had not found this second purpose uppermost in the authorities' minds. But he does observe that the priests – unusually – always treated exiles as human beings.

Father Simeon Kazanshy, Priest Simon, for instance, 'wandered for years through the island, even without roads, on sledges, boats, on foot, getting frozen, snowbound, tormented by mosquitoes and bears, bathing in cold water. He was an excellent companion to officials and soldiers, a legendary figure'. There were four parish churches at Aleksandrovsk, Douai, Rykovo and Korsakovsk, each with a priest. Some convicts were known to fast at Lent and attend church services, though given their rations and conditions this can hardly have helped their health. But unskilled convicts did not usually go – on days off they rested or hunted for berries. Chekhov went to a church service in Aleksandrovsk, in the front were prison officials, then soldiers and overseers, free women, soldiers' and overseers' wives, and then at the back some settled exiles. He asked if a convict with a shaved head could attend – no one answered. Settled exiles could receive communion, get married and baptize their children in church if they lived close to one, if not then priests would travel. The church seemed to offer what respite it could from the hell.

Chekhov went to a burial:

> The freshly dug grave was a quarter full of water. The grave-diggers puffed and panted, their faces covered with sweat, carrying on a loud conversation that had nothing to do with the burial as they dug. When the hole was deep enough, the convicts lugged a shoddy box made of unpainted boards to the edge of the grave. 'Well?' said one. They lowered the coffin swiftly. It squelched as it landed in the water, and shook as the convicts shovelled lumps of clay onto its lid, the water splashing as they continued talking about some business of their own. (Chekhov, 1895: 270)

Chekhov described five schools on Sakhalin, (not counting one with 222 children but no teacher). They were poor and precarious, and directed by an official 'who is king but does not rule'. Teaching was done by exiles who were cheaper than qualified teachers. He found 29 per cent of males were literate (adults and children), but only 9 per cent of females, all of whom were at school. He was not impressed.

The guards were no better – they even corrupted the convicts. Rather than simply condemning, he details the guards' miserable conditions and overwork. He counts 1,548 lower-ranking soldiers on the island and suggests that all were working far beyond their physical and intellectual ability.[3] The Sakhalin soldier was 'meek, taciturn, obedient and sober as well as coarse, mentally underdeveloped and inarticulate'. It is from these that the next rank up, the overseers, were taken, with predictable consequences. Prison overseers were frequently fined or dismissed for theft, dereliction of duty, lack of intellectual ability, receiving stolen goods, selling on of kit and romantic liaisons. Such people, he thought, who were brutal, hard drinking, played cards with convicts and enjoyed 'the love and alcohol of female convicts' could possess 'a negative kind of authority'. They were promoted without any idea of what they should be doing.

The 'educated classes' were arguably even worse off. 'Punishing one's fellows, being able to suppress disgust, the remoteness, derisory salary, boredom, constant proximity of shaved heads, shackles, executioners . . . and, most of all, consciousness of one's powerlessness in the struggle with encircling evil; all have made service exceptionally arduous and unattractive'. People came only out of necessity and those that stayed either went downhill through drink, out of their minds, killed themselves or, little by little, the environment dragged them down into its filth. Judging from the official accounts, he concludes that in the 1860s and 1870s the educated were outstanding in their sheer moral worthlessness, prisons were havens of debauchery and people were corrupted and flogged to death.

Then, in 1878, a new superintendent arrived, an excellent administrator and an honest and intelligent man. Though he was academic, 'writing in his study' as the prisoners lived as badly as before, he did at least leave behind a *Dossier on the Administration System on Sakhalin Island* which was a good basis for subsequent progress. A year later the Voluntary Fleet began sailing to the island and European Russians began to head east. A few years later, with new regulations, more educated, cultivated officials arrived with their families. By 1888 there was even an amateur theatrical group in Aleksandrovsk (Chekhov, 1895: 279ff). Despite the bestiality of many older officials, there was hope.

I repeatedly met intelligent, good natured and noble officials . . . a guarantee that a return to the past is no longer possible . . . . Good people and good works are no longer rarities. By reducing the overwork, by education and by the development of social life the percentage of lunatics, alcoholics and suicides will be reduced.

Alas, from his account, it seems that enlightened officials were in the minority.

In the next chapter he considered the exiles themselves. 'Some prisoners bore their penalty with fortitude, acknowledging their guilt; others staggered on with "a lack of spirit, look of dejection, and whine, weep and despair". Under the same roof are died-in-the-wool villains, sadistic monsters and those unfortunates falsely convicted' (Chekhov, 1895: 283). In a footnote he quotes Mr Kamorsky, a prison inspector,

If out of 100 convict labourers, 15–20 decent ones ultimately emerge, we are obliged for this not so much to the corrective measures we utilize, as to the Russian Courts, which dispatch into hard labour such a large number of the good and trustworthy element of society.

With such a mixture, conclusions about morality were confused and tangled. In addition, he observed how exiles had their own criminality, their own statutes and that some offences we might consider trivial were serious on Sakhalin, for instance debt or drunkenness, while other crimes, for example, theft and burglary, were so common as to be unrecorded.

He detailed the 'vices and perversions of exiles; characteristic of those subjugated, enslaved, starved and in constant fear; mendacity, cunning, cowardliness, lack of spirit, thieving, secret vices; these form the arsenal the degraded put forward against authority' (Chekhov, 1895: 283). Even when describing their vices he also suggested that they were driven to be like this. 'Prisoners hurl themselves at anything not nailed down, thieving in prison, off each other, from settled exiles, convicts, from a captain, and on ship "even the port holes and compass . . ."' The sole mental pleasure was playing cards, and one prisoner infected the others 'gambling has taken control of prisons, clouding the mind like a narcotic, so that some lost all food and clothing and yet felt neither hunger nor cold . . .' He wrote of how 'even when loading a ship with coal, when the waves are pounding and people green from seasickness, there was a game of cards in the barge'. In Aleksandrovsk, he asked how many prostitutes there were, 'As many as you like'. Officially there were thirty, all inspected as disease-free once per week by a doctor. But, he observes, that this profession was impeded neither by some girls' youth nor by others' tertiary syphilis.

The government records of 1890 (there were some) showed that recidivists, those convicted by the regional court for offences on the island, were 8 per cent of the total, with some having three, four or even six sentences. Three per cent had been in penal servitude for over twenty-five years. But he questions the statistics; many were attempted escapes by those who had never been tried and just kept under house arrest instead (though how was not clear). He shows how the justice system on Sakhalin was failing, with poor records, underfunding and a huge volume of cases. After escape, murder was the next most frequent offence. But investigations might take up to seven years, by which time the details would have been lost. Most of his account on 'morality' actually concerns the conditions driving exiles to these extremes. His criticisms were directed less at individuals as at the systemic failings which led to such appalling social conditions. After one murder, four men were arrested and kept in cold, dark cells. Three were released and the other put in irons, given 100 lashes and kept starving till he confessed.

On Sakhalin officials could, by law, and without trial, birch, imprison and send to the mines anyone, making the court have a 'purely formal significance'. Punishments were severe, and humiliated and embittered the convict, coarsening morals and mores. 'The birch and lash, chaining to wheelbarrow, are employed widely . . .' In Aleksandrovsk in 1889, 282 convicts were punished, 265 by birch. Grounds for birching included failure to complete the day's work, drunkenness, rudeness and disobedience. One official birched if handed an unworthy petition (for an improvement in conditions), while another flogged everyone. What was not allowed in European Russia was accepted on Sakhalin, despite what the governor general had said, though to be fair, other parts of Siberia may have been as lawless too. The vast size of the country was one of several reasons for its laws and policies being diluted and flooded by corruption. Chekhov found that flogging was so frequent that it almost became devalued. He made himself watch one flogging:

> The man was white as the doctor examined his heart to make sure he was able to endure, which did not take a minute. A certificate was issued. The man does not know if he has been brought here for the escape or for his original offence. The Governor tells him that his original sentence included 90 lashes which was commuted and that today he would have them. He had tried to be too clever.

Apart from the lashing, the open wounds afterwards frequently became infected. Flogging carried a serious chance of becoming a death sentence.

> The executioner, Tolstykh, a tall sticky individual with the build of a circus strongman, nods to the prisoner who lies down. His trousers are lowered and he is bound to bench by hand and foot. Tolstykh delivers the first blow. Initially Prokhorov is silent and then a convulsion of pain and a sound rings out.
>
> After every 5 blows the executioner walks to the other side and has a short rest. Prokhorov's neck is swollen, his body crimson and dark blue, skin splits from each blow. He cries out for mercy, retches, wheezes, bellows; the overseer calls out 42, 43 . . .

Chekhov had to leave. When he went back the overseer was still counting. After ninety, his teeth chattering, his face yellow and wet, his eyes wandering – they led the prisoner to the sickbay.

That's for the murder, there'll be more for the escape.

'I love to see them getting punished', the military doctor says joyfully. 'I love it; such villains they should hang them' (Chekhov, 1895: 291–4)

For once Chekhov's comment seems superfluous: 'Those who carry out the punishments become callous, hardened and embittered'. The beating was designed to inflict pain, but it left open wounds, so before antibiotics there was a fair chance of dying slowly from septicaemia afterwards.

He detailed a hanging too, though he did not see it. In the Korsakovsk District, eleven men were sentenced to death for the murder of some Ainos. 'All through the night before the execution, the officials and military officers did not sleep but kept going to each other's quarters to drink tea . . . nobody knew what to do with themselves. Two of the condemned men poisoned themselves with aconite'.

'11 men were condemned to death, yet I see only 9,' demanded the District Governor. 'Where are the remaining two?' 'Look, hang me. Hang me,' muttered the commanding officer.

It was a morning in early October, dismal, cold and dark. The faces of the condemned were yellow, and their hair was standing on end from horror. An official read the sentence, trembling with agitation, and constantly stammering and hesitating over it because he could not see properly. A priest in a black chasuble gave all nine the cross to kiss and whispered to the District Governor: 'For God's sake, release me, I can't go on . . .'

The process was a long one: each prisoner had to have a shroud put on and to be led to the scaffold. When at last all nine had been hanged, the effect was of a 'whole garland' in the air.

When the executed men were taken down, the doctors found that one of them was still alive. The chance occurrence had an especial significance: the prison — including the executioner and his assistants — which knows all the secrets of all the offences committed by the inmates, was aware that this one who was still alive was not guilty of the crime for which he had been hanged.

'He was hanged on another occasion,' the District Governor concluded his story. 'Afterwards I couldn't sleep for a month.' (Chekhov, 1895: 297)

Not surprisingly, people tried to escape, or as Chekhov suggested laconically 'everybody, during their sentence, arranges a holiday'. Though Sakhalin was an island, convicts knew it was possible to walk to Siberia in winter across the ice, while in summer people sailed in makeshift or stolen boats. But it was not easy:

> the taiga, mountains, mosquitoes, the damp, the mists, bears, lack of humans, frosts and storms are the true allies of surveillance. Walking 5 versts per day is difficult. Escapees often, after a week or two, exhausted by starvation, diarrhoea and fever, bitten all over, legs battered and swollen, wet, filthy and ragged, perish somewhere in the taiga, or drag themselves back. The driver is both a love of home and loathing for Sakhalin. One old lady, a convict, went into ecstasies over my suitcase, books and quilt, purely because they were not from Sakhalin.

> At the Korsakovsk Post convict-in-exile Altukhov, an elderly man of sixty or more, escapes in the following manner. He takes a hunk of bread, locks his cabin and, walking not more than half a verst from the post, sits down on a hill and gazes at the taiga, the sea and the sky; after sitting like this for 3 days or so, he goes back home, draws his provisions and goes back up the hill again. . . In the past, they used to flog him, but now they simply laugh over these 'escapes' of his. Some abscond with the intention of roaming at large for a month or a week, for others a single day is sufficient. 'It may be only a day or two — but they are mine.'

> Sensible, unassuming people with families flee with no clothing, no bread, no purpose and no plan, with the certainty that they will be caught. Escape reflects hopelessness and that things could not be worse, a perverted safety valve. (Chekhov, 1895: 298ff)[4]

Inevitably there was sharp practice, with the rewards for capturing escapees sometimes shared out. Several convicts would flee to an agreed spot and be led back by a guard who would give the convicts part of the reward. 'It is comical to see a young puny Gilyak, or a private not distinguished for his sturdy build, leading back 6, 7, 11 broad shouldered imposing vagabonds'.

There were rumours of escape. The son of an Archpriest was sent to Sakhalin for murder, fled to European Russia, committed another murder and was sent back. Assuming he walked, that was six to nine years on foot. Chekhov found the main deterrence to escape was repression – in 1889 15 per cent escaped from Aleksandrovsk prison but only 6 per cent from Voyevodsk and Douai, with their armed guards. He pointed out – given that Siberia was hardly a Shangri-La – that more humane measures, simple things like better bread, might be more effective. After all, the aim was to establish a colony. Those in the south seemed less escape minded, partly due to the geography – they were much further from Siberia – but also because conditions were better.

One surprise in the book, especially since Chekhov wanted to submit it for an MD thesis, is how little conventional medicine it contains. He tried to use hospital and parish registers to try to find prevalence of disease, though he felt these unreliable and that the causes of death had 'a lot of fantasy in them'. He listed 632 convicts of both sexes who were, in 1889 'feeble and incapable of labour; 10.6% of the total . . .'. He could trace only 194 deaths in 1889, or 1.25 per cent of the population. So low a death rate leads him to ask, with none too delicate sarcasm, if Sakhalin is the healthiest place on earth. In contrast, in the same year 11,309 applied for medical aid, that is, everyone did at least once (or fewer people did more than once) (Chekhov, 1895: 311).

He itemized diseases, in part to highlight the hopelessness of medical reporting. There were eighteen deaths reported from smallpox over ten years. More common were typhus, typhoid and enteric fever with twenty-three outbreaks and 30 per cent dying. 'Croupous pneumonia' was mentioned twenty-seven times in 1889, with again around 30 per cent dying – parish accounts had 125 mentions of this in ten years. Dysentery or 'the bloody flux' was recorded five times while 'imprecisely diagnosed feverish illnesses' were reported seventeen times, mainly in the winter and its cousin, 'intermittent fever', 428 times.

There were 271 cases of scurvy, of which six died. Most had just arrived on the island, whether by walking or on ship, having had a poor diet deficient in vitamin C for months or years. On arrival, prisoners fell ill 'in whole crowds'. Since the aim was to settle Sakhalin as a colony, such poor attention to convicts' health was counterproductive.

Tuberculosis killed a surprisingly low number, 15 per cent, who were mostly young adults. Infant mortality was also allegedly small, 3 per cent under twenty, with 43 per cent dying between ages twenty-five and thirty-five and 27 per cent between the ages of thirty-five and forty-five, and only 8 per cent over fifty-five (figures not age matched). Such a small infant mortality is suspicious. Syphilis was mentioned 246 times in 1889, with five deaths. One man, a 44-year-old Jew, was singled out as having both syphilis and TB. Syphilis was most common in Aleksandrovsk because of the large number of newly arrived prisoners and troops. The measures to combat this included examining the convicts twice a month, and weekly examination of 'women of dubious morality', though a considerable number 'slip through the net'. There was no mention of the dubious morality of the men, officials and convicts, who imposed such conditions on the women, nor of how syphilis was treated.

Since TB and syphilis were long-term infections with which you could live, declining, for years, they occupied unique places in people's collective fear and resignation. Rayfield, (personal communication), has suggested that TB tended to kill earlier, in one's thirties and forties, while syphilis took you later, in the fifties. Death from bleeding and respiratory complications was considered preferable to a long syphilitic fall into chronic insufferable pain and dementia. Chekhov knew he had TB, of course, and may well have presumed – correctly – that he had syphilis too, given his frequenting of brothels.

Neurological disease was not neglected, with 'brain inflammation' a cause of twenty-four deaths and stroke in ten. Epilepsy was mentioned thirty-one times and mental health twenty-five. Sciatica was considered hysterical. Over ten years he found 170 registered unnatural deaths – twenty hanged, twenty-seven suicides, two non-judicial hangings, poisonings, shootings, drowning and one 'torn to pieces by a bear'. Since there are accounts of suicide, often from aconite poisoning throughout his book, these numbers seem low. Within the paucity of statistical records and the patchy reporting of disease, Chekhov points towards the mediocrity of medicine on the island.

The three hospitals did not impress either. Despite Aleksandrovsk Hospital being new, the medical care was poor, and the staff 'exasperating'. Only one person, Vasilii Iakovlev Sozi, a 31-year-old convict and ex-medical assistant from Vilan, seemed adequate. Outpatient doctors sat behind a wooden grill, like in a bank, to avoid getting too close to patients. There were also a medical assistant and an overseer with a revolver.[5] Given the degrading conditions patients were subjected to, he comments that many would not seek medical advice at all. Arguably his most savage criticism was directed towards fellow doctors.[6] Chekhov saw a boy with a boil which needed to be lanced. The scalpels were blunt, there was no cotton wool, no washbasin, no decent scissors and not even a decent amount of water. He detailed the expense of the hospital and compared it with the smaller cost of far better hospitals back in Moscow province. He does not need to elaborate the cause for such differences – corruption.

Chekhov's detailing of Sakhalin's medicine is at the end of the book and brief, though typically telling in detail and leaving little room for ambiguity about his opinion. But the data are comparatively brief, especially for an MD thesis. It is clear that Chekhov viewed his survey as being as much about matters beyond conventional medicine. There is now a distinction made between healthcare, what clinical staff do to improve those who are ill, and health and well-being itself, which is far more about avoiding the largely social conditions which underpin much of the differences in the prevalence of illness today. Chekhov saw that on Sakhalin public health and government policy – or neglect – was a driver of much of the deprivation and degradation he itemized. As we will see with the survey and his analysis, he did try to drag 'big data' (for the time especially) from his census, hoping to impress with science, but all the while he supported this with examples and with narrative. Chekhov was always most interested in individuals and stories and tried to harness those to his greater purpose. Indeed, one of the tensions in the whole work is between those two elements.

Another is his need to remain dispassionate, in part for the injunction to show and not tell, but also to remain onside with the authorities. Though Rayfield (personal communication) has suggested that censorship was not unduly restrictive, or efficient, Chekhov needed to be alert to its potential. This, despite being assured in Aleksandrovsk that he would see no floggings and no shaved heads, Chekhov details both. Without saying it overtly, he showed how poor the governor's knowledge was, based – as it was – on paper reports from corrupt officials; how guards and overseers corrupted convicts, that doctors were two hundred years behind the times compared with what he had been taught in Moscow, and that the whole island had such all-pervasive despair that any adult or young person who could leave did so. One can imagine that a posting to Sakhalin was not highly sought after by doctors, officials or even priests. Though he does not go into this in detail the mettle of the staff, like that of the guards and officials, must have been severely tested. Climate, soil and the prison system, with its punishments, hard labour and haphazard distribution of people in settlements, all conspired not only against the convicts and exiles but against Sakhalin becoming a self-sufficient colony. Any other conclusion, one suspects, he would have found 'totally incomprehensible'.

In this, Sakhalin was probably at a severe disadvantage compared with those other parts of Siberia which were settled (though those also had decidedly mixed results (Beer, 2016). Chekhov's criticisms appear to be addressed at how Sakhalin was an unsuitable place for colonization, for a number of carefully elaborated reasons, rather than against colonization in mainland Siberia, difficult though that was.

Yet, along with this careful, clinical assembly of evidence, Chekhov also praised some of the more enlightened officials and the priesthood. He pointed constructively towards ways in which improvements might be made, both for prisoners and for the colony, and finds some optimism in the new educated class of administrators. Though the effect on him of seeing the utter depravity and breakdown in order and humanity was profound, his account still had room for dispassionate analysis and, just about, for hope.

## Notes

1. Average life expectancy in Russia, skewed by high infant mortality, was thirty years at the time.

2. In the footnotes, he details the holders of the Inspector of Agriculture Class VI post. One, after two years produced a small academic inconsequential report, with conclusions not outstanding for their accuracy. Another tried to show it was impossible to farm Sakhalin. He was 'honest, erudite but crazy'. A Pole embezzled his travel expenses and so was forgiven to leave, while a German drove to a village, asked why there was a frost and then drove off again (Chekhov, 1895: 404).

3. In the footnotes, he quotes a police report from 1870 of lower ranking soldiers, 'poor disciplinary record. One was arrested for drunkenness and insolence, whilst others were "lazy," "a moron," and "a thief"' (Chekhov, 1895: 421).

4. Kennan describes how the prisoners in Siberia, lived outdoors in summer and, at the onset of the cuckoo, tried to escape, up to 30,000 of them. One old man could not resist trying to escape at the sound but knew he was too old, so pleaded to be locked up.

> There is something pathetic in this inability of the worn, broken old convict to hear the cry of the cuckoo without yielding to the enticement of the wild, free, adventurous life . . . He knew he was feeble and broken; he knew he could no longer tramp through forests, swim rapid rivers, and subsist on roots . . . (Kennan, 1958: 182ff)

It is unclear if escapees went home or remained in Siberia. He also met one man who had escaped 4 times, which would be eight times across; another knew of a man who escaped 16 times. (Kennan, 1958: 128ff)

5. We were told during a visit to Sakhalin that the assistants turned the patient with a stick, though this was not mentioned by Chekhov.

6. This came out in his subsequent literary writings as well as in *Sakhalin Island.*

# References

Beer, D. (2016). *The House of the Dead*. London: Allen Lane.

Chekhov, A. (1895). *Sakhalin Island*, translated by Brian Reeve. London; One World Edition. 1993, 2007, 2014. (Throughout translations are from the 2007 edition).

Kennan, G. (1958). *Siberia and the Exile System*. Abridged from the First Edition, 1891 (New York: Century). Chicago and London: Chicago University Press.

**Figure 1** Aleksandrovsk. This view is from just across the river, looking north. Much of the town still has low rise wooden houses, though the centre is now built up. Krasnov, I. N., photographer. *Vid posta Aleksandrovskogo s ptich'ego poleta*. Russian Federation Aleksandrovsk Sakhalin Oblast Sakhalinskiy, 1890. [Sakhalin, post Aleksandrovskiĭ: publisher not identified, konet͡s XIX-nachalo XX vv] (Photograph) Retrieved from the Library of Congress, https://www.loc.gov/item/2018684022/.

**Figure 2** A settlement. Trees cut and houses built in an orderly row. What is not clear is how the settlers would then survive. Chekhov noted that the locations chosen for settlements were often inexplicable. One official article stated that colonists should be given timber for cabins, but this just meant that they had permission to cut down trees themselves. Krasnov, I. N., photographer. *Poselok Krasnyĭ I͡Ar na ostrove Sakhalin*. Russian Federation Sakhalin Oblast Krasnyy Yar, 1890. [Sakhalin, post Aleksandrovskiĭ: publisher not identified, konet͡s XIX-nachalo XX vv] (Photograph) Retrieved from the Library of Congress, https://www.loc.gov/item/2018684041/.

**Figure 3** Convict types. From 1880, before Chekhov's visit. Note how their facial features differ. As he wrote, there was little attempt to put men from the same area together. Pavlovskii, I. I., photographer. *Tipy Ssyl'nokatorzhnykh*. Russian Federation Sakhalin Sakhalin Oblast, 1880. [Dui: Publisher Not Identified, to 1899] (Photograph) Retrieved from the Library of Congress, https://www.loc.gov/item/2018691401/.

**Figure 4** Convicts at work. The composition of the photo suggests a degree of staging, perhaps. They wear summer clothes and uniforms. Note the troops with fixed bayonets. Krasnov, I. N., photographer. *Raboty Katorzhnikov*. Russian Federation Aleksandrovsk Sakhalin Oblast Sakhalinskiy, 1890. [Sakhalin, post Aleksandrovskii: publisher not identified, konets XIX-nachalo XX vv] (Photograph) Retrieved from the Library of Congress, https://www.loc.gov/item/2018684050/.

**Figure 5** Douai coalmine. Douai is a steep valley at right angles to the coast and a few miles south of Aleksandrovsk. Voyevodsk Prison was a kilometre or so to the north of the mine, so convicts would walk down the beach to work. Chekhov itemized the mines output, and its dubious methods. Pavlovskii, I. I., photographer. *Duĭskiĭ kamennougol'nyĭ rudnik. Alekseevskai͡a shtol'ni͡a.* Russian Federation Sakhalin Oblast Due, 1880. [Dui: Publisher Not Identified, to 1899] (Photograph) Retrieved from the Library of Congress, https://www.loc.gov/item/2018691423/.

**Figure 6** Escaped convicts. Note their half-shaved heads and their summer clothes. Winter escape bids were also attempted, since the sea between island and mainland froze. Pavlovskii, I. I., photographer. *Ssyl'nokatorzhnye Korsakovskoĭ ti͡ur'my, poĭmannye iz begov.* Russian Federation Korsakov Sakhalin Oblast, 1880. [Dui: Publisher Not Identified, to 1899] (Photograph) Retrieved from the Library of Congress, https://www.loc.gov/item/2018691403/.

**Figure 7** Golden hand. Sonya 'was famous in Russia and around the world: a swindler and murderess. It was like theatre. Photos of her were sold abroad'. Once released, she left for the mainland. But she was persecuted and it proved safer on Sakhalin. 'Two years later she died of the common cold.' Krasnov, I. N., photographer. *Sof'iā̃ Zolotaiā̃ ruchka'*. Russian Federation Aleksandrovsk Sakhalin Oblast Sakhalinskiy, 1890. [Sakhalin, post Aleksandrovskiĭ: publisher not identified, konets XIX-nachalo XX vv] (Photograph) Retrieved from the Library of Congress, https://www.loc.gov/item/2018684054/.

**Figure 8** Hauling coal at Douai. Pavlovskii, I. I., photographer. *Ssyl'nokatorzhnye na otkatke ugliā̃ vo dvorikakh Duĭskogo kamennougol'nogo rudnika*. Russian Federation Sakhalin Oblast Due, 1880. [Dui: Publisher Not Identified, to 1899] (Photograph) Retrieved from the Library of Congress, https://www.loc.gov/item/2018691404/.

**Figure 9** Hauling timber. The heaviest work was coalmining, road construction and timber hauling. These men were chosen from the strongest, and soon after Chekhov's visit, in the mid-1890s, and not before time, they were replaced by horses. Krasnov, I. N., photographer. *Perevozka Drov Katorzhnymi*. Russian Federation Aleksandrovsk Sakhalin Oblast Sakhalinskiy, 1890. [Sakhalin, post Aleksandrovskiĭ: publisher not identified, konets XIX-nachalo XX vv] (Photograph) Retrieved from the Library of Congress, https://www.loc.gov/item/2018684058/.

**Figure 10** Korsakov prison. Korsakov was in the south of the island, with 450 inmates when Chekhov visited and with another thousand or so working outside, mainly on roads. Pavlovskii, I. I., photographer. *Korsakovskaiă Ssyl'nokatorzhnaiă Tiŭr'ma*. Russian Federation Korsakov Sakhalin Oblast, 1880. [Dui: Publisher Not Identified, to 1899] (Photograph) Retrieved from the Library of Congress, https://www.loc.gov/item/2018691421/.

**Figure 11** Tasks for convicts. These four wintry photographs showing convicts hauling a sled. No horses used it seems: the effort is apparent, especially in the right image. Note the armed guards in attendance. Krasnov, I. N., photographer. *Raboty Katorzhnikov*. Russian Federation Aleksandrovsk Sakhalin Oblast Sakhalinskiy, 1890. [Sakhalin, post Aleksandrovskiĭ: publisher not identified, konetŝ XIX-nachalo XX vv] (Photograph) Retrieved from the Library of Congress, https://www.loc.gov /item/2018684026/.

**Figure 12** Wheelbarrow men. In Voyevodsk prison 'The Chasm of Sorrow', the worst repeat offenders chained to heavy, wooden wheelbarrows night and day, for years on end, by hand, foot and waist. Krasnov, I. N., photographer. *Katorzhniki, Prikovannye K Tachkam*. Russian Federation Aleksandrovsk Sakhalin Oblast Sakhalinskiy, 1890. [Sakhalin, post Aleksandrovskiĭ: publisher not identified, konetŝ XIX-nachalo XX vv] (Photograph) Retrieved from the Library of Congress, https://www .loc.gov/item/2018684067/.

# CHAPTER 8
# NUMBERS

Chekhov had already written hundreds of short stories and several plays, and established himself as a literary figure, so his ability to write about the experiences of those he saw was not in doubt. To be awarded an MD thesis required more than eloquence, however – he needed facts and figures and numbers. While public opinion might be awakened by harrowing reportage, he also knew he needed hard data to change government policies. Of course, there are limits to what one man, with three months' field work, on an island as large as Sakhalin and without much assistance, might achieve. He was also hampered by the inadequate records, for instance when researching escapes, he could only find six complete years of statistics since 1877 (Chekhov, 1895: 304). Much of his work was exploring the limits of the available knowledge and what he could say with any certainty. Nevertheless, the book, though rooted in observation and description, as well as the fruits of his research beforehand, is also packed with numbers both in the main body of the text and in his extensive footnotes.

As we have learnt, Chekhov used the census to become more closely acquainted with the exiles . . . 'in the settlements . . . I went round all the cabins and noted down the heads of the households, members of their families, tenants and workmen'. Though his aim was 'not its results but the impressions received during the making of it', and despite him wondering if it could even be called a census, 'its results could not be said to be distinguished for their accuracy and completeness . . .', it does contain interesting data. He wondered if, 'in the absence of more reliable data, either in the literature on the subject or in the Sakhalin offices, my figures will perhaps be of some use'. As Laffitte suggests this was the first large-scale census in Russia (Laffitte, 1976: 136), and Chekhov probably underplayed its significance and his work in assembling it. Later work, however, has not repudiated its findings. He also used the cards to generate some simple statistics himself.

He writes that he saw everyone on the island (except all but a few political prisoners), and filled in 10,000 cards from those living outside the jails.

Rosamund Bartlett suggests that there were 8,710 completed cards, with 534 from Aleksandrovsk in the handwriting of a Buryat priest Chekhov befriended (Bartlett, 2004: 181–2). Of these 7,445 are now online.[1] With the financial assistance of Wellcome Trust we arranged for these to be translated into English by Alexander Iosad for, we understand, the first time,[2] and analysed them using statistical methods unavailable to Chekhov at the time.[3] The reasons for the slightly different numbers are unclear. Some cards may have been misplaced. Alternatively, Chekhov might have rounded up to 10,000, or possibly the difference reflects the political prisoners living on the island which he was prevented from seeing.

The twelve questions in the census were given earlier. The on-line cards have slightly different information. After each person's number there is the district, town, address and house number before the name. Then, we are given relation of the owner to their residence, age, religion, place of birth, year arrived on Sakhalin, occupation, literacy and marital status.[4] Comparison between Chekhov's figures and those from the translated cards is difficult because of the different sizes of the samples (Chekhov's being larger, suggesting some have been mislaid), but it does allow some confirmation of his figures. Where possible, current simple statistical models (from Microsoft Excel) have been used to re-analyse his data from the 7,445 census cards and his analysis within the book.

In his text, he does not mention the times when he used his census and when not but when, for instance, he gives the numbers of inhabitants in each town and village, this information was likely to have come from it. But equally he mentions that in May 1890, 1,279 convicts ate from prison cauldrons and slept the night in prison, whereas at the end of the summer that number had shrunk to 675, figures that one presumes came from official registers (Chekhov, 1895: 92).

He certainty did borrow from prison records and the official government register, so we read that Douai, up to 1890, owed 94,337 roubles and 15 kopecks, though for what is unclear (Chekhov, 1895: 131). On 1 January 1890, there were 91 exiles from the nobility and gentry, and 924 from urban ranks, merchants etc. (Chekhov, 1895: 223). He gives the age groupings of people on Sakhalin, under twenty-five – 25 per cent, twenty-five to thirty-five – 24 per cent, thirty-five to fourty-five – 24 per cent and finally twenty to fifty-five – 65 per cent[5] but is sceptical about their meaning: 'Even if the statistics . . . were outstanding for their perfect accuracy and were far more complete than those I have gathered, they would yield almost nothing.' He goes on to explain how they are dependent on the will of those in the prison department to fill them in, together with 'economic conditions and legal theories'. Then, he suggests, the small number of older men reflects the fact that all who can leave once their sentence is served do so (Chekhov, 1895: 237). He mentions mortality, but elsewhere is scornful of the official figures. Later he writes,

> one day rooting around office documents for figures is enough to give way to despair at the overblown figures, incorrect totals and overblown concoctions. [There was] nothing for 1886, some have in pencil, 'obviously untrue' at the bottom. (Chekhov, 1895: 424)

If the official statistics cannot be trusted and his other sources, parish records and hospital registers, are similarly patchy, then might his own census be a worthwhile source? We have used contemporary statistical analysis of the 7,445 cards, to see if it dissects the numbers better than Chekhov could by hand. This presumes reliability within the data he collected, something which has been severely criticized. For these reasons, Popkin, in an influential article written over twenty years ago, was very critical of the census and, indeed, of Chekhov's whole project (Popkin, 1992: 36–51). She itemized inadequacies in his census returns, suggesting that the answers are likely to be unreliable with convicts referring to themselves as workers, and people uncertain about their age or about their year of arrival on the island.

But Chekhov must have had a fair understanding of the people he was interviewing. The grandson of a serf, his father might well have ended up in exile after he ran from Taganrog to avoid bankruptcy. His writing was more about ordinary people than noblemen.[6] In one of the most revealing of his letters he wrote to Suvorin, on 7 January 1889:

> What upper class writers have always taken for granted, those from humbler origins must sacrifice their youth to acquire. Try writing a story about a young man, the son of a serf, a former shop boy and chorister, schoolboy and student, brought up to be respectful of his betters and to kiss priests' hands, to submit to the ideas of others, to be grateful for every crust of, who is constantly thrashed, who goes out without galoshes to tutor other people's children, who gets into fights, torments animals, savours the taste of good dinners with rich relations, unnecessarily plays the hypocrite before God and his fellows purely from a realisation of his own insignificance – and then go on to tell the story of how this young man drop by drop wrings the slave out of himself until, one fine morning, he awakes to feel

that flowing in his veins is no longer the blood of a slave, but that of a complete human being. (Bartlett and Phillips, 2004: 78)

Chekhov never forgot whence he came. If anything, as Rayfield suggests, Chekhov may have brought out the best in people; readers and indeed government officials on Sakhalin were surprised at how he managed to extract coherent narratives from a wide variety of otherwise uncommunicative convicts and guards.[7] So, while his census will contain some inaccuracies, it still pays close re-analysis, not least because this may reveal its inconsistencies or otherwise. The analysis allowed numbers in each group to be calculated, for example, arrivals by year, age, sex, occupation, but also for each category to be correlated with any other, for example, how many born on Sakhalin were still living there aged twenty-one.

## Null returns in census

The first question is how many returns were not filled it. Popkin is right to point to these null returns, though these appear for some questions and not for others. In the census the column, 'rank' i.e. status leading to transportation, has only twenty-four null returns from 7,445 cards. The category 'Free', showed 862 entries, mostly women, who freely followed husbands or partners to Sakhalin. Only three (named) husbands followed their wives, though Chekhov notes that one man who came with his wife was a fool (though why was unclear). Of the ninety-eight 'free' males, seventy-eight were the sons or grandsons of convicts, so these data are not entirely uninformative. Each card entry has a name, and though some are nicknames, time and time again families are clearly identifiable. Most people give two or three names, with given name, surname and patronymic – hardly acts of deceit. True, 'Nepomniashchii', 'no name', was among the commonest names, but then only given by 17 out of 7,445. At the time it was also adopted by some as their proper name. Nicknames were also common at the time, without necessarily implying deceit. It is difficult to falsify the idea of stolen identity, but since all going to Sakhalin were exiled forever the advantage of an assumed name may not have been as great as in Siberian camps, where there were fixed sentences with return home afterwards and different degrees of hard labour to avoid (Figure 13).

The entry under 'occupation' does have the largest null return, with 3,658 males and 2,310 females, though from this must be subtracted the children,

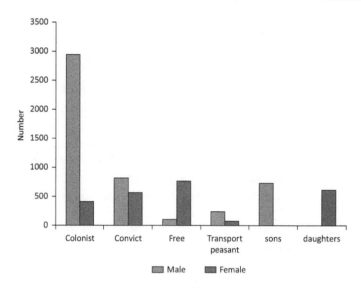

**Figure 13** Rank (type of person) arriving or born on Sakhalin, 1865–90. (Based on data from Chekhov's 1890 census.) Translation by Alexander Iosad, data available on-line at Jonathan Cole, Neuroscience and Narrative, https://jonathandcole.org.

of whom there were well over a thousand. Either adults did not consider themselves to have a single job or they were not prepared to answer this question. The age of the people interviewed was not given by 1,475, but many in this group also declined to answer any questions – they were not engaged either with the process or with the interviewer.

The duration of time on Sakhalin was not answered by a high number, 2,611, but over half of these, 1,376, were either born on Sakhalin or in transit and so probably arrived as children, and may not have answered for this reason. Of the remaining 1,235, many were once more multiple non-responders with, for instance, 745 not replying to the date of birth question. Popkin suggests that most people did not understand the term literate, perhaps unaware that Chekhov specifically asked about the reading of a book rather than the word itself.

There were 2,087 null replies under 'married' or 'single', but 1,496 were under twenty years old, leaving just 600 adults who did not answer. Of those who replied that they were married at home, 2,676 of which 924 were women. Two-thirds of these also said they were 'free' – presumably they accompanied their convict husbands to Sakhalin. This leaves over a thousand men married at home and who were not accompanied by their wives and families. Twelve married in transit, and were still together on Sakhalin, while 383 married on the island. Over 600 described themselves as widowed, with 410 women of whom 346 had found new partners on Sakhalin.

Overall, there were around 14,000 null returns, mainly in occupation (5,900), year of arrival (2,600), literacy and marital status (around 2,000 each). That is around 20 per cent of the total possible returns. If one removes the 1,626 children under the age of twenty from the sample of 7,445, since the main unanswered questions are age related, then the percentage of nulls falls to 15 per cent. Given the conditions under which Chekhov was working and the population surveyed this may not seem too bad.

## Origin of people in the census

Of the 7,445 total, 1,288 were born on Sakhalin, so 6,157 were sent there between 1865 and 1890. There were 3,365 colonists (412 female), 1,371 convicts (560 female), 71 peasants transported against their will, and 812 free people or free peasants. Colonists would have been transported as convicts, and spent years living in prison or houses before being released to be settlers, living relatively freely in their own dwelling, though of course they were never allowed home.

Analysis of where in Russia people were sent from was given by Chekhov himself as a note, from a sample of 5,791 (Chekhov, 1895: 389). They came from all over Russia and beyond, with no clear picture. His aim was, in part, to give the details of the origin of exiles, but also to point out the heterogeneous mix of settlers scattered around the settlements he visited, 'a randomly assembled rabble' (Chekhov, 1895: 223). 'Every year, some arrive, others leave . . . they have little in common and are alien to each other . . . They have different religions and different languages. The old men ask laughingly what sort of society was possible if in one and the same village live Russians, Ukrainians, Tatars, Poles, Jews, Chukhons, Kirgizes, Georgians and Gypsies.'[8] How much better it might have been to put people from similar areas and common languages together.

Chekhov addressed the social class from which convicts came, though here the census adds very little given the small numbers in the survey. It mentions sixty different jobs. A few were educated; three scribes, one teacher, one surveyor, a doctor, one nobleman, a lieutenant Colonel, Mine Manager and Court Councillor. Most of these entries were from

Aleksandrovsk and Douai, so some may be erroneous and the cards filled in by his assistant. Of the remainder, there were 207 farmers, 128 carpenters, 84 cobblers, 37 scribes, 21 tailors, 22 blacksmiths and 14 locksmiths. There were single entries for mullah, mower, gardener, sailor, fisherman, jeweller, brick-maker, clockmaker and comb-maker, two choir singers and three makers of cigarettes. The numbers are very small, however, since 3,537 did not answer this question.

## Year, status and gender of arrivals on Sakhalin

The census sampled twenty-five years, from 1865 to 1890 in terms of the year of arrival on Sakhalin (Figure 14). Very few people came in the first few years of the colony. As can be seen, the peak year was 1884, and over 60 per cent of people arrived in the 1880's. Early on they also sent some forcibly transported peasants, but this practice petered out.

There were 856 people who chose to enter exile voluntarily. Of these 762 were women, either wives or partners, travelling with their men. There were ninety-four 'free' males, but most of these were sons and dependents. Only 3 adult males in the 7,445 sample were free and of those one was single and one married on Sakhalin. In other words, only one man accompanied his convict wife or partner to exile (forty-year-old Ivan Fedorov Zhigulin who accompanied his convict wife, Avdot'la Stepanova Zhigulina aged forty-nine from Tambov, with both arriving in 1886). Of the 560 women convicts, 136 had been married at home. The number of free people arriving increased

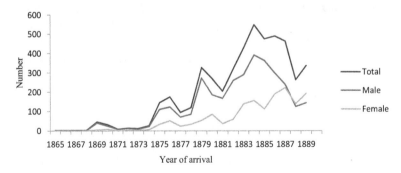

**Figure 14** Gender of arrivals on Sakhalin 1865–90. (Based on data from Chekhov's 1890 census.) Translation by Alexander Iosad, data available on-line at Jonathan Cole, Neuroscience and Narrative, https://jonathandcole.org.

towards the end of the period, presumably as it became more possible for wives and partners to accompany their men in the later years of the colony by sea. There were sixty-five free women under the age of twenty of whom twenty came with their parents (i.e. they were not born on the island). All of them were married or had a partner.

The average age of the whole sample was thirty-one. But this includes those born on Sakhalin and other dependents under the age of twenty-one. Once these are removed, the average age rises to thirty-eight for the sample of 5,500 or so. The average year of arrival for convicts and colonists was 1883. Since 1883 is seven years before 1890, we can suggest that the average age of convicts when they reached Sakhalin was thirty-one. Chekhov suggested it was slightly older, something we will come to later. The oldest in the census was ninety-one, a woman who accompanied her son to Sakhalin, was born in 1799 and arrived on Sakhalin in 1869, aged seventy. She was born in Kamenets-Podol'sk Governorate, in eastern Ukraine. There were sixty-one babies under one year old and 857 children under the age of five. One hundred and thirteen children were born 'in transit'. (Figure 15).

The number of colonists falls closer to 1890, which may reflect the fact people left for Siberia when they could. Chekhov suggests that men spent around ten years as a convict, though from the census it seems less than that. It is interesting that while the number of men arriving decreased from the peak in 1884, women continued to increase, so that in 1888 and 1889, there was a small majority of women arriving. Women were more able to travel to Sakhalin to accompany their husbands with the Voluntary Fleet. This does not explain the whole increase, however, and in a footnote, Chekhov discusses how women are no more moral than men, but that the difference in their lives leads to differing crimes. Men's strength is required for plundering the mail and for highway robbery, they serve in the military and so can desert, while some crimes like rape and 'unnatural vices' concern men alone. Women, in contrast, murdered more, especially by poisoning, where the rate was found to be twenty-three times greater than in men. Of the 560 women convicts, from the 7,445 sample, 392 had arrived during or after 1885.[9]

Chekhov mentions around forty settlements in the census. The largest were Aleksandrovskii fort, with 1,337, Aleksandrovskoe (95), Andree-Ivanovskoe (364), Derbinshoe (632), Douai (274), Malo (177), Novo (445), Palevo (283), Rykovskoe (1266)[10] and Verkhnii (175). Much of his book concerns the beginning of his visit in and around Aleksandrovskii, and near

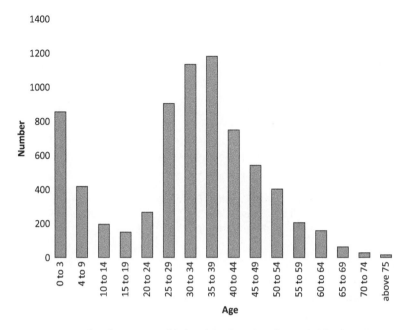

**Figure 15** Age distribution on Sakhalin. (Based on data from Chekhov's 1890 census.) Translation by Alexander Iosad, data available on-line at Jonathan Cole, Neuroscience and Narrative, https://jonathandcole.org.

Douai; the census shows this was not necessarily misrepresentative since most people lived in these areas.

Of the roughly 1,300 census cards for convicts, only 11 – men – were living in prison (Figure 16). It seems that he had easier access for the census to those living outside prison. These men may also have been considered less dangerous and so have been moved to colonist status earlier. This might explain the discrepancy between the time as a convict from the census, five years or so, and Chekhov's suggestion in the text of this being nearer ten years, since he was reflecting his conversations in prisons. It may be confusing to have census data from outside prison, almost exclusively, and yet include over a thousand convicts, who are in part defined by living in prison. But to be fair to Chekhov he anticipates this and states that the 1,332 cards of convicts he had available for analysis (he had more than are now present), represent 23 per cent of the total number of convicts on the island, which makes around 5,800 convicts,

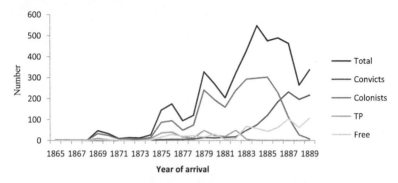

**Figure 16** Status of arrivals on Sakhalin. (Based on data from Chekhov's 1890 census.) Translation by Alexander Iosad, data available on-line at Jonathan Cole, Neuroscience and Narrative, https://jonathandcole.org.

with 4,500 in prison, at least during the summer months he was on the island (Chekhov, *Sakhalin*: 213).

Colonists lived on the island and were expected to build their own houses. This might be seen as an improvement in their lives, but remember Chekhov quoting one governor 'hard labour does not begin in hard labour, but in settled exile afterwards'. The 307th article stated that colonists should be given timber for cabins, but on Sakhalin this just meant that they had permission to cut down trees themselves. Being transferred from living in a prison to becoming an independent colonist was akin to being a castaway.

## Women and children on Sakhalin

No female convicts lived in prison. As Chekhov wrote, 'there is no convict work for women; the prison has totally yielded up its convict women to the colony, for bearing children and running a farm holding'. Nearly all women became the wives, or partners of colonists on arrival as we have seen.

Of the 560 convict women, 136 were married at home, 47 married on Sakhalin, 66 were single and 254 widowed from their marital status entry (with some entries empty). Yet, their relations once on Sakhalin were very different. There were 374 who were the partner of a house and seventy-one who were married to either an owner or tenant. Only fourteen were owners themselves and twenty-five tenants in their own name, with the remainder mothers, mothers-in-law and maids (five).

There were 1,435 children (aged under fourteen), with roughly equal numbers of sons and daughters, 733 to 692, but only 198 aged fourteen to twenty, of whom thirty-five were born on Sakhalin and twenty-three were born in transit. Chekhov bemoaned the absence of teenagers and young adults, suggesting that those young people born on Sakhalin left as soon as they could. It is certainly the case that there were only three Sakhalin-born young adults, all aged twenty-one. But it is unclear, from the census at least, whether there were more who had left or that people on Sakhalin only started having children in the years after 1870 or so. The numbers of women on the island were less than forty per the census before 1875. In that year, there were thirty-four women arrivals and one birth on Sakhalin. Between 1875 and 1880, 134 women arrived and during that time forty-eight children were born who survived to 1890. Given the circumstances, the fertility and survival rates seem good.

As Chekhov suggested, the distribution of women throughout the colony was not uniform. In Aleksandrovsk Post, with first pick, there were 1,337 people: 713 men, 388 women and 133 boys and 103 girls under the age of fourteen; in Derbinskoe, 315 men, 180 women and 137 children, and in Rokvoskoe 588 men, 322 women and 356 children. Some small settlements seemed even better; in the Arkovo settlements there were 80 men, 72 women and 73 children. Set against this were places such as Bol'shoe with 49 men, 11 women and 8 children, Khomntov; 25 men, 10 women and 3 children, Maloe Takoe; 35 men, 9 women and 4 children, Mauka; 33 men, 5 women and no children, and Uskovo; 54 men, 9 women and 5 children.

Chekhov was especially concerned about the children, and their literacy and education. In comparing literacy rates between the adults and children on Sakhalin one must first define the age at which literacy might be attained. The census details a number of children aged six and seven who are literate, so an age of six was chosen for the present purpose. Of the adults 58 per cent were literate. There were 679 children and young adults aged six to twenty, of whom 31 per cent were literate. Of those born on Sakhalin between those ages, only 25 per cent were literate. However, within this sample, 45 per cent were not recorded. From Chekhov's concern, it seems likely that most of those null returns were illiterate, so that the literacy rate was lower in those born on the island than in those sent there, but one cannot be sure.

Chekhov did not expect his census, if indeed he felt it could be called that, to yield anything valuable. Despite his suggestion, it does add some sociological detail to the development of the colony on Sakhalin. The picture it paints is, however, relatively bloodless compared with the measured indignation of his written account of his visit and its 'extreme and upmost form of human degradation'. Our translation of the census may capture most of the data, but the remaining cards might alter some results. For instance, he writes in the book of how the settlement at Voskresenskoye is 'almost twice as large as Uskovo (and yet) . . . There are 183 inhabitants, 175 men and eight women and just one little girl'. This settlement does not appear in the census and presumably it is in the remaining cards not analysed here.

But what the census does achieve is to reinforce just how hard Chekhov worked on Sakhalin and, since he met around 8,000 convicts inside prison and settlers outside, as well as guards and officials, how his written account was distilled from a huge number of interviews and impressions, and from a near indigestible mass of notes and cards. We do not know whether he spent time trying to squeeze information from the cards, or gave up fairly soon on his return. He was concerned that they might be useful for later generations and, despite their possible inaccuracies, they are now a genealogical resource – or at least an object of curiosity – in the new museum to his book in Yushno-Sakhalinsk, which would no doubt amuse him.

In summary, there were a number of null returns, 5,600 for occupation and 2,600 for year of arrival, but these formed a minority. He showed that most people had arrived in the 1880s, with mainly men initially but with a subsequent increase in women, both as convicts and free travellers, accompanying their husbands, with few men following their convicted wives. As he wrote in his free text, there were few older children and young adults. While there were 1,435 children under the age of fourteen who had been born on the island, he only found 3 people aged twenty-one who had been born there (though he could not distinguish whether this reflected emigration or a low birth rate around 1870 or so).

Chekhov presumably wished to use of the census to generate numbers and impress for his doctorate. He also used the census to support several of his conclusions. One was that after eight years labour on the island, convicts when released were too old to colonize outside, and anyway too demoralized as well (Chekhov, 1895: 213). Elsewhere he uses the census to suggest there are insufficient women to populate the island (53 to each man outside prison, 25 to 100 overall), while the data on children highlights their poor schooling and the way in which they appear to leave the colony if they can, depriving it of the very population of young adults it needs (Chekhov, 1895: 225). Though a morass of detail, understandable given the numbers of cards and the difficulties in analysis, Chekhov managed to drag some data in support of his thesis from the census.

Meeting so many people in such a short and difficult time must have meant they became a blur. Chekhov's instinct, though, was to focus on the person and the individual. In his memoir on the death of his wife, Julian Barnes writes that 'grief is the place where statistics run out' (Barnes, 2013: 109). Statistics do indeed run out. The impression is certainly that Chekhov preferred individual narrative to dry statistics, feeling that numbers though useful, needed fleshing out as well. This may have reflected his literary background, but also, as we have learnt, his medical training.

## Notes

1. www.findrussianheritage.com/news/russian-imperial-census-1897/ and http://www.chekhov-sakhalin.ru/people/1. The rest of the cards are in the State Library, Moscow. They have also been published in book form (in Russian).

2. Alexander Iosad, a student at the time in Oxford, translated the cards into XL spreadsheets and these were initially available on Andy Dawson's website for the project which is no longer maintained. So I have arranged for them to be accessible at my own site, www.jonathandcole.org.

3. Though he was not supposed to see political prisoners, there appear to be two census cards from this group.

4. This gives over 110,000 entries with 15 categories and 7,445 individuals. It is clear that he did not use the census to diagnose disease. In the cards he only noted disease in around fifty subjects; five were interviewed in alms houses and presumably infirm (all in their 60s or 70s), six were blind, two deaf, four had respiratory illnesses and six were mentally ill or insane – most of the latter were exiles who had their own houses and were single. Only one was diagnosed with TB, seven with syphilis and one unfortunate man with both, a single Jewish convict aged forty-four. Both diseases would have been common on the island, though not always easily recognizable during a short conversation. Remember that Chekhov was not looking for illness when interviewing people. Indeed, he may have avoided medical matters since if word got round that he was a doctor then he might have been inundated.

5. In his footnotes he gives a more detailed breakdown of numbers, for each five-year age range for each gender, for a sample of 8,040 people. Interestingly this does not tally completely with a similar analysis of the translated cards sample of 7,445. The main difference is that Chekhov's larger sample has more children.

6. He only wrote one story set in St Petersburg which details the lives of government officials. It is told from the perspective of a shadowy man, a presumed infiltrator. *An Anonymous Story*.

7. Rayfield, D. The original suggestion is from an official on Sakhalin, Feldman, 'Chekhov has a remarkable ability to gain prisoners' confidence'.

8. Some were from even further, with Austria sending two, Persia two, Poland four, Prussia seven and Turkey one. At the time the major populations were to be found in Moscow and St Petersburg, which – arguably – were under-represented among the exiles.

9. One woman had arrived in 1873 and seems to have still been classified as a convict, though this might have been to avoid settler status and lose her allowances.

10. Rykovskoe is on the Tym River on the Pacific coast side of Sakhalin across from Aleksandrovsk.

## References

Barnes, J. (2013). *Levels of Life*. London: Jonathan Cape.

Bartlett, R. (2004). *Chekhov*. London: Simon and Shuster.

Bartlett, R. (2004). *Anton Chekhov: A Life in Letters*, translated, Bartlett, R. and Phillips, A. London: Penguin Classics.

Chekhov, A. (1895). *Sakhalin Island*, translated by Brian Reeve. London; One World Edition. 1993, 2007, 2014. (Throughout translations are from the 2007 edition).

Laffitte, S. (1974). *Chekhov*. London: Readers Union/Angus Robertson.

Popkin, C. (1992). 'Chekhov as Ethnographer; Epistemological Crisis on Sakhalin Island', *Slavic Review*, 51(1), 36–51. See also Chapter 11 for further discussion.

# CHAPTER 9
## MONDAY TO WEDNESDAY

He had returned to Moscow with a trunk full of notes, all his census cards, and enough memories to haunt a lifetime. He had done the field work, now was time to write the thesis, repay his debt to medicine and improve his chances of an academic medical position. It did not turn out quite that way. For starters, he returned with a cold, an exacerbation of his haemorrhoids, which made sitting down painful, and had a disquieting heart arrhythmia.[1] Unsurprisingly, the trip had worsened his TB and his health never recovered to pre-Sakhalin levels. Back at home he was too ill to leave the house for a month. Despite this, once well enough, he wrote letters and a short story *Guzev*, based on an event which happened at sea soon after he had left Sakhalin.

He described to friends his memories of his journey to 'heaven and hell'. He had been alive in a way he had not before, as he had hoped, and boasted of his dalliances with dusky women.[2] In a letter to Suvorin:

Sakhalin appears complete hell . . . [In contrast] Ceylon was paradise. I travelled more than seventy miles by train, and enjoyed my fill of palm groves and bronze skinned women. When I have children of my own I shall boast to them, 'Well, you little sons of bitches, once upon a time I had intercourse with a black eyed Hindy girl . . . in a coconut grove, by the light of the moon'. (Heim and Karlinsky, 1973: 173–5. Letter to Suvorin, 9th December 1890)

And to a friend, Leontiv, 10 December 1890.

'I have lived! It is enough.' I have been to Hell, represented by Sakhalin and in heaven, that is to say the island of Ceylon. (Bartlett and Phillips, 2004: 255. Letter to Leontiv, 10 December 1890)

Once well enough, and after nearly a year away, he was understandably desperate to play and to catch up with friends. Early in January 1891 he went to St Petersburg for three weeks, getting drunk and objectionable at parties, playing the field and resuming his romance with Lika Mizinova. He also found time to start writing *Sakhalin Island*.

He went back to Moscow, where soon afterwards Suvorin appeared. Chekhov decided that they should go to Europe, a journey postponed previously. They set off with Suvorin's son, in mid-March, by train on a two-month jaunt which included Vienna and the tourist sites and nightclubs of Venice, Rome, Naples, Nice and Paris. Not only making up for lost time, he seemed to be seizing life while his health allowed. Despite these trips and the Chekhov family's several changes of address, the next year and a half were extraordinarily productive for his literary output. And, throughout, he worked steadily on his Sakhalin project, though progress in that appeared at times worrying slow.

Once back in Moscow, the whole family decamped for the summer to a cramped dacha. Despite Lika's renewed attentions and the small quarters, he, finally, settled down to write, getting up at 4.00 am and working up to fifteen hours per day and at times sleeping only for a few hours.[3] He was regimented in approach; Monday to Wednesday he wrote on Sakhalin, on Thursday to Saturday he worked on what he called his novels, or major stories, and then on Sunday he would write his shorter stories. One reason for his pace was that he and his family needed money, since Chekhov had earned little for over a year and was dependent more and more on Suvorin.[4]

That summer he finished *The Duel*, the publication of which eased his financial worries, and an initially anonymous attack on the conditions in Moscow Zoo called *The Tricksters*, which was influential in its rebuilding. It was only after publication that he asked the zoo to take the increasingly difficult mongoose and civet, which must have made things interesting.

In the autumn, Chekhov was distracted from writing by another good cause. The harvest failed in central Russia and the resulting famine, about which the government discouraged discussion and failed to intervene in, together with the severe winter, led to perhaps one million deaths. He campaigned for funds and in January 1892, after the usual drunken partying in St Petersburg, went to the famine area and set up a scheme to prevent peasants from slaughtering their horses for food, since that left them without for the next year's work. He raised funds to buy the horses, look after them and then sold them back when the peasants were able to buy. Once back at home, sick once more from tramping around muddy fields and far-off farms, he found that much of the money raised had been embezzled. He also wrote *My Wife* in which a saintly doctor works for famine relief despite his obstructive, estranged wife. It may lack subtlety or nuance, but was very effective in mobilizing publicity and aid.

In February, Chekhov and his family bought an estate, Melikhovo, with 600 acres and a small, dilapidated house and some outbuildings. The plan was to give Chekhov privacy and a place to write, and for them to live more cheaply.[5] The reality was that the estate had been neglected and the house needed fumigating, cleaning and re-decorating. It also needed a proper water supply and sanitation. They had to buy horses and hay and straw, poultry, seed and ploughs. They found that their Tolstoy-style back to land idyll turned sour as local peasants, happy to be hired were equally happy to swindle. Chekhov set up free clinics to win them around (and over the next few years saw a thousand or more patients).

Initially it must have been a nightmare though he grew to love it. He stocked the cleaned-out pond with every freshwater species of fish he could find, and planted fifty cherry trees (the real orchard preceding the theatrical one). He would fish, garden and play his much-loved croquet, even rigging up lanterns to allow games at night.

In the summer of 1892 work was again interrupted, this time when cholera broke out in the district and was expected in Melikhovo. He gave up writing completely to work as an unpaid zemstvo physician, ending up as physician for twenty-three of the surrounding villages, treating syphilis and worms as well as cholera with a variety of efficacious drugs, including castor oil, calomel (a mercury-based purgative), scalding hot tannin enemas, and a subcutaneous salt solution which occasionally 'paralysed the heart' (Heim and Karlinsky, 1973: 238. Letter to Suvorin, 1 August 1 1892). He also shamed the owners of a tannery into cleaning up their pollution of a river. Some of the material for his stories on the effects of industrialization may be traced to this period.

In his collection and analysis of Chekhov's letters, Karlinsky entitles the period from late 1891 through 1892 as part of 'The Busy Years' (Karlinsky, in Karlinsky and Heim, 1973, *Chekhov's Life and Thought*: 201). He had swanned around Europe, arranged famine relief (risking his life and health going through central Russia in mid-winter), moved into and renovated the dilapidated estate at Melikhovo, and worked as a physician fighting cholera. At the same time, he had also written some of the 'greatest masterpieces of Russian prose even written, all in the span of sixteen months' (Karlinsky, in Karlinsky and Heim, 1973, *Chekhov's Life and Thought*: 203). And there was still time for partying and women.

It is not surprising that progress on *Sakhalin* stalled, and though it was never forgotten or dropped, his staccato progress alternately frustrated and consumed him. To Suvorin he wrote, 'writing my Sakhalin, and I'm bored, so bored' (http://www.gutenberg.org/files/6408/6408-h/6408-h.htm #link2H_4_0008), and yet only forty-eight hours later, 'There are times when I want to spend three to five years on it, slaving frantically and times when I am depressed and want to chuck it all' (http://www.gutenberg.org/files/6408/6408-h/6408-h.htm#link2H_4_0008).

Soon after he started the zemstvo work, in August, 1892, he wrote again to Suvorin, who may have given up hope of a *Sakhalin* manuscript,

I have not time to give even a thought to literature . . . When you read in the papers that the epidemic is over, you'll know I've begun to write again. But as long as I'm working for the zemstvo don't think of me as a writer. You can't run after two hares at once.

You write that I have given up Sakhalin. No, I can't give up that particular brainchild. When fiction begins to bore or oppress me, I enjoy taking up something nonfictional. And I am not particularly concerned with when I'll finish Sakhalin and or where I'll publish it. As long as Galkin-Vrassky sits on the throne, I don't feel like releasing the book. Of course, if I had to publish it or starve, that would be a different story. (Heim and Karlinsky, *Letters*: 241)

His problems, though, were not just due to his clinical work, which he continued after the end of concern about cholera, mobilizing support for famine victims, or with Galkin-Vrassky – he was struggling to find the right tone for *Sakhalin*. At one level, he was overwhelmed with the sheer amount of data and notes he had made. But he was also haunted and appalled by what he had seen. Nothing he had seen or read, in Kennan, in Dostoevsky or elsewhere prepared him for the complete absence of law and humanity he met on Sakhalin.

My brief Sakhalin past seems so enormous that whenever I try to talk about it, I scarcely know where to begin, and it always seems to come out wrong.

I shall try to describe in some detail the situation of children and young people on Sakhalin. It is quite extraordinary . . ., I saw starving children, girls as young as thirteen acting as kept women, girls of fifteen pregnant. girls start prostitution before menstruation. (Heim and Karlinsky, 1973: 179)

He had to come to terms with it and then find a way to show others, without them thinking he was exaggerating, or even imagining the horror. *Sakhalin Island* took two years or more before it was serialized in *Russian Thought* in 1893–4, with the book published a year later in 1895. For someone who had once boasted of never spending more than a day on a story early in his career, this was an immense gestation.

I saw everything. The question is now, not what I saw but how I saw it. I don't know what will come out finally, but I have done quite a lot. There is enough for 3 dissertations. I have been getting up at 5 every morning, going to bed late, and spent every day on the thought that there is still a great deal I haven't done. I have a feeling as if I have seen everything and missed the elephant.[6] There is not a single convict or settled exile on Sakhalin who has not had a chat with me. The census of the children has been especially successful. (Chekhov, 1895: 497)

In his previous writings, he had taken from real life, frequently basing characters on real people and events on real events (and sometimes got into trouble for this). He was a master at implying emotions and feelings between the lines, exploring what was happening off stage and in people's minds. On Sakhalin there was no subtlety, no nuance, just overwhelming, unimaginable depravity; how could he express it? He had to step back from his previous methods and portray Sakhalin's bleak, foreign world from the outside, like an anthropologist in Hades. Even then some of what he saw and heard of on Sakhalin was too depraved to be included, though some found its way into his later fiction.

In parallel with this was another, almost insuperable, concern that he never fully escaped. To Suvorin, 'I have the feeling that my trousers don't hang right on me, that I am not writing it as I should, that I give my patients the wrong medicine'. He was no stranger to cruelty and injustice in his life, but on Sakhalin he had witnessed hell, 'utter degradation beyond which it was impossible to imagine', cruel and corrupt officials and a complete absence of morality as people, focussed on survival, lost their dignity and their humanity. If to reveal this was one problem, the second was how to express *Sakhalin* without condemnation. How could he write of a hell created by the indifference of the authorities without judgement and without telling people what to think? As Rayfield wrote:

> Sakhalin, his magnum opus, he suspected there was falsehood or a wrong note in the work, namely its didactic intention. (Rayfield, 1997, 2010, *Chekhov – A Life*: 117)

He detected his insincerity in trying to make it instructive and felt relieved when he realized there really were swine on the island and that he did not need to be scrupulously fair handed. Supressing his outrage, as he assembled his thesis, his conclusions were clear, though these were wrapped, as best he could, in facts rather than opinions, detached conclusions rather than moral indignation, as he itemized, for instance, crop yields, the problems with settlement sites and the living conditions and convicts' morals. Where possible he made constructive suggestions, for instance the advantages of releasing convicts from prison earlier. Rather than condemn, he tried to understand, to explain and to blame the system rather than its victims, whether convicts or their guards.

In the end, the form and structure emerged as he wrote. It began with his travelogue on the journey out, full of description, personal observation and anecdote. This was relatively straightforward and a short step from his previous work. On arrival, there are chapters of reportage on what he saw in the northern and then southern settlements. The next five chapters are observations and conclusions on settlers, women and children and on diet and food production before he ends, in the published book, with four chapters on the guards, morality, escapes and health that were not published in serial form in *Russian Thought*.

*Sakhalin Island plan.*
From Siberia – 9 short chapters of travelogue.

1. Journey from Siberia along Amur etc.

   *The North*
2. Arrival in Aleksandrovsk, geography and meeting people
3. Census
4. Aleksandrovsk
5. Aleksandrovsk prison
6. Yegor's story

7.  Korsakovskoye
8.  Arkovo and Douai
9.  Tym valley
10. Rykoskoye
11. History and Gilyaks
    *The South*
12. Journey to Korsakovsk
13. Around southern settlements
14. South, Ainu and Japanese
    *Thesis assembled*
15. Transfer to settle status
16. Women and children
17. Population by age, marriage, birth, children
18. Farming, hunting, fishing
19. Diet, church, literacy
20. Overseers and the educated
21. Morals and punishment
22. Escapes
23. Morbidity, mortality and medicine

(The book sections in italics have been added. The book in Brian Reeve's translation has 322 pages of text and 123 pages of notes and references.)

He finished with a patchwork of travelogue, narrative, census, biography and prose poetry, combining meteorology, anthropology, agriculture and fisheries, his collation of facts and figures, as best he could assemble them, all worked towards conclusions, some explicit and others wrapped in subtlety and irony. More than that, however, he showed how a breakdown in decency, law and feeling towards fellow men, might emerge and lead to, for him, a previously unimaginable heart of darkness.

They had thought him mad to go, mad to travel and risk the 6,000 miles there and then to spend all that time with the convicts. On his return, he had boasted about prostitutes and showed off the civet cat. But he had been less forthcoming about what he saw – the disease, depravity, prostitution, beatings and sheer utter desperation. In the end, to tell this dispassionately, to show a breakdown of all the humanity that he held precious, he was clinical, effacing his own views, trusting his medical and scientific descriptions and the human stories to move people to action.[7] He was never sure he had succeeded.

> Chekhov's modesty underestimated the sheer magnitude of his achievement . . . he remained convinced he had seen everything but missed the elephant. (Rayfield, 1997, 2010, *Chekhov – A Life*: 96ff)

On publication, as we shall see, the book raised a predictable mixture of public outrage and tempered response by the authorities. Since then, it has both amazed and puzzled, convincing some more than others. But before considering its reception, we consider the stories he wrote while grappling with *Sakhalin Island*, since these may betray his preoccupations more clearly than his letters. While some are short and fun, others are among his best and most revealing. The next section, then, moves from an analysis of *Sakhalin Island* to a consideration of his literary output as he was writing it before moving on to the critical reception the book received on publication in 1895 and since, and then to an analysis of how the journey affected Chekhov subsequently. It moves from direct analysis and exposition to wider interpretations.

## Notes

1. This could have been a number of different rhythms, from atrial fibrillation in which the heart beats irregularly to a supraventricular tachycardia. Such beating can induce a feeling of unease, with some also feeling nervous and anxious, with butterflies in the stomach. This is mentioned in his short stories and, right at the beginning of *Ivanov*, Borkin describes his heart beating irregularly too. Chekhov mentions his irregular heartbeat in the letter to Suvorin and goes on, 'Every minute my heart stops a few seconds' (24 December 1890). The cause will remain unclear.

2. Before setting out for Sakhalin with Andrew Dawson his wife, Sarah, said to me, 'You're going for an adventure; to feel more alive'.

3. His father retired in April 1891 and found his new life difficult, taking it out on his wife. One reason for working so early in the day was to take advantage of the peace and quiet.

4. During the trip to Europe he was, in his own words, like, 'a kept woman' completely dependent on Suvorin for funds.

5. For the grandson of a serf to own an estate would have been unimaginable a few decades earlier.

6. This phrase, so overused in England now, was in currency then too. Heim and Karlinsky suggest it originates from Krylov's fable, 'The Inquisitive Man', in which a visitor to a museum who is so absorbed looking at preserved insects that he fails to notice the stuffed elephant (Heim and Karlinsky, *Letters*: 172).

7. He also omitted some of the worse examples of inhumanity, though these emerged later in his short stories.

## References

Bartlett, R. (2004). *Letters*, translated Bartlett, R. and Phillips, A. London: Penguin Classics.

Chekhov, A. (1895). *Sakhalin Island*, translated by Brian Reeve. London; One World Edition. 1993, 2007, 2014. (Throughout translations are from the 2007 edition).

Heim, M. and Karlinsky, S. (1973). *Letters of Anton Chekhov*. New York, Evanston, San Francisco and London.

Karlinsky, S. Introduction, in Heim, M. and Karlinsky, S. (1973). *Letters of Anton Chekhov*. New York, and London; Harper and Row.

Rayfield, D. (1997, 2010). *Anton Chekhov – A Life*. London: HarperCollins. 1997, 2010. Second Edition, London: Garnett Press. 2021.

# PART IV
## INTERPRETATIONS

# CHAPTER 10
## BUSY YEARS

The preparations for his trip and the visit itself took two years or so, and it took another three years for *Sakhalin Island* to be published. After the year away he and his family badly needed money, so Chekhov returned to fiction. There was no Great Russian Novel on penal conditions – the times were not right and, in any case, what he saw was too dark – but instead a series of stories, some short trifles which he wrote on Sundays, and others written on Thursday to Saturday which were among his finest and most important. Maybe Sakhalin spurred him to go deeper and further than previously, maybe he was more aware of how little precious time he might have left.

His letters throughout his life detail what he did and sometimes what he thought, but only a very few tell what he felt. One such is on why he was going to Sakhalin, another details his lost childhood and a third, to be reproduced later, gives his philosophy on life. Despite the trip, many of his letters from the time are routine. There are clues, however, in his feelings from the more substantial novels from this time, as he balanced *Sakhalin* with his other writing.

Before this, were two short stories, *Gusev* (published soon after his return in December 1890) and later *In Exile* (May 1892) directly related to his trip.

*Gusev* is a fictionized account of the death and burial at sea of two men on the boat coming home. He had written to Suvorin:

> Two people died on our way to Singapore . . . thrown overboard. When you see a dead man wrapped in sailcloth somersaulting into the water, it is a shocking realization that the bottom lies several miles below . . . (Heim and Karlinsky, 1973: 173. Letter to Suvorin, 9 December 1890)

The short story has two protagonists: Gusev a discharged private soldier, a batman, who has been in the East for five years and is now sent home with TB, and Ivanovich who is more educated. Both are in the sickbay and mortally ill. They chat but scarcely understand each other. Ivanovich dies first and then Gusev. Chekhov contrasts the peasant's simple acceptance of his fate with the more educated man's useless railing against it. All this, however, seems pale compared with the description of Gusev's burial at sea and Chekhov's uncharacteristically poetic description of it.

> Gusev slides down the plank, flies off headfirst, does a somersault in the air and vanishes beneath the waves . . . He sinks eight or nine fathoms and then moves more slowly, as if trying to make up his mind.

> Pilot fish stop dead and turn tail and vanish before pouncing on him like arrows. Then a shark . . . ponderous, reluctant and apparently ignoring Gusev it glides under him... then it turns belly up and languidly opens its jaw, plays with the body and tears the sailcloth. One iron bar falls out, scares the pilot fish, hits the shark and goes swiftly to the bottom.

> Overhead, clouds are massing on the sunset side, one like a triumphant arch, another like a lion, a third like a pair of scissors.

> A green shaft of light breaks through . . . a little later a violet one, then a gold one and then a pink one . . . The sky turns a delicate mauve. Gazing at this sky so glorious and magical, the ocean scowls at first, but soon takes on gentle, joyful, passionate colours for which human language may well have no name.

Here Chekhov's poetic description stretches his credo of writing with clinical precision.

*In Exile* is set in Siberia and tells of how to survive there. 'Foxy', sixty, lean, toothless and drunk, is talking with 'The Tartar', young and new to exile, as they wait for a ferry. The Tartar looks forward to his mother and wife joining him. But Foxy insists he would be better off alone: 'You don't need anything, no father, no mother, no wife, no freedom, no nothing . . .'. He tells a story of another young man whose wife came to join him. They had a daughter but then the wife fled back to European Russia with her lover and their daughter faded from consumption. For the Tartar, even three years of marriage was better than none and he breaks down thinking of his own wife left at home. Foxy replies he will settle down in time. 'Things ain't so bad in Siberia, it's a life of sorts' – less of a Tolstoy-like purity than an acceptance of a minimal life worthy of Beckett.

Other stories are free from his Sakhalin preoccupation. In 1891 he produced several stories, *My Wife*, as we have learned, was inspired by his work on the failed harvest in central Russia, and is about lost love, and donating money for famine relief. Its main aim, which was very successful, was to increase awareness of the famine. *After the Theatre* concerns a girl swimming in young love. In the more substantial *Neighbours* a young girl runs away from her family to live with an older married man who cannot afford to divorce his wife. The girl's brother goes over to remonstrate with his sister about the unhappiness she has caused at home. Once there, he understands their situation and realizes his own impotence to do anything more than meddle and make things worse – a classic liberal dilemma.

In three other short stories Chekhov obviously had fun. *The Story of a Commercial Venture* concerns a man who attempts to bring culture to a town by opening a book-shop. After three weeks, the first customer arrives, and he wants not books but pencils. As a result, the shopkeeper stocks up with stationary. Other customers ask for stamps, satchels, games and Christmas decorations. Nappies, tea, paraffin and groceries follow. The shop prospers as a general store and he eventually sells off the books at 3 roubles per hundredweight. Chekhov's views of the cultural life of provincial towns are clear.

In *From a Retired Teacher's Notebook* the old teacher muses, 'when teaching science one should ensure that pupils have their books bound; one cannot bang them on the head with an unbound book. Children! What bliss it is to receive one's pension!' This from a man who loved education, who built several schools himself and raised money for schoolbooks to send to Sakhalin and elsewhere.

*A Fishy Affair* concerns a carp which falls in love with a young girl. When she swims in his pool the carp kisses her feet, even though he knows there is no chance of reciprocity. Instead, the carp buries himself in mud, writes a diary and tries to engineer his death by the hand of his girl. Later he mistakes a young poet for his love and kisses his back, infecting the poet with his lovelorn pessimism. He returns to St Petersburg and, in turn, infects his fellow poets, which is why they all write gloomy melancholic verse. This may not have endeared him to the literati and intelligentsia of that city.

These stories must have been welcome diversions from writing on Sakhalin. His difficulties in finding the right voice for his Sakhalin experience are reflected in three more substantial stories – or what he sometimes called 'novels' – from this time, *The Grasshopper*, *The Duel* and *Ward Number 6*.

The difficulties of communication between the two cultures, art and science, are explored in *The Grasshopper* (January 1892). Chekhov described it, drily, as 'a sentimental love story for family reading'. His earlier titles, *The Philistines* and then *A Great Man* are more revealing.

It begins after a wedding. The bride's friends wonder quite why the pretty young Olga has married such a plain boring man – a doctor. He worked hard at two hospitals, had little private practice, and there was 'nothing more to say about him'. In contrast Olga's friends were all distinguished, one a 'histrionic, eloquent, and modest' actor, while Ryabovsky, a painter, was twenty-five, and inevitably successful and dashing. There was also a cellist and a writer . . . all free, artistic, spoilt favourites, who 'only knew of doctors when they fell ill'.

While Dymov, the doctor, worked, she spent – on clothes and decorations for the house. She got up at 11.00 am, played the piano, painted, went to her dressmaker, called on a friend, before going onto a painter's studio and then sang or acted. She worshipped and dreamed of the famous. After dining with her husband at 5.00 pm she went out again and returned only after midnight. On Wednesdays, she gave extravagant parties for her exclusively male circle. At 11.30 pm Dymov would appear to announce supper. Though he ate with the artists, he was ignored.

One summer she and her artists went to the country to paint. A few weeks later Dymov visited, looking forward to seeing Olga and, after a day's travel, to dinner. The artists did not recognize him while she made him return immediately, without eating, to send a pink dress for her to wear at a country wedding.

Chekhov describes Olga's seduction by Ryabovsky in over-ripe prose worthy of Barbara Cartland.

On the deck of a steamer, the black shadows on the water were not shadows but dreams, the water was magical, with a lambent sheen, with a fathomless sky and sad, pensive river banks, it would be good to forget everything, to die, to become a memory . . . her heart filled with unaccountable joy as she stood with a great genius, one of God's elect. She was chilly so he wrapped his cloak round her,

'I feel I'm in your power. I'm your slave. Why are you so adorable today? Say the word and I will stop living. Love me, love me . . .'

Her heart beat violently.

They sent for wine. The story picks up three months later. The day is overcast, dull, drizzling and cold, as her affair is becoming and, eventually, she returns home. Realizing that her interest in artists went well beyond their art, Dymov starts to bring a medical friend to dinner and they bore Olga with their chat.

As Ryabovksy's affections decline, she becomes less cautious in her affair and more demanding. Months pass. Dymov explains that he had just defended his thesis and suggests he might be offered a prestigious post. 'From his blissful, radiant face, had she been able to share his triumph, he would have forgiven her anything. But she did not know what it all meant and was afraid she was late for the theatre . . .'

Ryabovsky meanwhile is having another affair. Distraught, Olga goes home to find that Dymov has diphtheria. In the only medical part of the story we – and Olga – learn that it was from 'suck[ing] out the fibrinous exudations from the throat' of a little boy.

She is kept from him to avoid infecting herself, as doctors arrive to nurse him instead. As he deteriorates, a colleague tells Olga what a waste it was – Dymov was a great man, remarkable, an inspiration to them all, a moral force and future professor, despite having, the friend continues, to look for private practice and sit up all night doing translation work to pay for her rotten rags. She runs to him in his study, but it is, of course, too late. She wanted to explain her error, her mistake, how everything would now be different, how she would worship him and feel a sacred awe of him. In another room the doctor friend arranges the funeral.

The story satirizes a woman attaching herself to famous artists and delights in parodying the romantic descriptions of overblow artistic (in) sensibilities. It lays bare Chekhov's suspicions of marriage, and of women in general as distracting from deeper work. This is probably why Tolstoy – by now espousing chastity and sexual abstinence after an enthusiastic early romantic life and thirteen children – loved it. But one of the main contrasts is between his relentless focus on the wife and her art and feelings, with the almost complete absence of the work and inner life of Dymov. Medicine and science seem, he is saying, to be impenetrable and inexpressible compared with literature. Remember him writing of how medicine was his lawful wedded wife and art his mistress. This story has elements of criticism towards artistic frippery compared with the dull, worthy, methodical work of medicine. And self-criticism maybe too, since Chekhov, after all, had chosen writing and was not immune to the overblown praise and adulation of young women admirers.

At the time though this was opaque, at best, and the story produced a more immediate furore. He had always sailed close to the wind, assimilating material from friends and acquaintances into his work – artists are merciless magpies. This time he overstepped himself. His close friend, the painter Levitan, was teaching the wife of a doctor, Sofia Kuvshinnikov, and having an affair with her. They went off on a painting trip to the Volga; she gave weekly parties for her male artist friends at which her husband would announce that supper was served. Fortunately, Dr Kuvshinnikov did not die from diphtheria, though another doctor had, with considerable debate as a result.

Levitan had first met Michael Chekhov at Moscow School of Painting, Sculpture and Art in 1875. When Chekhov moved to Moscow they became friends. Levitan was to become one of Russia's foremost landscape painters. He was also, probably, a bipolar depressive and, not unlike Chekhov, hugely attractive to women. Chekhov and he became close friends, and for three summers Levitan stayed with the Chekhovs, in part because Anton was concerned about his health. He even asked Levitan to go to Sakhalin with him. Though that did not come to pass, Levitan was one of the party who saw Chekhov off at the station on his journey East. In his depth of feeling and descriptive power, Levitan painted landscapes as Chekhov wrote about them. He also proposed to Anton's sister Maria, something she – an unmarried, lifelong keeper of her brother's legacy – disclosed in 1953 four years before she died (Gregory, 2015: 221).

Levitan had many affairs and seemed unconcerned to keep them private. The enduring one was with Sofia Kuvshinnikova. Gregory suggests that Chekhov did not approve of her open adultery, nor that she rather fawned over him. Even so, for Chekhov to have been quite so clear in using their affair in his story must have been unexpected and was less than sensitive to a friend and someone he had helped through depression. To add spice to the story's genesis, Lika tried to make Chekhov jealous by staying with Levitan and Sofia. Not surprisingly, Levitan took exception to his affair being exposed to the whole of Russia, and initially wanted a duel. They fell out and did not talk for several years. Lika was amazed a man as sensitive as Chekhov could be so blind to others' suffering. A friend told Chekhov that 'you really do not care how people will take what you write'. Sofia and her husband the doctor never spoke to Chekhov again. Chekhov hardly helped by denying it, on the grounds that his grasshopper was a pretty young girl, like Lika, whereas Sofia was neither pretty nor young. In Chekhov's defence, if 'defence' is appropriate, he had suspected Levitan of cuckolding Chekhov with Lika. She was equally hurt, but as Rayfield suggests, was in love and therefore more understanding (Rayfield, 1997, 2010: 269).

Fortunately, he and Levitan were reunited nearly three years later by a young woman writer, Shchepkina-Kupernik. Though their rapprochement was welcomed, Chekhov and Levitan were never as close again. Ironically, Shchepkina-Kupernik used this episode for the basis of a short story herself, though one published in 1911, after they had both died. Levitan died in 1899, probably of an enlargement of the aorta and failure of the aortic valve of the heart, which may well have been caused by syphilis.

*The Duel* (published in November 1891) is more substantial, in terms of the story, its revelations about Chekhov's changes of heart and mind following his trip and indeed its length. It begins with a preliminary skirmish about women between Laevsky, who has come to the town in the Caucasus with his married mistress, Nadezhda, to start a new life, Tolstoy style, on the land, and a military doctor, Samoylenko, about what you should do when, after two years, you no longer love your mistress. Laevsky soon found working on the land too hard, so takes a civil service job and lives beyond his means. He wants to leave Nadezhda, quoting Tolstoy's ideas about the wickedness of women as justification, but the doctor suggests there is a duty to remain with one's partner. If Samoylenko is the kindly if innocuous doctor, Laevsky is a self-styled 'Superfluous Man', by then a rather tired Russian literary fashion originating in Pushkin's *Eugene Onegin*, a man, somewhat talented, usually wealthy and privileged, who is naturally bored, cynical and dissolute, with a penchant for cards, duels and women – what in English might be a wastrel or cad. Laevsky continues that he needs someone else's theories about life to guide him and cites Tolstoy as 'the great man'. Samoylenko agrees, though he has never read him, despite 'meaning to every day'. Samoylenko is fond of Laevsky, even though he dislikes most things about him – his extravagance, bad language, card playing, debt, his wearing slippers in the street and his feelings for Nadezhda, which 'would be insulting to a dog'.

Laevsky learns that Nadezhda's husband has died – he must either marry her or dump her. He will not marry for duty but to leave her he needs money and so asks Samoylenko. Now he, in turn, has two paying guests, a deacon and Von Koren, an evolutionary zoologist, studying the 'embryology of jellyfish'. A Darwinian evangelist, he is as strong in his views on natural selection as he is keen on admiring himself in the mirror. One cannot think of such figures today.

Von Koren hates Laevsky.

If that man was drowning, I'd take a stick and give him an extra shove. Drowning him would be a public service . . . He's a great a threat to society as cholera . . . In two years, all he has done is 'taught people to play bridge, drink beer and flaunted his adultery . . . Flabby, feeble and senile . . . I'd ignore him [but for] his success with women, so he threatens to have descendants. Primitive man was protected by the struggle for existence and natural selection. Modern civilisation has made this less intense. We must attend to extermination of the sickly and unfit ourselves.

At one point when asked if he would exterminate Laevsky he replies, 'without hesitation'.

Only later do we hear that Von Koren studies on his own and is a tyrant who wants to rid academe of its intrigues and mediocrity. Not, perhaps, an ideal way for Chekhov to describe an institution he was dependent on for the success of his thesis. Meanwhile Nadezhda is secretly pleased at Laevsky cooling towards her, since she is not enamoured with the Caucasus and has her own debts which she is reducing by prostitution, entertaining two men, one of whom is the chief of police.

Laevsky tells Nadezhda of her husband's death and then immediately goes to Samoylenko for money, who in turn approaches Von Koren. Realizing who it is for, the Darwinian imposes conditions – that either they leave together or that Nadezhda goes first, since he knows she will be deserted otherwise. The duel between Laevsky and Von Koren is finally achieved over Samoylenko's honour.

The night before the duel, Von Koren has time to lecture the deacon on the perils of loving people, and how the strong had to exterminate the weak. When 'force' wants to destroy the feeble, scrofulous, degenerate breed, 'don't try to stop it with quotations from the Gospels'. In contrast, that night Laevsky discovers his mistress with another man.

The next day, no one knows the rules for a duel, so they try to remember from Turgenev's literary description, life imitating art. As they count the steps, the deacon watches from a riverbank. Laevsky takes aim, deliberately high, and misses. Von Koren aims to kill but is put off his shot by the deacon's well-timed shout . . . the Darwinian's aim frustrated by the man of God.

It turns out Von Koren found trying to shoot someone repulsive. Laevsky on reaching home, and having escaped death, rather than being indignant and angry at Nadezhda, is the reverse, loving and kind, realizing what has driven her to it. Laevsky finds a proper job and marries Nadezhda. Three months later Von Koren, just before he leaves, apologizes to Laevsky for being wrong about him.

For Donald Rayfield this story is more dramatic even than his plays, with serious argument interspersed with meals – and humour – and with its action arising through and from dialogue. It also has a dramatic climax followed by a conclusion. Chekhov duels with, and partially disowns, two of his heroes. After writing that obituary in praise of Przhevalsky, the explorer and man of action, Chekhov must have learned more of his hard-line social views. The pistol fight is a farce and merits far less description than the duels between Von Koren and anyone who will listen – mainly the deacon – to his views on natural selection and social Darwinism. Von Koren was based on (though also disguised from) a Moscow zoologist, Vagner, that Chekhov had met in Bogimovo, But the character also in part represents Przhevalsky, who was uncompromising in his view that the abnormal must be wiped out for the love of humanity. Post-Sakhalin Chekhov saw Przhevalsky for what he was and foresaw the excesses of social Darwinism which were both so fashionable and so disastrous in the early twentieth century. He had seen, at first-hand, society dealing with convicts, their families and their children, how social structures perverted and degraded both the punished and the punishers. There was a delicious irony in his ex-hero missing with a shot, since Przhevalsky always practiced shooting and took the finest guns and rifles on expeditions, mainly to intimidate and subdue the natives. Sakhalin cured Chekhov of any ideas about the merits of social Darwinism and the survival of the fittest. As Rayfield suggests, Chekhov had worshipped Przhevalsky in 1888, but by 1891 he was 'disabused of heroics' (Rayfield, 1997, 2010: 106).

The other duel was gentler. Around this time Tolstoy's influence on Chekhov waned. He wrote a little later, in 1894, an oft quoted letter to Suvorin:

Tolstoy's moral philosophy has ceased to move me . . . [It] moved me deeply and possessed me for six or seven years . . . not so much his basic postulates . . . it was his way of expressing himself his common sense and probably some sort of hypnotism as well. But now something in me protests. Prudence and justice tell me there is more love for mankind in electricity and steam than in chastity and abstention from meat. War is evil and the court system is evil, but it doesn't follow that I should wear bast shoes and sleep on a stove alongside the hired hand and his wife. (Heim and Karlinsky, 1973: 261–2. Letter to Suvorin, 27 March 1894)

Before going he was a little in awe of Tolstoy, for his style perhaps more than for his morality or verisimilitude. In *The Kreutzer Sonata*, as Donald Rayfield suggests, the hero is destroyed as a force for good by a bourgeois marriage, by the twin evils of music and female sexuality and by the 'experiences of the bedroom'. Chekhov was impressed, though not blind to the great man's slack medical knowledge:

Even without mentioning its artistic merits, which are in certain passages astounding . . . as you read it, you can barely keep from shouting, 'That's true.' It has some very irritating faults . . . the audacity with which Tolstoy treats topics about which knows nothing and which out of obstinacy he does not wish to understand . . . syphilis, foundling homes, women's revulsion for sexual intercourse . . . expose him as an ignorant man. (Heim and Karlinsky, 1973: 156. Letter to Pleshcheyev, 15 February)[1]

While Laevsky might be considered to parody some of Tolstoy's ideas, leaving the big city to work on the land (initially at least), against this, other aspects of his life and, in particular, his relations with women would not have appealed to Tolstoy. But these aspects are but a part of the increasing ambivalence Chekhov felt for Tolstoy's philosophical outlook, though he always admired his writing. As Coope suggests, Tolstoy was suspicious of experts, and professionals who he thought were motivated by self-interest (Coope, 1997: 75–94). Progress for him was about moral advancement or it was about nothing. The gap between this and Chekhov's belief in progress through science was unbridgeable.

Though always suspicious of ideas and intellectuals, Sakhalin cured Chekhov of theoretical ways of improving people. He had seen, in his mind, the evils of the most severe human degradation imaginable as a consequence of 'justice', of how systems degrade both convict and guard, and implicitly the judges and lawyers too. On Sakhalin, he had listened, without judgement, to psychopaths, murderers and sadistic guards who responded to his openness with an honesty and humanity. As Kataev suggested:

In his book, The Island of Sakhalin, and in other Sakhalin works, he exposed not only the horrors of penal servitude, but the lies about it, both officially and in superficial denunciatory literature. He was also interested in how people judged these . . . educated society blamed the red-nosed governors, but he felt it was not the governors who were guilty, we all are. On Sakhalin he saw how claims to reform humanity might lead to disasters, and how unconditional application of universal concepts such as the law, crime and sentence to individuals might lead to multiplication of evil rather than its destruction . . .

When the logical application of laws and decrees comes into contact with the concrete reality of human existence, the consequences may be inhumane in the extreme – of that Chekhov had become totally convinced on Sakhalin. (Kataev, 2002: 110ff)

On his return, he was rid of the supremacy of an idea or an ideal, rid of heroes indeed. In a letter to Suvorin, 'How wrong of you to tell me not to go . . . before the journey "The Kreutzer Sonata" was an event for me; now I find it ridiculous and senseless. Perhaps I've matured; perhaps I've gone mad . . .'[2]

After Sakhalin his narratives became more complex and morally ambiguous, with dual or multiple –and often conflicting – perspectives. We are left to ourselves to decide, if indeed decision is the word. He wants to show life as it was, without judgement, or moral stance. Chekhov was on his own, and asked us to see that we all are too. To take such a stance cannot have been easy at the time and that apparently throwaway question to Suvorin about whether he was more mature or just mad was not entirely in jest.

His next major work comes as close as he ever did to a fictional account of Sakhalin. Ward Number 6 (June 1892) about a mental ward of a hospital, is saturated with imagery and events from Chekhov's visit. Rayfield suggests it is his most famous story in Russia and has inspired many other similar works where a ward or confined area is explored both for itself and as a metaphor, one recent example being Solzhenitsyn's Cancer Ward. One of his most powerful stories, it stands alone in its bleakness and sparseness. This truly is Sakhalin-made literature and, incidentally, the story terrified Lenin.

Ward Number 6 is a distant, isolated, forgotten nightmare of a mental ward of a hospital – a bare, man-made world completely unimaginable before Sakhalin. The story begins by inverting Chekhov's use of nature as beauty, with 'a jungle of burdock, nettles and wild hemp, a spiked fence and a doomed air peculiar to hospital and prisons'. Inside, the hall is filled with rubbish – tatters of clothes and old mattresses on which sits a caretaker, Nikita, who believes in the 'efficacy of blows'. The ceilings are black with soot – in winter the stoves belch smoke and poisonous fumes. There are iron-barred windows, the floor is carpeted with splinters and the place smells of sour cabbage, bed bugs and ammonia.

The ward has five long-term patients. The main character, Gromov, has persecution mania, his broad face tormented by incessant struggle and fear. His speech is confused and febrile, and yet you are aware of both the madman and the man within. We learn to understand that his madness followed the loss of his family – first his father, then his brother died, the latter of TB. After his mother's death, he lost his job as a teacher. Despite being friendless – possibly related to how he talked of his town being boring, with its violence, debauchery and senseless existence rather than schools and theatre – people liked him. He loved women 'though he had never been in love'.

His paranoia began one autumn morning, when he saw some prisoners and thought he might be dragged to prison too. Though not guilty of any crime, might he have done one by accident? After all, miscarriages of justice were common and people were never safe from poverty or prison. Judges, policemen and doctors (a neat group to choose), 'whose attitude to human suffering is strictly official and professional, become callous, as the peasant who slaughters sheep . . .'. A judge requires only one thing to deprive an innocent man of civil rights and sentence him to hard labour – time.

More and more paranoid, Gromov is admitted by the doctor, Ragin, to Ward 6 and within a year everyone had forgotten about him. His books, dumped on a sledge under an awning, are then carried off by urchins. On Ward Number 6, we learn, as Chekhov had learned on Sakhalin, the worst thing about the beatings is that the inmates do not shout or move, but just rock side-to-side like a heavy cask. Nowhere in the world was life as monotonous as this.

When Dr Ragin had been appointed to the hospital, young, keen and innocent, he had found it impossible to breathe for the stench in the wards, while cockroaches and bedbugs made life unbearable. Echoing Sakhalin, the whole hospital had only two scalpels and no thermometer. The townspeople knew all this but did not worry – after all only peasants and tradesmen were admitted, as most people were unconcerned about exile on

Sakhalin. Dr Ragin had wanted to close the hospital, 'an immoral institution highly detrimental to the health of those who lived in it'. But he could not – he had no authority and anyway it would only move somewhere else. So, once in post, he became indifferent, lacking the strength of character and confidence to assert himself.

Initially, he worked hard at medicine, seeing 12,000 outpatients in a year, but became increasingly disillusioned and lazy – this simply meant he deceived 12,000 people: 'To treat them in accordance with science was impossible; there was no science. And what did it matter if people died 5 years early and, anyway, could we not achieve perfection by suffering? If mankind alleviated suffering by pills it would give up religion and philosophy'.

He lost heart and stopped going in every day, or went home early to read. His only friend was the postmaster with whom he conversed about how the mind is the only place of pleasure and how he was forced into medicine by his father. Otherwise he could have been, 'in the middle of an intellectual movement. Life is a snare and an illusion, a trap from which there is no escape until death comes, "against his will"'.[3]

The hospital's work, he relates, was based on theft, gossip, favouritism and charlatanism, though he knew, in the last twenty-five years, medicine had undergone a miraculous change. It was no longer alchemy and metaphysics but science – antiseptics, heredity, Koch, Pasteur, hygiene, statistics, and even psychiatry.[4] No longer was cold water poured over the heads of lunatics. Like Sakhalin, Ward Six was years behind the times.

His sloth is noticed and a deputy appointed; Khobotov. Then, bored, Dr Ragin starts to visit the ward and engage in conversation with Gromov who asks, 'Why keep me here? Scores of madmen walk about unmolested, because you are incapable of distinguishing them from healthy people. Where is the logic?'

Ragin replies:

Morality and logic have nothing to do with it. It's chance. Those put here, stay here, those not put here are free. If I let you go you'd be stopped by the townspeople. Reconcile yourself that your stay here is necessary. Once prisons and lunatic asylums exist, there must be someone to be there. If not you, it's me. Have patience, in some far way time prisons and asylums will cease to exist. You are an intelligent and thoughtful man; you can discover peace of mind in any environment. Diogenes lived in a barrel and yet was happy.

'He was a damn fool.'

Ragin persists with his theories.

> Even if sentenced to exile or Siberia, you'd be no worse off. There is no difference between a warm, cosy room and this ward. A man's peace of mind and contentment are not outside him but within him.

> 'Go preach that philosophy in Greece, where is warm and the air full of perfume of orange blossom.'

> Marcus Aurelius said, 'Pain is merely a vivid conception of pain, change this by an effort of will, shake it off and the pain will disappear.' That's true. A sage has contempt for suffering.

Gromov replies:

> I must be idiot, for I'm suffering . . . I respond to pain with tears and cries, to baseness with indignation. To my mind that it is what's really called life. To be content one needs to . . . be so hardened by suffering to have lost all susceptibility to it - or in other words to have ceased to live . . . In contrast Dr Ragin, he says, has seen nothing of life, has stopped working, and just reads and drinks, never interfering when he sees evil. A peasant woman comes with toothache, well pain is just a concept . . . we're kept here behind iron bars, tortured, allowed to rot, but all this is wonderful and rational, for there is no real difference between this ward and a warm, comfortable study. How expedient.

Gromov goes from being shy talking to Ragin to becoming open and then adopts a condescending irony. Meanwhile people had noticed these visits and were becoming increasingly worried both by Ragin's behaviour and by his drinking. He is called to see the mayor and given a mental examination. His friend suggests he rests and that they take a trip. On their return his deputy has taken his job and his flat. Then, after Ragin loses his temper with his friends, Khobotov gently admits him to Ward 6.

He puts on hospital clothes, 'pants too short, shirt too long, smock stinking of fish'. That night he looks out under a cold crimson moon to the nearby prison and a glue factory – all terrify him. He approaches Gromov for comfort, only to be jeered at. 'How about a spot of philosophy?' He asks to be let out and argues with Nikita who punches him in the face and body.

Tasting blood, Ragin lies on his bed unable to move for the pain. Previously 'he had neither known pain, nor had a conception of it'. Next day he dies of a stroke.[5]

One motif in *Ward Number 6* concerns the relation between the real and the imagined, between false posturing and real pain, between what Ragin talked of before his incarceration and what overcame him when admitted, between the intellectualized theories of those in Russia and what Chekhov saw on Sakhalin. In Ragin's lack of resistance to evil and non-violence, he was also parodying Tolstoy's views again, as well as Schopenhauer's (Rayfield, 1999, *Understanding Chekhov*: 10). Michael Finke also suggests in his consideration of Ragin and Gromov, and by implication on Sakhalin, that environmental and biographical or psychodynamic factors may be of greater importance than inherited ones (Finke, 2005, *Seeing Chekhov*: 111ff). Chekov spends time detailing how Ragin was forced into medicine by his dominating father just as Gromov's paranoia followed family loss.

*Ward Number 6* was written over eight months as Chekhov struggled to find a way to write about Sakhalin and the 'utter hell' he had seen. As Rayfield has suggested, the journey to Sakhalin proved by action what Chekhov refused to do by writing – his commitment to alleviating human suffering. But he had to demonstrate the substance of his commitment by writing. In *Ward Number 6*, as on Sakhalin, there were no evil people, just systems which create them. The story is not only a brilliant dissection of a mental hospital, which leans heavily on Chekhov's experiences of medicine on Sakhalin, some saw it as an allegory of Russia at large and the politics of the day.

Chekhov referred to working on his novels on Thursday to Saturday and his stories, for relief on Sundays. By novels he meant the more substantial works of fiction of which *Ward Number 6* and *The Duel* are two. But this is not to suggest that his short stories were insubstantial. The last of the works written as he wrote up *Sakhalin*, was *Terror* (1892). Though a short story with an unnamed narrator, a drunk and an affair, all these are almost incidental to the heart of what he wrote, which is a cri-de-Coeur of a man depressed, and indeed terrified, by the everyday.

A graduate, Silin, gives up a civil service job to work on the land, Tolstoy style (again). But the work is backbreakingly hard and his friend (the narrator) does not see Silin as a farmer, but likes him instead for his 'philosophy, intelligence and kindness'. We learn Silin tends to confide in his friend rather too much. The narrator is also extremely attracted to his wife, Marya, but thinks she only sees him as her husband's friend.

A year and a half passes. The two men are shopping (cheese that smelt of soap and petrified sausages that smelt of tar – like those described on the journey to Sakhalin). They go for a beer while they wait for the horses to be shod and are joined by a drunk with an odd surname, Forty Martyrs (more echoes of Sakhalin), who they have both sacked in the past. Silin begins to talk, his 'eyes sad, truthful and a little frightened'.

. . . in moments of depression I have sometimes pictured to myself the hour of my death.... I don't understand life and I am afraid of it. It seems to a sound healthy man that he understands everything he sees and hears, but that 'seeming' is lost to me . . . it seems to me that [even] its [a beetle's] life consists of nothing but fear.

'I am afraid of everything . . . chiefly the common routine of life from which none of us can escape. I am incapable of distinguishing what is true and what is false in my actions . . . my whole life is nothing else than a daily effort to deceive myself and others. We are unjust, we waste all our powers on trash we do not need and which hinders us from living . . . I don't understand men. It frightens me to look at peasants and I don't know for what higher objects they are suffering and what they are living for. If life is an enjoyment, then they are unnecessary superfluous people. If the object and meaning of life is to be found in poverty and unending hopeless ignorance, I can't understand for whom and what this torture is necessary.

'if only you knew how afraid I am of my ordinary thoughts. I distract my mind with work, and try to tire myself out that I may sleep soundly.' He turns to his family life. He plays the fool, has a lovely wife and children, but his happy family life is 'only a grievous misunderstanding . . . my chief misery and my chief terror'.

He is madly in love with his wife, but she not with him, his low self-esteem reflected in the way he describes their relationship. 'Because I don't understand our relations, I hate, sometimes her, sometimes myself, sometimes both at once. I torment myself . . .'.

The coachman arrives and breaks up his narrative. Silin goes to bed, while the narrator and Marya find they are attracted to each other. She goes to his room, only leaving at 3.00 am, which Silin sees. The next day the narrator leaves, to never see them again, though he hears they remain together.

Gromov's initial paranoia in *Ward Number 6* and Silin's anxiety – indeed terror – are Kafkaesque in being undirected towards any object, and infect and consume their whole being. Remember Chekhov writing that all had to be from real life. We cannot know how he came to write such works in 1892. But we do know he was working extraordinary long hours at this time, trying to come to terms with Sakhalin while writing some of his greatest fiction, and that at this time he was more than usually anxious and found it difficult to sleep – so difficult that he read *War and Peace* at night. He also wrote to Suvorin of 'horrid psychopathic moods'. His brother Mikhail, is also reported to have written that, 'in Melikhovo Anton Pavlovich's nerves got completely out of order due to overwork' (quoted from entry, *The Black Monk* – Wikipedia. Letter to Suvorin, 28 July 1883).

These narratives may also reflect Chekhov's concerns about how people would interpret his whole Sakhalin obsession. He, like Ragin, had gone voluntarily – he too had befriended the incarcerated – might he be alienated like Ragin, for going to and for writing about the colony? Might he too die earlier as a result? Might people think he too was out of his mind? *Ward Number 6* and *Terror* reflect Chekhov's response to Sakhalin and how he might explain what was going on, but also, arguably, his more personal concerns about how he might be viewed. He was right. Suvorin read *Ward Number 6* and questioned Chekhov's sanity. Reading *Sakhalin Island* a hundred years later, Popkin also questioned whether his sense-making abilities had deserted him too, as we will see.

## Notes

1. In fairness to Chekhov he then finished, 'Nevertheless, these faults disperse like feathers in the wind; the worth of the work is such that they simply pass unnoticed'.

2. A letter to Suvorin, 9 December 1890, describes 'his soul as being in a ferment'. http://www.gutenberg.org/files/6408/6408-h/6408-h.htm#link2H_4_0008

3. 'I was born here and I will die here, against my will'. Bob Dylan, *Not Dark Yet*, from *Time Out of Mind*, 1997. Dylan has been quoted as basing one album on Chekhov's stories.

4. There was no department of psychiatry when Chekhov was at medical school. Finke, *Freedom from Violence and Lies*: 103).

5. Though one can see why such an immediate death after incarceration was necessary, there is surely another story had Ragin been a patient for longer, adapting to the appalling conditions in some way.

# References

Coope, J. (1997). *Doctor Chekhov; A Study in Literature and Medicine*. Chalk: Cross Publishing.

Finke, M. (2005). *Seeing Chekhov*. Ithaca: Cornell.

Gregory, S. (2015). *Antosha and Levitasha; The Shared Lives and Art of Anton Chekhov and Isaac Levitan*. Illinois: North Illinois University Press.

Heim, M. and Karlinsky, S. (1973). *Letters of Anton Chekhov*. New York, Evanston, San Francisco and London.

Kataev, V. (2002). *If Only We Could Know*. Chicago, IL: Dee.

Rayfield, D. (1999, 2010). *Understanding Chekhov*. London: Bristol Classical Press/Bloomsbury.

Rayfield, D. (1997, 2010). *Anton Chekhov – A Life*. London: HarperCollins. 1997, 2010. Second Edition, London: Garnett Press. 2021.

# CHAPTER 11
## CONSCIENCE, IRONY AND UNDERSTATEMENT

As we have described, Chekhov itemized the failing of the colony, from its climate to the ignorance and indifference by officials as well as their officiousness, as they falsified crop yields rather than confront their superiors. All led to a generalized, overwhelming neglect and powerlessness. If people back home only knew what was going on, he thought, things must change. How then was the book received and how has it been interpreted since?

Too controversial for one of Suvorin's journals, serialization took place in *Russian Thought*, the same journal which had attacked his lack of morality before he left, but which later feted him with dinners. It attracted some interest from newspapers.[1] As a result, people made contributions to Sakhalin's schools, libraries and children's homes. One lady even left St Petersburg to go to Sakhalin to help, though what happened to her is not recorded. Journalists, inspectors and physicians followed. No one disagreed with Chekhov's findings and such was the scandal that the government set up a secret committee to discuss the future of the colony (Beer, 2016: 265–9). Any idea of the island as a sustainable colony was lost as its cataloguing of the pervasive corruption, appalling conditions and hopeless administration was put before people. The sexual exploitation, especially fathers selling their daughters, was emblematic of the destruction of family life, itself a symbol of Sakhalin's corrosive and complete inhumanity. A physician, Podubsky, produced an account of the conditions for women and children which was discussed by the prison administration and the Society for the Care of Families of Penal Labourers before being forwarded, in May 1899, to the Minister of Justice, Muravyov. Apparently, a lady-in-waiting pressed a copy into Nicholas II's hand in St Petersburg. Its findings were also discussed publicly, having been published in the weekly legal journal *Right* and the official *Prison Herald*. One early change was that settlement in Siberia from the island, which had been restricted in 1880, was allowed once more. In 1894, 220 left but by 1898 this number had risen to 2,000, out of a total population of 22,000. These modest improvements took years.

As Chekhov had suggested, the real culprits were the authorities for failing to administer and resource the island properly.[2] Sakhalin dragged down the rest of the state's plans for combining penal settlement and colonization in Siberia. But, despite the reports and the visits, the outcry and the indignation, inertia was a powerful defence. Some even thought Sakhalin remained salvageable. The state had spent more than 20 million roubles on it since 1879; to abandon it was humiliating and expensive. Aleksandr Salamon, head of the prison administration, suggested during a visit in 1898 – six years after Chekhov's account started to come out – that the shortcomings might be addressed through 'hard work'. On his return, however, even he had to admit that the prisons were destructive and the only industries on the island were gambling, vodka and prostitution. 'There can be no question of rehabilitation in the Sakhalin penal colony' (Beer, 2016: 267).

Things still dragged on and, finally, it was finished by war. Russia's expansion east and its construction of the railway to Vladivostok led Japan to fear Russia's plans for Korea and Manchuria. In January 1904 Japan attacked the Russian naval base in Port Arthur, a deep-water port on the tip of the Liaodong Peninsula in Manchuria, and then destroyed the Russian fleet at the Battle of Tsushima. They occupied southern Sakhalin in May 1905 and promised the convict settlers an amnesty if they fought the Russian soldiers. In the end, the Japanese and Russians from the north dumped the remaining people, 7,600 men, women and children, on the shore of the bay of De Castri opposite Sakhalin. They had to walk 60 kilometres through the taiga to Marinsk whence they were dispersed through Siberia. On 1 July 1906, the Russian government abolished the penal colony by decree. It was over.

Serialization and then publication of the book had one other effect – no one could doubt Chekhov's moral integrity ever again and, in Rayfield's words, he became, with Tolstoy, 'the conscience of the nation'. Most importantly in terms of the scientific aspect of the work, his findings were not disputed, and his methods vindicated.

His friend Rossolimo, by now a neuropathologist, asked him to lecture medical students. Chekhov felt underqualified without an MD. Rossolimo suggested he ask the Dean of Medicine at Moscow University, Ivan Klein, on Chekhov's behalf, whether *Sakhalin Island* would be acceptable as a medical dissertation.

> As soon as he gave me his consent, I met with the dean of the Faculty of Medicine. The meeting was a complete disaster. The dean's eyes widened, he looked me over with his glasses and without saying a word, he turned his back on me. I reported my failure to Chekhov, who laughed heartily. On that day, he stopped dreaming of becoming an academic . . .[3]

The professors may not have wanted to be associated with its findings.[4] Alternatively, Chekhov may have upset them too much in the past with his waspish descriptions of academics (Rayfield, *personal communication*).

Subsequently the book has more usually been defined by what it isn't – fiction or drama like the rest of Chekhov's work – than by what it is. It has perplexed and divided critics and biographers like none of his other work. Why did he do it, and how does it fit with the rest of his output? Some have nodded respectfully, though one suspects many have been put off by its indigestible length and breadth. Some have been more appreciative, some have all but ignored it, while others have just sunk their teeth in.

Among biographers, Sophie Laffitte, a beautifully sympathetic writer, mentions that though Chekhov was quite dismissive of it, his census was the first in Russia on a scientific basis (Laffitte, *Chekhov*: 136). In turn, Hingley suggests:

> Part dissertation and part travelogue, it is a harmonious work despite the mingling of genres. The style cool, light, objective, admirably controlled, free from pomposity and jargon; a model for thesis writers everywhere. (Hingley, 1976: 144)

One presumes some irony, knowing that Chekhov's work was dismissed as a thesis. Considering it in more depth, Rayfield finds,

> it has literary values of conscience, irony and understatement, and fits within a Russian genre that starts with Dostoevsky's Notes from the House of the Dead, and ends let us hope with Solzhenitsyn's The Gulag Archipelago . . . (Rayfield, 1999, 2010: 96)[5]

He also mentions Chekhov's impartiality and openness which were astonishing for its time:

> The most remarkable element about Chekhov's work on the island is that he established a relationship with the population of Sakhalin rather similar to that he was to establish with posterity. Brutalized psychopathic murderers and callous sadistic guards all responded with a frankness and humanity that astounded their colleagues when they read Chekhov's account. The work as a whole, like Chekov's best mature work, tends to emphasize the potential for goodness in every individual and the potential for evil in every hierarchy – by implication Chekhov became a guarded anarchist in politics after Sakhalin. (Rayfield, 1997, 2010: 96)

In his recent reflections Finke considers *Sakhalin*. While this chapter has 72 pages out of a total of 205, Sakhalin is only focussed on for ten pages, and then he rather dismisses the adventure and book; his focus, like most others, is understandably on his literary works (Finke, 2021: 77–150).

While many other biographers have been content to mention *Sakhalin* and then return to Chekhov's 'proper' work of stories and plays, academics have been more critical. In her penetrating account, Popkin lists past critical responses to what she describes as 'one of the strangest documents in any genre', in a footnote to her paper (Popkin, *Chekhov as Ethnographer*). Several critics excuse its problems, its scientific documentary character, its literary aspects and its fusion of genres (medical dissertation, artistic sketch, or documentary prose). Some acknowledge a dryness in the statistics but defend this as being part of its impact, with the avalanche of data 'sterile only to the superficial reader'. Most seek to explain its use of incomplete and untrustworthy statistics as the price of its impact. Others find the tedium of its detail 'an artfully constructed commentary on the grim realities' and that its strangeness might reflect 'Chekhov's response to the horrors he could not assimilate'. Popkin writes that only a few have recognized the book's oddness and not tried to defend it and its esteemed author.

In contrast, and offering no such excuses, she attacks the book to its very core. Though less critical of the first two travel chapters setting the scene, after that she writes:

> In the remaining twenty-one chapters is the repeated undoing of Chekhov's precious distinctions and ultimately the breakdown on

knowability itself . . . A kind of epistemological crisis, and the text itself reproduces the collapse of Chekhov's project . . . [His] great scientific project begins to fall apart almost immediately. (Popkin, 1992)

She points out, rightly, that Chekhov's aim was to be scientific, to assemble data and evidence for his thesis, and that in this he came up short. She quotes Chekhov himself admitting that the existing statistics were 'shoddily gathered, irresponsibly recorded and hopelessly inaccurate and incomplete' and yet, she says, he quotes them. On Sakhalin information is either unavailable or unreliable. Population figures haphazard, birth rate 'an unattainable luxury', nutritional data non-existent, even the herring catch is uncountable . . . There were no archives, so the past was utterly forgotten . . . when figures are available they were obviously falsified, with prison reports written by ignorant guards while agricultural returns were ludicrous or fraudulent and medical records fabricated or fantasy. She concludes that:

there is no knowledge on Sakhalin Island . . . Chekhov encounters a complete failure of the human sciences, the bankruptcy of sociology, geology, geography, topography, medicine, anthropology, psychology, demographics, statistics, economics, agronomy, meteorology, even linguistics and especially criminology . . . the convicts' world is not only unknown, but unknowable, not only uncategorised but uncategorisable, not only unrecorded, but unrecordable. (Popkin, 1992)

Quoting Foucault and Derrida, she suggests 'Sakhalin is some proto-deconstructive, post structuralist space in which distinctions fail and oppositions collapse'. In contrast, she praises the numbers in Kennan, of which there are many taken from official information which one hopes was more reliable. Chekhov had few such records to draw on, itself reflecting Sakhalin's breakdown in governance, and was sceptical of those he did find. He wrote from observation and from scouting for scraps, whether official records or those from hospitals, parishes or cemeteries. True, the lack of statistics did at one level undermine Chekhov's project. Yet, this very lack reflected how far Sakhalin had descended from standards in the prisons, mines and workhouses of Siberia. Chekhov would have known this and by highlighting the lack of data could well have been showing us too. Some scepticism towards the accuracy of the Tsar's bean counters might be appropriate too.

In his recent book, Daniel Beer suggests that 'in the absence of precise statistics', there were likely to be tens of thousands of exiles living in Siberia at the end of the eighteenth century dispersed among 360,000 natives and 575,000 Russian and European migrants (Beer, 2016, *House of the Dead*: 28). Over the course of the nineteenth century exiles rarely exceeded 10 per cent of the overall population. By the time of the census in 1897 (which did not find Sakhalin very different to Chekhov's survey), he estimates that Siberia housed 300,000 exiles among 5.8 million people overall. Sakhalin was very different, with around 10,000 exiles plus 1,000 guards in 1890 and a total of perhaps 22,000 by 1897. Siberia had prisons, mines and its work parties, but the convicts were a minority and not too far removed from settlements and areas of law. In contrast Sakhalin had a majority of exiles, far from anywhere.

Popkin then details the failings of some of his distinctions between species of trees, classification of the Ainu and Giliaks, between various settlements, between convicts and settlers, the sick and the well, and between forced and free labour.

She also writes that the tale of Yegor – the only convict allowed to tell his own story – is 'confused, uninformative and boring . . . Yegor's inability to control his material is not unlike Chekhov's'. In fact, Yegor's story is startling in being the only extended narrative in the book and the only one with its own chapter. Within it Chekhov appears himself to keep interrupting, asking Yegor to get a move on, writing in the first person and so revealing himself, apparently, to be short-tempered and abrupt.

Yegor is introduced as a wood-cutter, barefoot, awkward and lumbering, and at first sight, with a rather stupid face and a 'mouth like a turbot'. Though a little slow, he was always working and looking for something to do, and only slept two or three hours per night. On holidays and days off he would stand at a crossroads and stare, which he called 'taking a stroll'. He had built his own cabin, tables and cupboards and, since his arrival, had never been in a fight, nor struck anyone.

Most unusually and against the advice he was given, Chekhov asks why he was sent to Sakhalin. 'For murder'. Chekhov asks him how it happened and Yegor relates his story in his own simple words. He had been bargaining for firewood. On the way back his friend suggested a drink or two. When he gives details of what drink and how much, Chekhov asks him to be briefer, but Yegor will have none of it. So much for Chekhov's authority.

'Now wait, don't go buttin in, Yer Excellency'. He goes on more about the drinking session.

'You just tell me about the murder.'

'Ang on.'

Eventually he tells of how in the morning someone had walloped his friend, Andy, who then died. They all knew a friend, Sergey, had done it. But he went to the police and fabricated a story about how Yegor and his two brothers had plotted to kill Andy. In court his brothers had an alibi and so got off – Yegor did not and so was convicted. He relates months in the local gaol and then being marched to Novgorod where they took his papers, shaved his head and put him in irons. Thence to Moscow prison to rot some more before travel to Odessa from where he sailed for Sakhalin. En route the boat nearly sank after striking a rock, which they thought was a giant fish. They survived and carried on in another boat. On Sakhalin during the summer he had dug ditches, brought logs, dug waterholes, made hay, and in what spare time he had, made sandals for sale. Once back in prison for the winter he had been loaned out as an unpaid workman.

Chekhov asked, 'Are you homesick?'

'No – there's only one thing – it's a shame about my children. They're not too bright. I prayed to God, to send them some brains.'

'Why didn't you bring your wife and children with you . . .?'

'Because they're happy enough at home.'

The chapter unfurls over six pages and little or none of it is straightforward. Juras Ryfa writes that though it was written as a single story, it was actually assembled from the census and many convicts' accounts as a composite and prototypical narrative (see Ryfa, *The Problem of Genre and the Quest for Justice in Chekhov's* Island of Sakhalin: 147). Chekhov wrote,

I purposely included Yegor's Tale so the reader may judge how colourless and barren were those hundreds of similar stories, autobiographies and anecdotes I heard from prisoners and other people . . .' (PSSiP Works, v 14–15, 743. Ref 7 Chekhov letter to Semanova)

The narrative carefully skewers the failings of Russian justice and Sakhalin's law. Yegor, innocent of the charge and unable to defend himself, was convicted on a mistake by the judge and with the indifference of the officers of the court and the jury. The ways in which the convicted reach Sakhalin, after long periods in jail beforehand, are exposed. Once on the island, mowing hay, he is proud of never having been beaten – so revealing beatings as common – and is never paid despite working as a settler (widespread but illegal). Then, as winter comes and in prison, he is made to do unpaid slave work (again illegal). The account has been carefully assembled by Chekhov, and framed within a narrative of a convicted exile, to challenge the indifference of society towards the fate of innocent victims, to reveal failings in the criminal justice system and to show the mistreatment of convicts on the island.

Popkin then criticizes his impressions, which 'defy logic, are riddled with contradictions'. Convicts live in abject misery and yet have relative freedom; Ainu are noble and wondrous and yet dirty and repulsive, women are forced to cohabit and are abused and yet also cherished, are fecund and then not fecund – and that children are both regarded as punishment but also loved. Some of these contradictions may sit ill within the rigour of an academic paper but still exist in the realities and messy flow of life. Parents may not want another baby, but once born she or he creates their own love and becomes richly valued and enjoyed. Abject misery and relative freedom are not necessarily mutually incompatible, nor are nobility, dirt and repulsiveness (as anyone familiar with the English upper class will testify).

Popkin quotes the poet Seamus Heaney 'he has found the right tone – not tract, not thesis', disapprovingly. After praising Kennan's account and criticising Doroshevich's sensationalism (Doroshevich, 2011),[6] she returns to Chekhov:

> He manages to raise Sakhalin not *from* obscurity, as he intended, but *to* an obscurity of even greater proportions . . . Chekhov's is one of the most terrifying accounts of senseless and horror . . . we see vividly what happens to his sense making capacity . . . and readers of his account we begin to despair for our own. (Popkin, 1992)

He was made to invent a novel method, that cannot be reduced to pure science or to narrative, as he strove, through a balance of the scientific and the literary, to create a reliable account of the colony. As he suggested 'Are landscape sketches, lyricism, richness of intonations considered indications of functionality? . . . Rigid scientific limits turn out too narrow for *The Island of Sakhalin*' (Ryfa, 1999: 71).

Other critics have been more forgiving. Igor Sukhikh suggested it was a new genre 'beyond the directly understood dilemma of scientific-documentary-fictive . . . the important thing is not the sum of the facts but an image of the world . . .' (cited in Ryfa, 1999: 69). Ryfa is also more understanding and balanced:

> In a sense, Chekhov failed in producing a truly scientific document . . . [but] he succeeded as a writer who raised his voice against social injustice . . . There is nothing like Sakhalin Island, and it is not focussed on enough as people look at [his] plays and stories. It is a serious study of inestimable impact on its readers of the time . . . It was a heroic deed, an apotheosis of his entire social and writing career, and reflects his basic moral principles. (Ryfa, 1999: 5)

He shows how Chekhov, in part, was writing in conversation with Dostoevsky and his book *The House of the Dead*, which detailed his period as a convict in Siberia where, incidentally, conditions were far kinder than on Sakhalin.

When in his late twenties, Dostoevsky was arrested in 1849 for discussing books critical of Tsarist Russia, he was initially sentenced to death but then instead sentenced to four years' hard labour in a Siberian prison camp. After that he had six years of compulsory military service, which was also in Siberia, so he could only restart writing in 1860, the year of Chekhov's birth. He kept notes of his time as a convict and then developed these into 'The House of the Dead', part novel, part autobiography, but with a documentary's realism and sparseness (Dostoevsky, 1860, 1985). Though far richer in dialogue and with prolonged detail, the book has, therefore, a somewhat similar feel to Chekhov's book. There are other similarities, for instance Dostoevsky begins by describing the prison and its conditions, as Chekhov did both in *Sakhalin Island* and *Ward Number 6*, suggesting Chekhov was echoing Dostoevsky, even as he showed how much harder life was on Sakhalin.

Some things had not changed between Dostoevsky's time and forty years later on Sakhalin – the food was appalling, floggings were frequent, convicts had their half their heads shaved (weekly), and swopped identities on the walk to Siberia. Others feigned madness to avoid punishment. Consumptives died in chains, the lice were fat and bed bugs endemic. Some of his insights were echoed by Chekhov:

> I came to understand that in addition to deprivation of freedom, in addition to forced labour, there is in a convict's life one more torment,

one that is almost more powerful than all the others. That is *forced communal existence*. (Dostoevsky, 1860, 1985: 44)

Dostoevsky described how penal labour was not that hard, but that its cruelty lay in part from it being forced and compulsory, but also 'to crush and destroy a man entirely, make him work utterly devoid of usefulness and meaning' (Dostoevsky, 1860, 1985: 81). The men worked on their own at night making various items for money, and to work at something for a reason 'convict implies a man without will, but when spending money he has it' (Dostoevsky, 1860, 1985: 109). In contrast, on Sakhalin, will seemed to be in short supply.

Initially the author of *The House of the Dead* was shocked by what he saw, but gradually he found a way to exist and use the system. Though he states that 'no convict feels at home in prison', that 'convicts are afraid of everything in prison', later on companionships are formed and a newcomer becomes at home (Dostoevsky, *The House of the Dead*: 128, 78 and 306, respectively). As a nobleman, we read that there were certain privileges, but also that they were hated by the other convicts. But in a passage towards the end of the book, Dostoevsky writes how noblemen and the others were actually no different.

It is difficult to gauge the soul . . . by the application of fixed criteria. Not even education is a reliable indicator . . . I have encountered signs of the most advanced spiritual development among the . . . oppressed and unenlightened.' 'The reverse also happens: education sometimes cohabits with barbarity, such cynicism that you are filled with disgust. (Dostoevsky, 1860, 1985: 306)

Overall, conditions were better than those on Sakhalin. As Beer relates, some interaction occurred with settlements for trade, and that money made life more bearable, with some having their own tea, their own cook, their own bed and bedding and even their own samovar. Vodka was plentiful and, as ever, prostitutes available for those who could pay. Unlike on Sakhalin, the doctors appeared to have been admired and sometimes acquiesced to men having a week in hospital as respite. The authorities are even praised at times and overall appear firm but fair. Christmas was celebrated with some men managing to have their own meals cooked, and villagers sending alms. Though animals were not allowed, they had dogs, geese and a goat, and even for a while, an eagle. There was even a theatrical stage show put on by the convicts to which townspeople came.

Dostoevsky's voice becomes more apparent as the author reflects on his time there. His terrible isolation becomes cherished, since it allowed him to review his life and 'perhaps even bless fate for having sent me such isolation', since it allowed him to reflect. 'I swore to myself that in my future life there would be none of these mistakes'. 'I remember only a passionate desire for resurrection, for renewal, for a new life' (Dostoevsky, 1860, 1985: 339–40). Chekhov relates no such sentiments on Sakhalin. His description of a breakdown of decency and morality markedly contrasts with Dostoevsky's account.

Ryfa suggests that both were interested in exploring the origins of crime and punishment, and the corrupting effect of punishment and penal servitude on prisoners and administrators. But whereas Dostoevsky saw his time in Siberia as a form of a spiritual Christian resurrection, Chekhov was far more detached and dispassionate. Dostoevsky saw evil within man, bound up with the instincts for power, acquisition and sexual aggression. Chekhov, in contrast, while not dismissing a person's character, saw how the moral norms on Sakhalin were in part determined by people's exposure to violence as an everyday phenomenon. He thought that if social and environmental conditions improved then so too would people's morals and, therefore, their lives. Social change, he hoped, might then occur through an awakening of society's interest and through the work of the new intelligentsia he found on Sakhalin.

Ryfa concludes his account of Chekhov's book by suggesting it is a new genre – documentary prose. 'As a doctor, traveller, journalist, humanist, and first and foremost a man of letters, Chekhov entered that dark corner of the Russian Empire, brought it from obscurity and fulfilled his obligation toward his country and his readers' (Ryfa, 1999: 208).

More recently two eminent authors have also praised the book, and both incidentally in the *New Yorker*. Akhil Sharma suggested it is the greatest work of journalism from the nineteenth century (Sharma, 'Chekhov's Beautiful Nonfiction.' *New Yorker*, 2 February 2015).[7] The book has not aged, he suggests, because it has space to develop characters and because Chekhov's main concern was with 'how human beings live their lives . . . He is willing to write about anything, and he is willing to see everything with compassion'. Sharma cites the pleasure of moving through the physical world of Sakhalin, even though it also 'retains the gorgeous prose and the deep compassion of the fiction'. Writer and physician Siddhartha Mukherjee agrees: 'Chekhov, in short, invented a new kind of literature at Sakhalin. It was a literature inflected with clinical humanity—a literature of keen, nearly medical observation about human nature and its imperfections and perversions, but also a literature of expansive sensitivity and tenderness' (Mukherjee, S. 'Love in the Time of Numbness: or Doctor Chekhov, Writer.' *New Yorker*, 11 April 2017).[8] Picking up on Chekhov's letter about stagnation in his soul, he considers Sakhalin was where he went to 'inoculate himself against the ennui that was slowly destroying his soul'. Mukherjee also focuses on Chekhov as doctor and writer, in that order.

The anthropologist and ethnographer Kirin Narayan used Chekhov's book as the starting point to a long meditation on her craft. In one section she praises his approach and conclusions:

Sakhalin Island questions the social inequalities, capitalist rapaciousness, industrial growth, repressive state policies and environmental destructiveness of his times – and also the complexities of human hearts – Chekhov came up with new forms for stories, plays and non-fiction. As he wrote in his notebook, that was his storehouse of odds and ends to be worked into future projects, 'New literary forms always produce new forms of life and that is why they are so revolting to the conservative human mind.' (Narayan, 2012: 20)

But she was not slavish in her appreciation,

. . . he offers extended 'political-social-economic' commentaries around specific descriptions . . . [but] his call for 'total objectivity' to write as though simply observing lives, without persona judgment – is ironically reversed, if anything. By contemporary standards his objectivity is seen as ironic. Chekhov can be so frankly judgemental and unflattering in his descriptions of people living in Sakhalin that a contemporary ethnography squirms . . . His writing reveals the biases of his particular era [and] by including so many damning facts, building his case for outrage through sheer volume of documentation, he is hardly concise.

She concludes, however, that 'here as in his other writings, Chekhov upholds a standard for lasting originality that a writer of any genre might aspire to; writing something different and audacious… pervaded by a compassion for people's circumstances' (Narayan, 2012: 42–3).

*Sakhalin Island* was a new form, necessitated by what he saw and needed to write. One hopes that this work, which is cumbersome and at times puzzling, can find its proper place both within whatever multidisciplinary academic frameworks are appropriate, but also within assessments of Chekhov's work and his life.

As they and Rayfield suggest, the journey certainly changed Chekhov physically and in outlook (Rayfield, 1997, 2010: 96). His TB worsened so he knew he would not survive middle age; in 1895 he said that he would last between five or ten years – whether he saw a doctor or not. More significantly for his later work, Sakhalin was his first experience of irremediable evil, and irredeemable fall, which, from then on, banished any Tolstoyan morality from his work. On Sakhalin, he saw how social evils and individual unhappiness were inextricable linked.

The book's sweep is, at times, apparently interrupted – and enriched – by human and other detail. For Chekhov, however, describing conditions on Sakhalin, for convicts, guards, and the women and children, as well as the climate and soil, flora and fauna, history and politics as truthfully as he could, all contributed to the environmental medicine he had learned so well in medical school and which he practised. He struggled to convey to his audience back home the unimaginable breakdown of society and decency which he had witnessed and which, at times, he must have thought he alone was interested in. Beyond his census, facts and data were, for the most part, thin, but he still assembled an account, at times dry and impersonal, at other times humane and deeply moving, which conveys what Sakhalin was like. That this was achieved by one man, several thousand miles from home, working under unimaginably difficult conditions, remains an extraordinarily heroic act, whether one finds the resulting book 'confused, uninformative and boring', or full of 'conscience, irony and understatement'. Perhaps more importantly as we look back, it also changed Chekhov and his literary and philosophical development.

## Notes

1. Though Finke suggests the book was published to little acclaim (Finke, 2021: 114).

2. For example, he considers the failure of agriculture in chapter 18, 248ff, the poor diet in chapter 19, 260ff, and the quality of guards and overseers in chapter 20 (Chekhov, 1895: 272ff).

3. Rossolimo, in Sekirin, *Memories of Chekhov*, p.31. It was only after his death that a Russian professor wrote that *Sakhalin Island* would become a model 'when a department of ethnographical medicine, which we need so much, is opened up' (Chukovsky, 1945: 42).

4. The dean was a Professor IF Klein, who refused to consider it serious scientific research. But, in addition, Shubin suggested that 'the conferment of an

academic degree . . . would mean an official admission of this seditious book and the existence of those monstrous phenomena described in it' (Ryfa, 1999: 18. From Shubin, B.M. (1997). *Doktor AP Chekhov*. Moscow: Znanie, 97).

5.  Alas, the literature on Siberia has not stopped with Solzhenitsyn or Mandelstam. For instance, see Shalamov, Andrievich, etc.

6.  A journalist, Vlas Doroshevich visited the colony in 1897 and wrote an account in which it is clear that little had changed from Chekhov's time. His account was written in his 'feuilleton' style – short punchy essays akin to our present tabloid press. His writing was racy and popular, and led some more literary men to suggest his appeal was to unsophisticated provincials, while others suggested he was 'the basest of men' and 'an untalented scoundrel', in part for going to Sakhalin on a clearly commercial venture.

7.  I am grateful to Robert Prior, of MIT Press, for directing my attention to this article. He thought Chekhov lied about it being a medical thesis, using that as cover to reach Sakhalin and that it was a wonderful example of investigative journalism.

8.  See also: https://www.newyorker.com/culture/cultural-comment/love-in-the -time-of-numbness-or-doctor-chekhov-writer.

# References

Beer, D. (2016). *The House of the Dead*. London: Allen Lane.

Chukovsky, K. (1945). *Chekhov the Man*. London: Hutchinson.

Chekhov, A. (1895). *Sakhalin Island*, translated by Brian Reeve. 1993. Throughout translations are from the London; One World Edition, 2007 (updated 2014).

Doroshevich, V. (2011). *Russia's Penal Colony in the Far East*, translated by Gentes, Andrew A. Translation of Vlas Doroshevich's 'Sakhalin'. New York and London: Anthem Press.

Dostoevsky, F. (1860, 1985). *The House of the Dead*, translated by McDuff, D. London: Penguin.

Finke, M. (2021). *Freedom from Violence and Lies. Anton Chekhov's Life and Writings*. London: Reaktion.

Hingley, R. (1976). *A New Life for Chekhov*. Oxford: Oxford University Press.

Laffitte, S. (1974). *Chekhov*. London: Readers Union/Angus Robertson.

Narayan, K. (2012). *Alive in the Writing. Crafting Ethnography in the Company of Chekhov*. Chicago: University of Chicago Press, 20.

Popkin, C. (1992). 'Chekhov as Ethnographer; Epistemological Crisis on Sakhalin Island', *Slavic Review*, 51(1), 36–51.

Rayfield, D. (1997, 2010). *Anton Chekhov – A Life*. London: HarperCollins. 1997, 2010. Second Edition, London: Garnett Press. 2021.

Ryfa, J. (1999). *The Problem of Genre and the Quest for Justice in Chekhov's The Island of Sakhalin*. Studies in Slavic Languages and Literature, Volume 13. Lewiston and Queenstown-Lampeter: The Edwin Mellon Press.

Shubin, B.M. (1997). *Doktor AP Chekhov*. Moscow: Znanie, 97.

# CHAPTER 12
# HOLY OF HOLIES

To have made the trip – and survived – marked Chekhov forever. With the research beforehand and writing the book it occupied five years, a quarter of his most creative period. As we have learned, *Sakhalin Island* is also his longest piece of prose and his only biographical piece and, apart from some early court reports, his only non-fiction. One might have expected such an overwhelming experience to colour his subsequent literary work. Chekhov's readers, even his contemporaries, were puzzled, then, by the almost total absence in his work of direct reference to Sakhalin – the only specific reference in his fiction is the conclusion to the story *Murder* of 1895, where the convicted murderer is last seen three months after his arrival at Voyevodsk prison, working the mine at Douai. Within that short time, he had already tried to escape, been discovered, flogged three times and given a life sentence.

Sakhalin did influence his later work, though being Chekhov, not in any obvious and simple way – as we have seen there was no Great Russian Novel and only a few stories which mentioned prison colonies in general or Sakhalin in particular. To see the influences of Sakhalin on Chekhov, one needs both a subtler eye towards his writing and an awareness of how he viewed his life and work beyond literature – to look to what he did as well as what he wrote. It should also be remembered that Chekhov had begun to write in 1880, and had achieved enough success to largely support his family by short stories for popular magazines. Following Grigorovich's letter and with Suvorin's patronage he had matured by the late 1880s, and written several masterpieces. He had also been awarded that share of a Pushkin Prize for a volume of his stories. His reputation and literary style preceded Sakhalin.

Donald Rayfield has considered how his impressions of Sakhalin affected his subsequent literary development.[1] Chekhov's post-Sakhalin work surprised and indeed deplored some contemporaries for his – at times – brutal portrayal of Russian peasants, for example, in *Peasants* (1895) and *The Ravine* (1900). Before Sakhalin, Chekhov knew peasants, from summer holidays in the Ukraine with his grandfather, and later when he treated them in Melikhovo (where some swindled him). His early writings on the peasantry, though aware of their poverty and ignorance, have an idyllic, even condescending tinge. On Sakhalin, the convicts Chekhov interviewed and studied were not all peasants, but all were reduced to even worse penury than the most unfortunate peasants in European Russia. Himself the grandson of a serf – something he never forgot – he was especially sensitive to this and remarks in the book how prisoners are reduced to the state of serfdom with evident horror. But the resulting criminality and immorality, from cannibalism to incest, that he saw and which he omitted the worst of from his book, was seen in part as an indictment of the convict, but – more – of the system that reduced them to this state.

Further, Rayfield suggests that these fictional peasants still respected religion and were at least aware that what they did – stealing, fornicating and destroying other's lives – was wrong. On Sakhalin, there was a striking absence of conscience or remorse – neither the Bible nor the New Testament is mentioned once in the book, a compelling example of the complete breakdown he witnessed on the island of civilization, decency and its moral supports. The appalling crimes of his post-Sakhalin fiction – humiliation and rape of a woman, a baby scalded to death – echo what Chekhov heard and saw on Sakhalin and starkly differentiate the peasants of his pre-Sakhalin work from those of his later prose.

Rayfield also focussed on Chekhov's depictions of doctors pre- and post-Sakhalin. Before going, at least in the stories, they tended to be heroic and self-sacrificing, for instance the terminally ill professor of medicine in *A Dreary Story*. Immediately after Sakhalin, his few heroic doctors (Dr Dymov of *The Grasshopper* who dies after sucking diphtheria-infected tissue from a child, or the generous doctor in *The Wife* undermined by his uncharitable wife), serve other purposes – as a cipher for ineloquent science or to draw attention to the famine in central Russia. In contrast to Rayfield, Coulehan, himself a physician, has collected many of Chekhov's medical stories together, but does not distinguish between pre- and post-Sakhalin differences (Coulehan, 2003: xiii–xxv) There are callous, self-centred and narrow-minded doctors, as well as compassionate, kind and empathetic ones scattered in his stories both before and after his journey.[2]

In the plays, though he cannot approach the horrors seen on Sakhalin, Rayfield suggests that in later plays doctors become more flawed, and arguably more human. For instance, in *Three Sisters* (1900), the doctor, Chebutykin, announces that he has neither done any work or read a book since university, and forgotten his medicine: 'They think I can treat anything, just because I am a doctor, but I know nothing at all. I've forgotten everything'. There are also several hints he may have had an affair with the sisters' mother and indeed be Irina's father, while in *The Cherry Orchard* the unseen doctor fails to turn up to take the old retainer to a hospice, who remains trapped in the empty house. But even in his earlier, pre-Sakhalin plays doctors are figures of mockery and fun, if not tragedy. In the sprawling *Platonov* (1888), he writes that the doctor's speciality is 'the same as most. Presenting the bill' and in *Ivanov* (1887), that there is no difference between doctors and lawyers 'except that a lawyer will rob you, and a doctor will rob you and kill you'. Perhaps his saddest portrayal is of Astrov in *Uncle Vanya* (1899). True, Astrov is a prescient environmentalist, seeing a link between destruction of trees and climate change.[3] This may reflect in part Chekhov's medical school training, and in part the ideas current at the time. He also observed, though, that on Sakhalin bears were beginning to attack people as the salmon runs reduced in size. But Astrov, initially 'young and handsome' has aged and is 'no longer as good looking . . . and takes a drop of vodka'. By the age of thirty-five, he has also been worn down by the relentless work. In truth it is hard to see an influence of Sakhalin in the depiction of doctors in his plays. His portrayals of how people live were at times remorseless, but never as brutal as what he saw on Sakhalin, especially among fellow doctors. 'If the insane were burnt at the stake on the instructions of the prison doctors, even that wouldn't be surprising . . . the way things are done here are two hundred years behind the times' (1895: 111).

Coulehan discusses that Chekhov placed a doctor in each of his major plays, except *The Cherry Orchard*. Some were lazy, some burned out, some drunkards – few were heroes. He suggests that Chekhov knew too much to think medicine could heal many, and that as a result they often appeared impotent (Coulehan, 2003: xx). But there was no way to present what he saw in Sakhalin on stage, in part because the horrors were too appalling, but also because in his drama he was seeking to focus people's attention on themselves and their everyday lives. To seek any direct reference to Sakhalin in his plays seems overly simplistic. As he wrote:

> Really, in life people are not every minute shooting each other, hanging themselves or making declarations of love. And they are not saying clever things every minute. For the most part, they eat, drink, hang about, and talk nonsense; and this must be seen on the stage, a play must be written in which people can come, go, dine, talk about

the weather and play cards, not because that the way the author wants it, but because that's the way it happens in real life.

Let everything on the stage be just as complex and at the same time as simple as in life. People dine, merely dine, but that moment their happiness is being made or their life is being smashed. (Finke, 2021: 144)

So, while some direct influences of Sakhalin may be found in his literary work, they are few. The more profound changes were in his attitude and perspective in general. After Sakhalin, Chekhov's sympathies were more towards the oppressed, while his distrust of authority and systems increased. He showed a horror of judgement, in some cases quite literal, such as *The Head Gardener's Story* of 1894, in which a jury refuses to convict a murderer, despite the evidence of his guilt, as well as a suspicion of heroic seekers and a scepticism towards ideology, as we have seen, in *The Duel*.[4]

Chekhov's absence of judgement and refusal to instruct were not only criticized by Tolstoy but by many on the left and reflected the tightrope walked by Russian writers of the time, as we have touched on (Karlinsky, in: Heim and Karlinsky, 1973, *Letters*: 1–32). The tsarist's censors weeded out anti-government sentiment, and religious or sexual excess. One of his early plays, *On the High Road*, was even banned for being 'gloomy and filthy'. Perhaps more powerful and repressive, however, was unofficial censorship by anti-government liberal-leaning literary critics. Presaging the Soviet, Stalinist-era, writers had to be relevant and realistic, exposing social shortcomings for the greater good. Anything irrelevant, or imaginary, with psychological depth, joy or humour transgressed the ideological aim of literature.

It was not that Chekhov was unsympathetic to those wanting social justice, but he saw how those critics, and some of their supporters in the Russian intelligentsia, were in danger of becoming tyrannical and oppressive themselves – during the famine of 1892 he thought some were using the tragedy to foment unrest. He rarely advocated for social change, instead treating the sick, writing about Sakhalin and working in famine and cholera relief (Coulehan, 2003: xx). His refusal to be overtly political was much misunderstood by Tolstoy and by others. As Karlinsky writes, it took courage and vision to discern this oppressive strain in Russian dissent (Karlinsky, in: Heim and Karlinsky, 1973: 8–10). He even reflected this in his fiction.[5] Though his refusal to wear his heart of his sleeve may have sprung from natural reserve, it was also one of his cardinal literary principles. When faced with the ideological police of the time it also took real courage. As we have seen, it also led to huge soul-searching on his return from Sakhalin.

Sakhalin led Chekhov to distrust any proposal to transform human society. Even Tolstoy, whom he admired as a writer and as a man, lost his hold on Chekhov after Sakhalin. Rational science and technology became far more important than any faith-based ideals. His political stance was rarely explicit (except in his support for Dreyfus and his hatred of anti-Semitism), and he clearly had a distrust of all authority – after Sakhalin these views may have become clearer. Never a religious believer, after Sakhalin Chekhov forsook systems and organizations, and no longer accepted the moral authority of intellectuals, political parties, the press or the intelligentsia.[6] There were no heroes, just individuals doing their best under difficult circumstances.

> I have no faith in our intelligentsia; it is hypocritical, dishonest, hysterical, ill-bred and lazy. I have faith in individuals scattered here and there, all over Russia, be they intellectuals or peasants. (Heim and Karlinsky, 1973: 341. Letter to Orlov, 22 February 1899)[7]

This letting go of faith in justice, in theories, in organizations, in God and in intellectuals has led some influential commentators to suggest that Chekhov was a proto absurdist, prefiguring twentieth-century playwrights like Beckett, Genet and Ionesco. In his survey of Chekhov's plays, Gilman returns to this several times:

> In the way he chooses to circumscribe the situations his characters inhabit, he is closer to Beckett than any of his contemporaries ... In *Endgame, Uncle Vanya, Waiting for Godot, Three Sisters* ... there is nothing much to do ... Deprived of distractions, or having to rely on their own primitive, sadly provincial or solipsistic ones ... all of Beckett's characters and nearly all of Chekhov's are reduced to the essential tasks of getting through the days and nights making their way, with what is left to them, through time . . .' (Gilman, 1995, *Chekhov's Plays*: 79–80)

He notes how Chekhov, like Beckett, used the potential of boredom, with its undertones of ontological doubt, for dramatic interest.

> . . . like Beckett, Chekhov reveals characters who seem frozen in time and inaction . . . In *Three Sisters* they are laying out their own

existences, calling to mind Alain Robbe-Grillet's comment that in *Godot*, Didi and Gogo are thrown on stage, to 'ad lib for their very lives'. (Gilman, 1995: 158–9)

Chekhov, he concludes, is 'the anterior touchstone to Beckett', and to reinforce this he subtitles his chapter on *Uncle Vanya*, 'How it is', and *Three Sisters*, 'I can't go on, I'll go on', the latter echoing Beckett's famous line in *The Unnameable*. He also mentions that the three Prozorov sisters don't get to Moscow just as Godot never arrives. 'What's keeping us here?' Hamm asks in *Endgame*. 'The dialogue', replies Clov. The sisters, Gilman suggests, are kept by the text.[8]

Geoffrey Borny quotes several other writers and critics who have remarked on the similarities between Chekhov and the absurdists (Borny, 2006: 26). For example, Richard Corrigan suggested that 'Chekhov was the legitimate father of the absurd movement in theatre' (Corrigan, in Corrigan and Rosenberg, 1964: 145). Stein, memorably, wrote that Chekhov's 'heritage of pseudo comedy is being turned inside out in the dustbins of Beckett' (Stein, W. 1959–60. *Dublin Review*: 233: 381), and Esslin that 'There is only a small step from Chekhov's images of a society deprived of purpose and direction [deprived of God and an afterlife] to the far more emphatic presentation of a world deprived of its "metaphysical dimension" in the plays of Beckett, Genet . . . and Ionesco' (Esslin, in Clyman, 1985: 143–5).

In his critical study of Chekov's work, Rayfield also finds affinities with Beckett, and quoting 'Beckettian' lines from Chekhov:

In Vanya, 'It's nice weather today.' 'Its good weather for hanging yourself.'

Vanya again, 'The only hope is that when we lie in our coffins we will be visited by visions that may even be pleasant.' Astrov.

Firs at the end of Cherry Orchard, 'my life's gone by and it's just as if I'd never lived at all.' (Rayfield, 1999, 2010: 167, 175, 261)

He also finds overlap between the symbolism of trees in that play and the stunted tree of *Godot*. In *Godot* the tramps fumble and fidget similarly to many of those in *The Cherry Orchard*.[9]

Such a bleak view of Chekhov's work was not confined to those finding affinities with the absurdists. Leon Shestov, a Russian émigré critic, gave surely one of the bleakest interpretations of him – and any other author – in an influential 1916 essay. Chekhov was, he wrote,

> . . . a poet of hopelessness. Stubbornly, sadly, monotonously, during all the years of his literary activity nearly a quarter of a century long, he was doing one thing alone; killing human hopes. (Shestov, 1966: 4–5)

Chekhov was misunderstood during his life, overestimating people's ability to see through his apparent absence of polemic or instruction to the deeper enquiries beneath, for example not being able to see that stealing horses is wrong themselves without him telling them so. But this continuing misapprehension would surely have shocked him profoundly, for his aim was entirely different, not to extinguish hope but, simply and truthfully, to hold up a mirror. As Kataev wrote 'Chekhov was not killing hopes, he was killing illusions ' (Kataev, 2002: 169–70). To remain human in a hostile world that is essential. Kataev continued that 'the final conclusion Chekhov invites us to draw . . . is not one of hopelessness or pessimism, but of sober honesty'. Chekhov himself expressed another aspect of this misapprehension:

> You tell me that people cry at my plays . . . but that is not why I wrote them . . . all I wanted was to say honestly to people, 'Have a look at yourselves and see how bad and dreary your lives are.' The important thing is that people should realise this, for when they do, they will most certainly create another and better life for themselves. (Tikhonov, in Magarshack, 1980: 13–14)

He was no absurdist or, if he was, he was not their herald but rather the first *post*-absurdist. Yes, he did imagine a society without God and apparent purpose. Yes, he did focus on inaction and lethargy and yes, he did take us to the edge of hope. But in doing so his aim was not nihilistic but quite the reverse, to reveal, to liberate and to suggest doing something. Kataev once more:

> For Chekhov . . . writing about the meaninglessness or inadequacies of all manner of human activities and whose characters also have no idea of the final aims of their strivings and searchings, one of the most frequent and definite conclusions is that in spite of everything, one should not do nothing. (Kataev, 2002: 169–70)

Such a bleak interpretation of the absurdists, traced back to Martin Esslin's book of 1961 (Esslin, *The Theatre of the Absurd*), has been questioned by, among others, Michael Bennett. He uses Ionesco's definition:

> Absurd is that which is devoid of purpose . . . Cut off from his religious, metaphysical and transcendental roots, man is lost: all his actions become senseless, absurd, useless. (Bennett, 2011)

Bennett continues by suggesting that rather than being nihilistic or fatalistic, Beckett et al., by laying before audiences parables of their present situation, were inviting us all to find and make meaning in our lives, once its contradictions and false authorities have been recognized. His interpretation of *Waiting for Godot* for instance, is that it is life-affirming in its humour, its injunction to fill time (by theatre and talking in particular), but also in its contemplation, friendship and in hope. Such an interpretation might then allow Chekhov to qualify as one of the first of this group, even though Bennett does not mention him.[10]

Pertinently though, Chekhov's solution was not contemplative. However pessimistic his characters may appear, his aim was to challenge his audience to see themselves as they truly are and, having done so, to change. Unlike the absurdists – or 'parable-ists' – his meaning was to be found not in talking or contemplation or friendship but in action and so, arguably, in his own life, through medicine and humanitarian work.

Perhaps the severity of his clinical gaze has led audiences and critics to find his work bleak, perhaps it was his experiences, whether on Sakhalin or elsewhere, that led him to be so uncompromising, perhaps the depression which he endured throughout his life captured some of him.[11] It should not be forgotten that he lived most of his life with TB and counted off the years he had left, parcelling them out. He rarely talked of it and even more rarely expressed any bitterness, but it was there. Discussing an acquaintance, he is recorded as saying,

> 'Yacobi will die soon.'
> 'Why?'
> 'He wants to deceive himself. He will tell anecdotes. He laughs. But in his eyes there is death. In any case we are sentenced.'
> 'From birth?'
> 'No. I am talking of myself. And yet I know I so much want to live, to write more. It's hard to be a doctor you know.' (Coope, 1997: 142)

Later he wrote:

> To live in order to die is not amusing, but to live knowing that one must die prematurely is absolutely stupid. (Coope, 1997: 145. Quote from Khizniakov, VV. (1947). *Anton Pavlovic Chekhov, kak Vrach,* Moscow: 5)

Before his marriage he was examined by a Dr Shchurovsky. The notes, in a mixture of Russian, Latin and German,[12] mention TB and the peritonitis he had as a young man, as well as syphilis, gonorrhoea, malaria, migraine[13] and a temporary partial blindness which was either migrainous or due to vascular insufficiency in the brain. He also complained of haemorrhoids and loose bowels much of the time. We might therefore forgive his gaze for being so acute, even severe – Shestov described his 'merciless talent' (Bunin, 2007: 65) – seeing people wasting their time when he had so little. 'I despise laziness, as I despise weakness and inertia in mental activities' (Chekhov, in Shakh-Azizova T. (1980). 'A Russian Hamlet,' *Soviet Literature,* Vol. 1, January, p162). And, given his condition and medical knowledge, we might understand him suggesting, through Sonia in *Uncle Vanya* that 'Not knowing is better'.[14] Yet, despite his personal health, his aim was not nihilistic but affirmatively, heroically, ironically, comically, deeply humane. He thought that once people saw themselves and the way in which they lived, then they must change. This is the hope from Sakhalin – surely no civilized man, or civilized society, could know of this and do nothing?

The sort of change he valued – deeply and passionately – is clear. This is what *Sakhalin* is about, what his medicine is about, Chekhov showing us how he thought people might live, not through philosophical ideas, or religion as Tolstoy and others suggested, but through science and medicine, progress, whether engineering or in environmental work – planting trees and preventing famine.[15] 'Science and technology are now going through a period of greatness, but as for us [artists] this is a precarious, sour, dreary period' (Heim and Karlinsky, 1973: 243. Letter to Suvorin, 25 November 1892). As we have seen, there was, 'more love of humanity in steam and electricity than in chastity and abstention from meat . . .' (Bunin, 2004: xlii. Letter to Suvorin, 27 March 1894). He was not – and could not be – overtly political. But he believed that if social factors and education were improved then this would improve people's lives. If art held up a mirror to us all, it was through science that we might improve in living standards, health and education. Read Pinker and you might think Chekhov was right (Pinker, 2016).

If the material conditions under which people lived were better, then other social factors might also improve. In one of his few, great, explanatory letters he gave his creed:

> I am neither liberal, nor conservative, nor gradualist [in evolutionary debate], nor a monk, nor indifferent. I would like to be a free artist . . . and regret that God has not given me the strength to be one. I hate lies and violence in all their forms . . . I cultivate no particular predilection for policemen, butchers, scientists, writers or the younger generation. I look upon tags and labels as [badges of] prejudices. My holy of holies is the human body, health, intelligence, talent, inspiration, love and the most absolute freedom imaginable, freedom from violence and lies, no matter what form the last two may take. Such is the programme I would adhere to if I were a major artist. (Heim and Karlinsky, 1973: 109. Letter to Pleshcheyev, 4 October 1888)

Dotted around his work, too, are further clues. In 'A Sad Story', Professor Stepanovich says:

> . . . with my last breath, I shall continue to believe that science is the most important, the most beautiful and the most vital thing in human life; that it always has been and always will be the highest manifestation of love . . .[16]

One can decide how much Chekhov agreed with those sentiments. Through science came progress in people's living conditions, health, welfare and behaviour. And in *An Anonymous Story*, written soon after his return from Sakhalin, he wrote,

> 'I have now really grasped both with my mind and in my tortured heart, that man either hasn't got a destiny, or else it lies exclusively in self-sacrificing love for his neighbour . . .'[17]

This might be high-blown rhetoric, empty words from a writer and clinical spectator on the world. Except that his activities in medicine and in education reveal to us much about how, in acting out what he could not say, he lived what he thought a good life. Remember that he did not equate writing with doing – he needed to achieve in the real world as well as on paper. Neither did he elevate writing to some status above others:

Why should one be a writer? Our society needs all kinds of professions. To be a good doctor, a good shepherd, a good soldier or a good farmer – all these professions should be as respected as being a good writer. (Sekirin, 2011: 149–50)

If his writings held up a mirror for those around him – without preaching or taking sides – then how he felt we should live is revealed in his other life and his other work, in medicine, in education and perhaps above all in *Sakhalin Island*. Without an understanding of this our appreciation of his literary canon is partial – without an understanding of both sides to his work and life, literature *and* medicine, we cannot know Chekhov. His sadness, his melancholy, his Chekhovian gloom was for how we live now, not for how he thought we could all live if we only opened our eyes, and embraced progress through science and technology.

Throughout his post-Sakhalin life, he was not only writing stories and plays – he was active in medicine, education and more.[18] Medicine was not a hobby but a part of him in action. During the famine of 1891 he raised funds and, to the surprise of many, persuaded Suvorin to become involved – famine relief not being a usual pastime for rich conservatives. Remember that in November of that year, when too weak to move, he wrote a short story about the famine, *The Wife*, for the serious liberal journal *The Northern Herald*, despite the famine being a politically taboo subject. As Rayfield suggests, though the story is not his strongest, it generated 'more publicity for famine relief than any manifesto' (Rayfield, 1997, 2010: 259). In 1892 Chekhov worked in one of the most advanced zemstvo hospitals in Russia during the cholera epidemic. He wrote to Suvorin that:

At the Nizhni Fair miracles are performed which may cause even Tolstoy to adopt a more respectful attitude toward medicine and toward the general participation of educated people in life. It looks as if a lasso had been thrown over cholera. We country [zemstvo] doctors are ready. (Hellman and Lederer, 1955: 166. Letter to Suvorin, 1 August 1892)

In the good old days when people fell ill and died by the thousands, no one could have dreamed of the astounding victories taking place before our very eyes. It is a pity you are not a doctor and can't share my pleasure . . . (Heim and Karlinsky, 1973: 240. Letter to Suvorin, 16 August 1892)

He spent from August to October of that year in charge of twenty-six villages and saw maybe 1,000 patients.[19] It was hands on, with him treating not only gastrointestinal upset but worms, syphilis and TB, all of which were endemic among peasants. He prepared statistical reports for the sanitary bureau, as well as lecturing on hygiene to peasants and supervising sanitation at a monastery. He inspected factories and shamed a tannery owner over pollution of a river. Grateful patients gave him a pedigree pig and suede gloves. His enthusiasm and energy led to him becoming medical officer of health and builder of bridges, schools, libraries, post offices, roads and bridges for 100 square miles (Rayfield, 1997, 2010: 275ff). It was then that he arranged the horse purchase scheme. He wrote to Suvorin 'While I serve the zemstvo, don't think of me as a literary man' (Tulloch, 1980: 57–8. Letter to Suvorin, 16 August 1892). 'Life has been nothing but hard work this summer, but I have the feeling now that I have never passed a summer so well' (from Tulloch, 1980: 58. Letter to Suvorin, 10 October 1892). He did similar work the next year, while between 1894 and 1897 he worked as a zemstvo doctor and attended medical congresses. There were small acts of kindness too, for instance one winter he saw a blind beggar and arranged for him to be housed; students were supported in their studies.

His medical work was not in isolation either. Throughout the 1990s he met leading members of the zemstvo movement and remained connected to it even as his health deteriorated. He was sent a telegram of support from Dr Popov on behalf of zemstvo doctors in November 1898 and was delighted to be made an honorary Academician in 1900, for his literary work. He read the medical journal *Physician* regularly. When *Annals of Surgery* was in financial trouble he interceded on its behalf, and persuaded Suvorin to rescue it.[20] He managed a similar trick with other journals too.[21] Had health permitted, he would have gone to the 9th Congress of Medicine in 1897 in Moscow and he was able to attend central zemstvo congresses and maintain contact with many progressive and left-minded doctors of the time.

He was also active in trying to improve medical education and lobbied for funds for a postgraduate medical education institution and a skin diseases research institute in Moscow. He helped found a biological station in the Crimea. His specialist interests were in psychiatry and medical education. He pressed for better training, to overturn the old women and their assistants who were in place in many peripheral clinics of the time and who had little or no training. He was in favour of freely available public medicine and critical of 'doctors who own villas . . .' (Tulloch, 1980: 72) – those city doctors, and others, who put their concern for money before their professional duties. *The Physician*, one of the journals he saved, was taken by one-third of doctors and was an important way of maintaining standards and education (Mandelker Frieden, 1981: 106ff).[22] His hands-on work in medicine, his public and private work on others' behalf and perhaps above all in his literary portrayals of doctors and of medical and environmental health concerns, led Mandelker Frieden to suggest that 'Chekhov's influence may have been of almost equal importance to that of *The Physician* in helping to legitimist physician's complaints and reinforce their sense of integrity and social worth' (Mandelker Frieden, 1981: 207ff).

His interests were not confined to medicine. He also pressed newspaper publishers to print articles on hygiene, forestry and agriculture.[23] But his other main interest was education. At a personal level, he supported several boy's school fees, one a distant relative in Taganrog. He was as concerned with teachers as doctors and said that they needed the same level of teaching as those in science, teachers were 'Ill-educated, starved, crushed, terrorized in being sent to small village' (Tulloch, 1980: 60).[24] He suggested that they should go to Moscow each summer for refresher courses, in science, horticulture and the potential of the natural environment.

This regard for education led him to raise money for, or often pay himself for, new schools. While at Melikhovo he built a new school and a lodging for the teacher in Talezh, and then another in nearby Novoselki which opened in the summer of 1897, and then in 1898 another in Melikhovo.[25] These were all direct hands-on projects for him, supervised actively even as his health deteriorated. When he left Melikhovo he kept a few books and sent the rest to Taganrog, and also sent books to other towns such as Serpukhov, Armaviz and Perm. He even began collecting information and data for a Sakhalin-style investigation into conditions in schools, which he never completed.

Gorky remembered Chekhov telling him, after he had been forced to Yalta.

> If I had lots of money I would build a sanatorium here for sick village teachers. A building full of light, very light, with big windows and high ceilings. I'd have a splendid library, all sort of musical instruments, an apiary, a vegetable garden, an orchard. I'd have lectures on agronomy, meteorology, and so on – teachers ought to know everything.

> He broke off suddenly, coughed, cast an oblique eye at me, and smiled his sweet, gentle smile, a smile which had an irresistible charm, forcing one to follow his word with the keenest attention.

'Does it bore you to listen to my dreams?' (Gorky, 1959: 134–5)

While there, and despite increasingly poor health, he sat on Red Cross committees and continued his work in famine relief. During a visit to Taganrog, in 1899, he saw a body covered in flies at the market and started an appeal for a mortuary (Rayfield, 1997, 2010: 493). He even told the council what trees to plant. As Karlinsky suggests:

> His life was one continuous round of alleviating famine, fighting epidemics, building schools and public roads, endowing libraries, helping organise marine biology libraries, giving thousands of needy peasants free medical treatment, planting gardens, helping fledgling writers get published, raising funds for worthy causes and hundreds of other pursuits . . . (Karlinsky, in Karlinsky and Heim, 1997: 26)

Medicine as a means to improve people's lives had limited effectiveness. So Chekhov, like others, pursued other means. He was probably engaged in more direct social and humanitarian action than any other writer, and as such was, in Karlinsky's words, one of the most profoundly subversive writers who ever lived. This radical perspective was less well known at the time in part because of his modesty and avoidance of publicity. When approached by an admirer while dining he told his companion 'Take her away, I have a knuckle-duster in my pocket' (Rayfield, 1997, 2010: 213).[26] He also chose, and so presumably preferred, practical action at a time when the Russian liberal intelligentsia, with whom he always had an uneasy relationship, was drawn to the social sciences, humanities and, occasionally, religion. While Chekhov valued their aims, his ideas and work for social involvement differed markedly from theirs. Tolstoy's ex-communication from the Orthodox Church and defence of religious sects, and Gorky's support of a revolutionary movement and fund-raising for outlawed political parties were dramatic, publicity seeking causes. Chekhov's work, in contrast, was in medicine and education, alleviating ill-health rather than pursuing political theories. For contemporaries, his efforts to prevent cholera, his Sakhalin project, his concerns over the mistreatment of Tatars, Gilyaks and Ainus, his alarm over the disappearance of wildlife and the effects of environmental damage and his lifelong concerns for children and their education were not as interesting as Tolstoy's open defiance of the tsarist government. *Plus ça change* one might think – now, as then, publicity seeking causes predominate over good solid work. *Sakhalin* was his one major public issue, and the serialization and then publication of his book did cause some fuss and lead to a government enquiry. Even then, Chekhov does not seem to have spent years lobbying for his cause. His Sakhalin adventure remains enigmatic, but can perhaps best be viewed as the largest and greatest of the humanitarian projects born in part out of a frustration with the limitations of conventional medicine. With hindsight, however, it is striking how prescient Chekhov was in many of his environmental, educational and even social concerns and conclusions.[27] His suggestions for the abolition of means tests for children's benefits, the use of food subsidies for children and pregnant women, and for those suckling, given directly to avoid men stealing it, have a feel of some recent and contemporary debates.

It is difficult now to think of him as anything but a playwright and author.[28] But there is good evidence that he saw himself at least as much a doctor as a writer. He was delighted when in January 1902 he was recognized by the editor of *Physician* as a doctor and great writer and arranged a performance of *Uncle Vanya* for a meeting of a progressive medicine group in 1902. In return they sent two telegrams: 'The zemstvo doctors from remote corners of Russia who saw the work of the doctor-artist greet their comrade and will keep the memory of January 11th ever fresh.' Chekhov replied, 'I felt like a prince. The telegrams raised me to heights I had never dreamed of' (Tulloch, 1980: 69–70).

The relative importance to him of leftward-leaning medical movements versus contemporary theatre must elude us at this distance, and when now, as then, theatre and the arts receive more publicity than medicine and science, but to be so lauded by the pre-eminent scientific/medical progressives of the time was deeply appreciated by Chekhov. Of course, we see him as a dramatist and writer, but remember, he thought his writing might last a few years. As we have heard, his friend and fellow author, Bunin, relates how one night they were walking under some cypress trees, past the ruins of a palace, when Chekhov turned to him and said 'Do you know how long people will continue to read my works? Seven years' (Bunin, 2007: 24).[29] He wanted to do something lasting and, one suspects, thought that might be as much in his building and medical work as in literature. Bunin also quotes a diary entry from Chekhov: 'how good it would be if each of us left behind a school, a well, or something similar so that our lives would not slip into eternity without a trace' (Bunin, 2007: xxv. From his diaries, 17, 171).

On several different occasions he also expressed a preference for being thought of as medical rather than literary. When he was first in Yalta, in

July 1889, the local newspaper listed eminent visitors and listed him as a writer.

Chekhov looked very upset when he went to the editorial office.

'Why did you say in your newspaper that I am a writer? First and foremost, I am a doctor, not a writer.' (Gorodetsky, in Sekirin, 2011: 149–50)

In this he did not change. In 1898 he wrote 'I am disgusted with writing . . . I'd take up medicine with pleasure, but I haven't the physical flexibility' (Chekhov, 2002. Letter to Avilova, 25 July 1898). As we have learnt, very near the end of his life, the director of the Moscow Arts Theatre, Stanislavsky, remembered how Chekhov always valued his medical work above his literary. 'I am a doctor by trade and sometimes I do literary work in my free time'. As Michael Finke relates, he held onto his medical books when he gave away others, kept his medical instruments on his desk, including a stethoscope pipe and reflex hammer, and dressed as a doctor (Finke, 2021: 185–6).[30]

When he married Olga Knipper in 1901 it was necessary to have your husband's status/profession on your passport. 'At first I wanted to list [you] as the wife of an honoured academician, but then I thought it would be more pleasant to have you as the spouse of a physician' (Bunin, 2007: 5, footnote 12. Letter to Olga Knipper, 4 September 1901).

Even allowing for some Chekhovian irony, these episodes, covering a long period, fifteen years or so at the end of his life, show how important to him was his identity as a doctor. Remember too Rayfield's remark that Chekhov thought his most important work was in relation to Sakhalin. Medicine and humanitarian work was crucial for him, even though now it is completely overshadowed by his literary genius. We need to assess his life from his own perspective, as a doctor and humanitarian as well as an author, as well as from ours.

His medical work infused and guided his writing, and improved it too, despite what Tolstoy thought. Bunin wrote:

He astonished readers not only with his talent but his knowledge of life and his profound understanding of the human soul . . . He loved to treat people, he valued his calling as a doctor highly. (Bunin, 2007: 5ff)

His medical training shaped his literary approach and his deep observation may, in part, have come from his medical studies. One of my own primary care doctors, a professor no less, was very knowledgeable, but rightly unpopular with his patients since he was a terrible physician. He knew everything, it seemed, but could not listen, and pre-judged rather than waiting for the clinical history to unfold. It takes a certain skill 'just' to listen, to efface one's own self and one's own thoughts and ideas to focus entirely on another and their experience before reaching a conclusion. Wittgenstein wrote that the most difficult thing is to observe without prejudice and Oliver Sacks – another great medical writer – wrote 'There is only one rule – always listen to the patient'.[31] Sacks listened, and was indeed loved by many patients too, as one suspects was Chekhov – listening and careful observation imbues and informs Chekhov's writing.

Doctors also observe dispassionately, with an appropriate clinical detachment. Graham Greene is famous for his observation that a writer needs ice in the veins, prepared to use whatever tragedies he or she sees for his art, without sentimentality. Chekhov's advice in this regard is even more apposite and pithy. Bunin recalls his advice to a young authoress:

Be colder . . . one may weep (and) share the heroes' suffering, but one should do so without letting the reader know. The more objective you are, the more powerful the impression. (Bunin, 2007: xl. Letters to Avilova, 19 March and 29 April 1892)

Later Bunin relates Chekhov saying to him, 'A writer should sit down and write only when he feels cold as ice' (Bunin, 2007: 21).

Of course, Chekhov was aware of the effects medical training had on not only his writing but his way of seeing the world, and he did not think it was all favourable. As Finke quotes Chekhov, medicine 'more likely interferes in giving away to free arts, in the sense of immediacy of impressions . . . As a simple person looks at the moon and is moved, an astronomer looks at it without illusions. I too as a medical man have few illusions and it tends to make life dry' (Finke, 2005: 3).

And yet, his approach to medicine and to literary was not really dry. His observations of others and his desire to understand them, in health and in illness, had a depth few could match at the time and which has resonances today. Kuprin wrote that:

If Chekhov had not been such a remarkable writer, he would have been an excellent doctor . . . And there would be nothing surprising if his diagnosis proved more complete and penetrating than a diagnosis established by some sorts of fashionable star [physician]. He saw and heard in a person – in his face, voice, movement – that which was hidden from others, which didn't give itself away, which eluded the eyes of the average observer. (Finke, 2005: 51. From Kuprin, A. (1986) *Pamiati Chekhova*)

Chekhov was well aware that his approach was not mainstream. When his friend Rossolimo asked him to teach medical students he replied 'If I were a teacher (of medicine), I would try to draw students as deeply as possible into the realm of the patient's subjective feeling' (Finke, 2005: 114). Finke continues that Chekhov thought that his understanding of how it feels to be ill came, at least in part, from his own ailments which caused him sufferings rarely comprehensible to a doctor. Finke continues 'Chekhov proposes applying in the medical sphere techniques he developed as an author of prose fiction . . . subjective narration'. This has modern resonances, as we have learnt, with more first-person narrative medicine championed by, among others, as we have described, Oliver Sacks ('we must employ an intersubjective approach, to see the world with the eyes of the patient himself'), and Havi Carel who, like Chekhov, has a chronic respiratory condition herself ('to fully understand illness it has to be studied as a lived experience . . .'). In this, as in his environmental concerns and his approach to social determinants of ill-health, Chekhov was astonishingly advanced for his time.

Despite Tolstoy's (correct) misgivings that medical work took Chekhov away from writing, Chekhov valued his medical work for itself, and for its usefulness in his writing.

I've no doubt that my work in medicine has had a serious impact on my literary output; it has significantly broadened the scope of my observations, and has enriched me with knowledge whose true value for me as a writer can be appreciated only by another physician. It has also had a decisive guiding influence: my intimacy with medicine has helped me avoid many mistakes. My familiarity with the natural sciences and scientific method has always kept me on my guard; I have endeavoured, whenever possible, to take scientific facts into account, and where this was not possible, I have preferred not to write at all. (Heim and Karlinsky, 1973: 365–7. Letter to Rossolimo, 11 October 1899)

Karlinsky commented:

> Chekhov's humanitarian concerns were focussed on the physical and biological realities of a man's existence and future rather than on the topical passions of a particular decade.

> Chekhov was aware of the importance of his training in the biological sciences for his literary approach. Instead of starting from a preconceived moral, sociological or religious position, he began with unbiased observations of life around him, and refrains from sweeping generalisation . . .

> While French contemporaries, e.g., Zola, used biological sciences and in doing so reduced peasants characters to level of lab animals, Chekhov's unfailing humanity and compassion led his approach to be like a doctor observing a patient, though he never prescribed solutions. (Karlinsky, in Heim and Karlinsky, 1973: 26ff)

Chekhov's work outside literature has, thus far, been considered in self-effacing humanitarian terms. But his strong conviction to work with and for others may have coexisted alongside more personal needs.

He was no saint – he despised and antagonized academics 'I have my knife out for professors. Like authors they have no caring and much self-importance' (Bunin, 2007: xxxiii. Letter to Suvorin, 27 November 1899), and compared intellectuals to slugs and woodlice. They, in turn, shunned him. At the least, diplomacy was not his strongest suit. His attitudes to women were also curious. His concern for their welfare was evident from his work on Sakhalin. In his personal life, he seemed irresistible to many women, and yet was ruthless, loving and leaving for the sake of his art, as though his formative years 'studying' prostitutes never left him. His courtship of, marriage to and then subsequent living arrangements with, Olga Knipper were also unusual and surprised contemporaries. As a working actress at the Moscow Arts Theatre, she continued to work there from autumn to early summer each year while he lived in Yalta, leaving them little time together, over summers and during his visits to Moscow. Yet, Anton and Olga wrote frequently, almost daily, with letters of exasperation if for any reason there were a few days between letters (Benedetti, 1996). His letters to her are at times passionate and deepen with time as they become first acquaintances, then lovers and finally man and wife. He variously addresses her as Sweetheart, Goose, Linnet, Doggie,

Boozer, Sweet Knipshitz, Actress, Crocodile, Horseykins and Sperm Whale. He also says she is 'a great and genuine artist' and in a letter dated 23 August 1900, two years after they first met and soon after they became lovers, he wrote simply and unambiguously 'I love you'. He also made an allowance for her in a will he wrote in August 1901, which also looked after his sister Masha and his brothers. (The will also mentioned benefits to Taganrog Town Council, a road in Melikhovo and ended, 'Help the poor, Take care of mother. Live at peace with one another'.) For some time after his death Olga continued to write to him (Pitcher, 1979: 154ff).[32] Despite the unusual living arrangements which were agreed between them, and after his previous stringing along of various women, there is evidence of a deep relationship.

He was also unrepentant in using the personal details of friends shamelessly in his writing. As we have seen in *The Grasshopper* he depicted his dear friend Levitan's affair. Separating his art from his life was difficult, with something of that coldness in the latter as well.

Chekhov lived most of his life with his parents and siblings. He sat at table with Tolstoy, confided and travelled with Suvorin, had many friends, and others clamouring to admire him. Yet on several occasions he described himself as lonely. His friend and fellow writer, Bunin, quotes from Chekhov's diary 'I will lie in my grave alone, just as I have lived alone throughout my life' (Bunin, *About Chekhov*: 58), and goes on to write 'I once ventured the opinion that Chekhov had never been friendly or on close terms with anyone. Now I know it to be a fact' (Bunin, 2007: 123) Elpatievsky, a friend, near the end of Chekhov's life, observed 'Solitude. He lived in solitude. He was surrounded by family and friends in Yalta, but he felt as if he lived in solitude' (Sekirin, 2011: 177). Writers, of course, are solitary in their craft, seeking peace and silence in which to create. As Hemingway wrote for his Nobel Prize acceptance oration 'Writing, at its best, is a lonely life . . . and if he is a good enough writer he must face eternity, or the lack of it, each day' (https://www.nobelprize.org/prizes/literature/1954/hemingway/speech/). And, like most people of genius, Chekhov saw the world differently, and more deeply, than those he lived with and loved.[33] Gorky, a young writer at the time and who Chekhov encouraged, remarked how Chekhov's solitariness might reflect how misunderstood he was.

It seems that Chekhov was not immune to depression (just see *Ivanov*), and one way to keep it at bay was activity. He was driven throughout most of his life not only by knowledge of his prognosis from TB, but by a need to keep busy at all costs 'a writer should be a pauper, knowing he will die of hunger if he succumbs to laziness . . . they should be placed under arrest, put in cells and whipped and beaten to make them write' (Bunin, 2007: 57). But there is also evidence that he found living with his creative abilities difficult at times to sustain:

> Unhappiness with self is a key feature of genuine talent. Talent is work. Talent is responsibility. Talent is conscience. An artist must do a lot of thinking . . . (Bunin, 2007: 126)

Bunin added, somewhat superfluously, that Chekhov was 'thinking constantly'. The responsibility he felt to his talent may also have been a burden, He wrote to a brother 'The loneliness of creation is a burdensome thing' (McVay, 1994: 33. Letter to Alexander Chekhov, 10 May 1886). This may have been an additional, more selfish, reason for his work in zemstvo medicine, famine relief and education – he needed to keep busy, but he also needed time away from writing and the demands of his genius. Throwing himself into medicine, seeing patients, working with other people, building schools – these not only allowed him precious time off from writing, but they gave him an identity within a team which, for a while at least, banished his solitariness and propensity to melancholia, and gave him refuge.

It is difficult, over a century later, to gauge his contemporary reach or fame. At times newspapers covered his movements, for instance his trip to France with Suvorin, and he had to avoid admirers waiting to see him, towards the end of his life, in the Crimea. But Donald Rayfield suggests that most of the Russian public made little connection between Chekhov's life, which was very private, except to a small circle, and his stories and plays, seen by a fraction of the number who read his stories. Both the dogmatists of the left and the nationalists of the right, especially in St Petersburg, disapproved of him, and insisted he was a naive provincial.[34]

Few people outside Chekhovians and scholars are aware of his visit to, and work in relation to, Sakhalin Island. In biographies it can be treated as a slightly marginal, curious episode in his journey from pot-boiling comic short story writer,[35] to mature writer and dramatist or even, as one literary agent put it, 'no more than a footnote'. The book, *Sakhalin Island*, is rather glossed over, it is long and a little tedious, and enigmatic in form and method, something to be 'got over' before he could return to being the Chekhov we know and revere. In five popular biographies, the pages devoted to Sakhalin average 6 per cent of the total. And, if Sakhalin was and is side-lined, his other work in medicine and education remains similarly neglected. Their importance, as we have seen, lies in revealing Chekhov in action, overlapping his literary perspective and its quiet humanity. For not only did he straddle the two cultures of the arts and humanities, and medicine and science, he embraced and contributed to both.

One purpose has been to show how his work on Sakhalin and in other non-literary projects were a central part of his life. The journey probably shortened his life and led to a permanent deterioration in his health. The whole adventure, as we have learnt, was the longest work of his career by far – literally his magnum opus. Chekhov really did consider it as repaying his debt to medicine. By medicine he did not mean attending the sick with little hope of changing illness, or establishing a healthy private practice for himself, as many did. It was actually a singular, massive attempt to alleviate suffering and alter the conditions of penal servitude. The methods used were all employed for that purpose, whether they involved what might now be called ethnography, sociology, agriculture and fishery, or the use of statistics, the appeals to justice and the use of narrative and even fictionalized documentation, as in the case of Yegor. All were guided by the environmental and social approach to medicine he had learnt at medical school.

Chekhov was also both a physician and artist – long before medicine-art projects existed. Indeed, as Coulehan observed, he saw no conflict between art and science (Coulehan, 2003: xviii). Though deeply insightful, he was not polemical. He wrote one of the first fusions between the medical and artistic worlds. *Sakhalin Island* is also remarkable in Chekhov's work because the writer, usually invisible in his fictional work, even in his protagonists' characters, is conspicuously present, not just as a reporter but as a man recording his own moods and reactions.

In his art he held up a mirror, at times too brightly for some 'the only aim of artistic literature is absolute, genuine truth. Man will only grow better when he has been shown to himself as he is' (Laffitte, 1974: 188. From his notebooks). Beyond that he would never tell us how we should live, but his deeds reveal what he could not say. His faith was not in God but in science, in medicine, in engineering and in environmental work to improve social conditions and, above all, in individual people 'To work for science and public ideals, that is personal happiness'. These were his creed and his life's work. To see this, to see the whole man, we need his literature, and his science and medicine and educational work as well. In *Sakhalin* we see his ideas and morality in deed and in action – this is how he chose to live.

When we were shown around the museum dedicated to his visit to Aleksandrovsk, Lydia, the guide, finished her tour, over two hours for four small rooms, thus:

Towards the end of his life, living in Yalta to avoid winter, the artists held a lot of parties. People read their works, artists showed paintings, musicians played, and Chaliapin liked to sing for Chekhov. And in the course of such a meeting, one asked Chekhov, 'Why do you never mention Sakhalin, are you trying to avoid it?' He tried to joke but it did not work. Then he came to the window and just looked out for some time. And then he turned back and said as if to eternity, and to no one,

'I think everything is filled with Sakhalin.' He never mentioned it was filled with Taganrog, where he was born, nor Moscow – he loved Moscow – nor Melikhovo his estate. But after those three months and three days, everything in his life was filled with Sakhalin.

Moreover, Anton Pavlovich, in the summer of 1904, goes to Germany to die. The month before, in May, in letters to two correspondents, one Lazareski, he wrote,

'If I feel maybe a little bit better, I undertake another journey to Sakhalin.'[36]

In 1904, nearing the end of his life he kept up with the war between Russia and Japan over Sakhalin which had just started, and even suggested he would volunteer when his health allowed (Altshuller, in Sekirin, 2011: 175). He never forgot Sakhalin.

If his *Sakhalin* book can be criticized for a lack of hard data, reflecting the chaos and desperation which prevailed, his account must also be lauded for still managing to convey a sense of its hell. The difficulties for one man in encompassing its despair, as well as details of its prisons and mines, guards and governors, forestry and agriculture, were huge. Chekhov's approach, observing dispassionately and where possible constructively, allowed him to show what Sakhalin was like remarkably given the size of the island and his relatively short time there.

Chekhov's gaze was cold and clinical. Like other writers he used friends and lovers mercilessly in his fiction – even Lika Mizinova found her way into *The Seagull*. He used and dropped women without warning and scorned intellectuals. Away from this, though, was another side. Sakhalin was no impetuous gap year interval – it was the largest and most obvious example of this other life, his second life, his medical and humanitarian work beyond literature which was so important to him. No crying at his plays, instead he asked people to look as he had looked, unflinchingly and yet with deep compassion (Karlinsky, in Heim and Karlinsky, 1973: 26ff). And then he invited them to do something, something better, something lasting.

Remember his saying that 'Medicine is my lawful wife and literature my mistress; when I get tired of one, I spend the night with the other' (Garnett, 1920: 99). Chekhov's first love, his wife, was medicine and humanitarian work and he never fell out of love with this, even though it is his mistress, literature, which has endured. Unusually, but perhaps typically, it was his mistress who was public while his wife, medical and other work, remained more hidden. It is hoped that the present volume has shown how one can view Chekhov's work in thought and action, literature – showing not telling – and medicine and humanitarian and educational projects – acting in the world in the hope of improvement – as a single whole. It seems he did.

## Notes

1. Rayfield wrote on this for an unpublished manuscript on Chekhov and Sakhalin by Cole, Turda and Rayfield which flowed from the Wellcome project on *The Russian Doctor/Chasm of Sorrow*, and I have quoted liberally from his work in this section.

2. Arguably as interesting or more so are the ways in which Chekhov describes medical conditions in his work. There are observations of depression, mania, pre-Kafkaesque anxiety, and possible early descriptions of autism and synaesthesia. Coulehan also mentions depictions of depression, psychosis and emotional detachment and then burn-out in doctors. Coope also goes into some detail about *Ivanov* being in part a study in depression, as well as it being depicted in *A Case History* (Coope, J. 1997: 33ff).

3. Later Astrov appears with maps of the degradation of their local area, which Rayfield thinks one of Chekhov's classic stage jokes, the prolonged preaching suspends the play's action for the sole aim of an encounter between Astrov and Elena. Rayfield links Astrov's environmental ideas to both the earlier play, *The Wood Demon* from which Vanya arose and to his stories of 1887 (Rayfield, 1999, 2010: 178).

4. Even here his sympathies were already established, In *Sleepy*, (1888) a thirteen-year-old girl strangles the young baby she is looking after. The whole

story is about how the girl was orphaned and then taken in and treated as a slave, caring for the baby, tending the fire, washing up and cleaning the whole time. Exhausted and sleep deprived she kills just so she can sleep. The reader's sympathies are directed to understand what drove her to infanticide. The alternative and more revealing title is *Let me Sleep*.

5. In *Three Years* (1895), he satirizes this movement 'A work of literature cannot be significant or useful unless its basic idea contains some meaningful social task . . .' (Karlinsky, Introduction, Heim. and Karlinsky, 1973: 8).

6. The extraordinary intellectual developments in nineteenth-century Russia have been elegantly discussed by Kelly, 1998. She focusses on the debates underpinning the work of Pushkin, Turgenev, Dostoevsky, Tolstoy, Gogol, et al. She rarely mentions Chekhov, perhaps reflecting his antithesis to intellectuals, and perhaps to their paucity of deeds.

7. Such faith in individuals was echoed by Vasily Grossman in *Life and Fate*, responding to Soviet excesses. 'The only true and lasting meaning of the struggle for life lies in the individual, in his modest peculiarities and his right to those peculiarities' (Grossman, 2006; x). Chekhov would have agreed and have liked the focus on idiosyncrasy.

8. Just as Chekhov, of course, could not leave Yalta for Moscow during his last years.

9. There is always a difficulty discussing embodied, physical acting within a play when engaged in critical analysis of the written text.

10. Bennett has a delicious quote from Beckett 'If I knew what Godot was, I would have said so' (Bennett, *Reassessing the Theatre of the Absurd*: 28).

11. *Ivanov* can be interpreted as being, in part, about clinical depression.

12. Dr Shchurovsky's medical note kindly supplied by Donald Rayfield.

13. 'Yesterday and today I've been plagued by a headache that began with an intermittent flashing in my eyes' (Letter to Suvorin, 8 April 1892, in Heim and Karlinsky, 1973: 221).

14. From his notebooks 'Solomon made a great mistake when he asked for wisdom' (Chekhov, 2002).

15. After one meeting with Tolstoy, Chekhov wrote to Menshikov (16 April 1897; Bartlett, 2004): '. . . we had a most interesting conversation . . . mainly because I listened more than I talked. We discussed immortality. He recognises immortality in its Kantian form, assuming that all of us (men and animals) will live on in some principle (such as reason or love), the essence of which is a mystery. But I can only imagine such a principle or force as a shapeless, gelatinous mess . . . I don't understand it and Lev Nikolayevich was astonished that I don't.'

16. Hero of *A Sad Story*, Professor Nicolai Stepanovich, written by Chekhov in 1889 and quoted from Laffitte, 1974: 89 (also known as 'A Boring, An Anonymous, or A Dreary Story'). Lenin, of course, famously said

that socialism depended on the organization of Soviet workers and electrification.

17. Laffitte, S. *Chekhov*: 135. Quoted from Chekhov's *The Story of an Unknown Man* (1893).

18. Coincidentally, medicine and education were both liberalized by the Tsar in his reforms.

19. Coope writes that between July and December he made 576 house calls and saw 453 patients (Coope, 1997: 109–10).

20. In his begging letter, he mentions that he might offer to publish it himself, but for the 1500 roubles he is spending building a school . . .

21. Including *Surgery* and *Chronicles of Surgery.*

22. Mandelker Frieden mentions how Chekhov has his Dr Ragin, from *Ward Number 6*, read the journal, and it alone, 'from the back', where the grievances and answers to critics were to be found.

23. He was passionate about trees and forests, planting them wherever he could 'A tree is beautiful, but what's more, it has a right to life; like water, the sun and the stars, it is essential. Life on earth is inconceivable without trees. Forests create climate, climate influences peoples' character, and so on and so forth. There can be neither civilization nor happiness if forests crash down under the axe, if the climate is harsh and severe, if people are also harsh and severe . . . What a terrible future!' (Letter to Suvorin 18 October 1888), https://todayinsci .com/C/Chekhov_Anton/ChekhovAnton-Quotations.htm. In some of his environmental concerns he may have been influenced by Humboldt, whose work he was familiar with (Pritchett, 1988: 85), and who he mentioned in his letters before setting out for Sakhalin.

24. His plays often portray one consequence of this effect of widening education – bright intellectuals being sent to provincial towns and villages to endure Chekhovian boredom.

25. He also supported a Moscow doctors' campaign against corporal punishment at this time.

26. A knuckle duster is a metal guard worn over the hand to increase one's fighting ability.

27. He thought that deforestation reduced rainfall and that the trees of the north of Russia ameliorated the climate, both widely accepted today.

28. He once described the relation between the two in familiar terms. 'For me, narrative prose is a legal wife, while drama is a posturing, boisterous, cheeky and wearisome mistress . . .' (Sekirin, 2011: 108. Letter to Pleshcheev AN. 15 January 1889).

29. Though he later admitted to Shchepkina-Kopernik a similar thing, he added that after a certain time people would begin to read him again.

30. Finke also mentions that Chekhov kept a travelling bag, as he had used for Sakhalin, on his bedroom wall (Finke, 2021: 87).

31. Sacks, O. *Personal communication.*

32. She and Maria Chekhov lived until the 1950s. Two years before she died, in 1957, Olga Knipper saw Peter Brook's *Hamlet* in Paris.

33. One of his two last stories, *The Bishop*, is among his most moving and clearly autobiographical. It is about a gifted son saying goodbye to his mother before he dies and how the bishop's eminence had created a barrier between mother and son. He stipulated that not a word of it should be changed after his death.

34. Rayfield, *personal communication.* He also suggested that the 'Sakhalin book was read by relatively few, but must have had some temporary effect on the authorities, who probably had only a hazy idea about his fiction'.

35. He was good at writing melodramas and pulp fiction of the time.

36. Rayfield comments that this originated in a memoir (not published until 1967) by the headmistress of the Yalta girl's school, Varvara Kharkievich. She has been dismissed by Ivan Bunin, who knew Chekhov well and had met her, too, as an 'exalted [*vostorzhennaya*] lady', but Rayfield suggests the reply is plausible (*personal communication*). 'Filled with Sakhalin' is frequently translated as 'Sakhalinized'. The direct quote was translated and recorded verbatim and then transcribed.

# References

Bartlett, R., Ed. (2004). *Anton Chekhov, A Life in Letters*, translated by Bartlett, R. and Phillips, A. London: Penguin.

Benedetti, J. (1996). *Dear Writer, Dear Actress; the love letters of Anton Chekhov and Olga Knipper*. London: Methuen Drama.

Bennett, M.K. (2011). *Reassessing the Theatre of the Absurd. Camus, Beckett, Ionesco, Genet and Pinter*. London: Palgrave Macmillan.

Borny, G. (2006). *Interpreting Chekhov*. Canberra: Australian National University.

Bunin, I. (2007). *About Chekhov The Unfinished Symphony*. Trans and Ed Marullo, TG. Evanston Il, Northwestern University Press.

Chekhov, A. (1895). *Sakhalin Island*, translated by Brian Reeve. London; One World Edition. 1993, 2007, 2014. (Throughout translations are from the 2007 edition).

Chekhov, A. (2002). *Personal Papers*. Honolulu: University of the Pacific Press.

Coope, J. (1997). *Doctor Chekhov: A Study in Literature and Medicine*. Chalk, UK: Cross Publishing.

Corrigan, R. (1964). 'The Plays of Chekhov', in Corrigan, R. and Rosenberg, J.L. (Eds), *The Context and Craft of Drama*. Scranton, NJ: Chandler Publishing, p. 145.

Coulehan, J. (2003). *Chekhov's Doctors*. Kent and London: Kent State University Press.

Esslin, M. (1961). *The Theatre of the Absurd*. Garden City: Anchor Books.

Esslin, M. (1985). 'Chekhov and the Modern Drama', in Clyman, T.W. (Eds), *A Chekhov Companion*. Westport: Greenwood Press, pp. 143–5.

Finke, M. (2021). *Freedom from Violence and Lies. Anton Chekhov's Life and Writings*. London: Reaktion.

Garnett, C., Trans. (1920). *Letters of Anton Chekhov to his Family and Friends, with a Biographical Sketch*. New York: The Macmillan Company.

Gilman, R. (1995). *Chekhov's Plays*. New Haven: Yale University Press.

Gorky, M. (1959). *Literary Portraits*. Moscow: Foreign Languages Publishing House.

Grossman, V. (2006). *Life and Fate*. London: Vintage.

Heim, M. and Karlinsky, S. (1973). *Letters of Anton Chekhov*. New York, Evanston, San Fransisco and London.

Karlinsky, S. and Heim, M.H. (1997). *Anton Chekhov's Life and Thought: Selected Letters and Commentaries*. Evanston, IL: Northwestern University Press.

Kataev, V. (2002). *If Only We Could Know*. Chicago: Dee.

Kelly, A. (1998). *Toward Another Shore. Russian Thinkers Between Necessity and Chance*. New Haven and London: Yale University Press.

Laffitte, S. (1974). *Chekhov*. London: Readers Union/Angus Robertson.

Magarshack, D. (1980). *Chekhov the Dramatist*. London: Eyre Methuen.

Mandelker Frieden, N. (1981). *Russian Physicians in an Era of Reform and Revolution, 1856–1905*. Princeton: Princeton University Press.

McVay, G. (1994). *Chekhov: A Life in Letters*. London: Folio Society.

Pinker, S. (2018). *Enlightenment Now*. London: Allen Lane.

Pitcher, H. (1979). *Chekhov's Leading Lady. A Portrait of the Actress Olga Knipper*. London: Murray.

Pritchett, V.S. (1988). *Chekhov a Spirit Set Free*. London: Hodder and Stoughton.

Rayfield, D. (1997, 2010). *Anton Chekhov – A Life*. London: HarperCollins. 1997, 2010. Second Edition, London: Garnett Press. 2021.

Rayfield, D. (1999, 2010). *Understanding Chekhov*. London: Bristol Classical Press/ Bloomsbury.

Sekirin, P., Ed. and trans. (2011). *Memories of Chekhov*. Jefferson, NC and London: McFarland.

Shestov, L. (1966). *Chekhov and Other Essays*. Ann Arbor: University of Michigan Press.

Skaftymov, A. (1993). 'Principles and Structures in Chekhov's Plays', translated by McCracken Young, G. in Jackson, R.L. (Ed.), *Chekhov. Reading Chekhov's Text. Studies in Russian Literature and Theory*. Evanston, IL: Northwestern University Press.

Stein, W. (1959–60). 'Tragedy and the Absurd', *The Dublin Review*, vol 233.

Tulloch, J. (1980). *Chekhov; A Structuralist Study*. London. Macmillan.

# POSTSCRIPT
## SAKHALIN NOW

In order to research our original outline, and supported by the small development grant, Andy and I went to Sakhalin one late September. Chekhov's arrived on Sakhalin at Aleksandrovsk, on the west coast of the middle part of the island, though northern in terms of settlement. To research his time on Sakhalin for the proposed play, Andrew Dawson and I did the reverse, landing at Yuzhno-Sakhalinsk in the south. What took Chekhov eleven weeks took us eleven hours, with a stop in Moscow.[1] The museum's curator, Katya, met us at the airport in the afternoon and took us to our hotel. She arranged to meet us for dinner, so to keep awake we wandered round Yuzhno, past memorials to the Patriotic War to a park and fairground with a tired paddling pool named, like much else, after Yuri Gagarin.

Katya was beautiful, slim, shy and sad. She, her mother and grandmother were all from Sakhalin. She talked of her twelve-year-old daughter, but not of a husband. Alex, our translator, grew up in Sevastopol and had several jobs before working in oil and gas. Times were good with Shell but then Gazprom took over and started laying people off. He took early retirement at sixty-two and went into freelance translation work. Businessmen were his usual fare, so two vague Englishmen wandering around after Chekhov's ghost were fun.

Next day we were directed to a backstreet in the north of Yuzhno. Surrounded by anonymous residential buildings was a small, apologetic old house with an unkempt lawn, on which – apparently at random – was left an old wooden wheelbarrow. The entrance had a green sentry box and a bust of Anton Pavlovich Chekhov. This was the 'Literature-art Museum of the book A.O. Chekhov "Island Sakhalin"', a museum not to Chekhov but to his book.

In the entry hall was an oil painting of a ludicrously young and handsome Chekhov standing in the taiga. We were introduced to Sonia our guide – serious and round-faced, she showed us around.

Downstairs were two small rooms stuffed with glass cases, photographs, a wooden model of a ship, a desk, a traveller's trunk, a scale model of the prison in Aleksandrovsk and moth-eaten mannequins. First, in a glass case, was a second edition of the book, from 1896. The 1880s, she explained, had been very difficult – not only had the Tsar died but so also Turgenev and Dostoevsky.[2] That left Tolstoy alone, so it was good that Chekhov emerged.[3] Big authors were famous throughout Russia and important figures, even if few people could read (and even fewer read serious fiction).

'Sakhalin was opened as a penal colony in 1864. It failed; they all died, harsh conditions', she began, 'then they organised it in proper manner, initially for political exiles and then as a prison and colony as well'. She became more serious and took a deep breath. 'Chekhov just cannot pass by Sakhalin. He starts careful preparation for the journey; he has a list of 65 literary sources for his book, but there were many more. He studies history, geography, law, criminology'.

She showed us a photo of Chekhov and his family, just before the journey.

Chekhov arrived without any official documents. He was here 3 months and 3 days and left on the boat, 14th October. There were two ways to reach Sakhalin. The route on land lasted several years; they walked all the way to Sakhalin and 10% perished. By sea was later.

The settlements he visited are shown on this map. We see three census cards, some with red slash; female. The census allowed him to meet everyone, regardless of exile, local resident or guard. He also used church registration books, for birth and deaths. The census was not entirely accurate; some people changed their identity and others even forgot when they were born and where they lived.

In one glass cabinet were a travelling bag and a cut-throat razor – his, we were assured, relics from the great man. Next was a model of the ship he returned in and, mounted on a wall behind in a case, his ticket of passage. Further round the room were photos of the estate in Melikhovo he bought in 1892 and a reconstruction of his desk with, upon it, photos of his parents, a small drawing of a street scene, an inkwell and pen, a blotter, magnifying glass and a paperweight. In front of these were pages from one of his manuscripts with immaculate handwriting with lots of crossings out. 'He worked hard writing and re-writing the book. It is his unbiased view and analysis. He tried to describe life from all sides, including the exiled people, convicts and their shackles and punishment cells'. In one corner, in a glass cabinet, was a first edition of *Ward Number 6*.

In the next room were a wooden model of the prison at Aleksandrovsk and a large oil painting of convict miners in a tunnel, either chained to wheelbarrows or half-shaved, with the beach at Douai behind. 'They slept with their wheelbarrow, got up and were taken outside to sit all day beside their barrows. No movement for years, they were let off to wash every two to three years'. On the far wall was a mannequin in Sakhalin clothes, and a smaller figure of the ferryman in a small square boat. 'He was obedient and never argued, so he survived a long time. Disobedient people were beaten'. Though the death penalty had long been outlawed, lashings left open wounds and infections killed people afterwards, slowly. In one community, a sentence of 100 lashes was passed on a man who was well liked, so 100 men took one lash each instead. Behind were photos of the wheelbarrow men, either individual or together like a grotesque team photo, standing with barrows in front, some half-shaven. Next to them was 'Golden Hand'. 'She was famous in Russia and around the world; a swindler and murderess. It was like theatre. Photos of her were sold abroad, in Russia and Europe as well'. We do love a murderess. Below these, in a glass case, was a camera, like the one Chekhov took, together with a photographic plate of the time. He took lots of photographs, but his brother wrecked the negative plates during development.

To the right were a trunk, like the one Chekhov abandoned before it could kill him in the open cart, and a spinning wheel. It was too cold for sheep – they spun dog hair which 'made good gloves'. Around were more recent stylized lithographs. One showed a group of convicts pulling a huge log with difficulty, while to the side, sitting down gazing on with notebook in hand, was Chekhov, strikingly handsome and immaculately dressed in a cream suit.

On the second floor was a collection of modern editions of the book and more mannequins dressed this time as gentlemen and ladies. Olga took over, slightly older and striking in appearance.

Our museum is the unique one; we cannot find such a museum in any other city because it is devoted to the book Sakhalin Island. We also have some memorial articles from the period, descendants of APC also contributed. This unique museum completely described and opens the book, and commentaries to it and we also have certain library of books, including translations into foreign languages.

Of course, we have books published at the time when Chekhov was still alive and we do really hard work to find other items for our exhibition.

As far as scientific and research work, I want to tell we have annually a scientific and practical conference held here philologists and scientists studying Russian language and ethnologists also participate.

You know some statistics of descendants of convicts are there, but a lot of people come here to try to find their ancestors. Not just from Sakhalin but from Siberia and rest of Europe.

She showed us foreign editions of the book and memorabilia from around the world, of lectures and theatre pieces based on Chekhov's visit. The museum had also just bought, from America, a first edition. She handed it to us and we held it with reverence.

She explained that the first editions of the book were incomplete, since the committee of censors had prohibited it. The Head of Prisons was strongly against the book and tried to supress it, partly because he was guilty. The government disliked it too and claimed it was a malicious joke. They knew the truth, as usual and as always – they had spies and knew what it was like – so they tried to laugh it off. His publishers were punished and though the reason given was something else, everyone knew it was for publishing *Sakhalin Island*. In the noble tradition of shooting the messenger, Chekhov did not get in trouble, just the publisher, because the publisher could have rejected it. After the great October Revolution in 1917 all magazines were closed, but Chekhov's book was published. It was not until 1980 that it was published in full, why then is unknown.

Some have suggested that he came to Sakhalin to write a big novel, to be a real author. But it was not the proper time, end of 19th century, to have something related to prison. The censors were too active.[4]

Regarding his unofficial census, a few years later there was a Russian census with little difference in its results. There were some inconsistencies over names because a few were afraid to give their real ones. Chekhov would be amused that his census was still consulted, since he wondered whether his figures might be of some use, in the absence of more reliable data.

Olga continued:

In our colonies, at least, the convicts were working for their country, doing useful things. In the US and England, they just locked them up and they did no useful work. Putting stones one on top of another, that is no use to the community.

We finished by asking Sonia and Olga what they thought of Chekhov. Sonia, so quiet and efficient during our tour, suddenly became alive, big eyes wide open:

> Chekhov is everything, so revolutionary and humane. He left his family, his home to help others, risking all, as a physician and honest person trying to help others. He looked at people and their situation clearly and showed us their situation and their soul. We owe everything to him.

> Having read his short stories, we understand ourselves, our lives, much better; the short stories could have been written about us. We can see the *Sakhalin Island* as an encyclopaedia of the nineteenth century. We understand aspects of life not – never – described in other books. For us living in Russia this is a great contribution not only to literature but to life itself as well.

> He showed to all society the problems of that time and of Sakhalin. It had a great effect, with reforms following the great book.

Olga just shrugged her shoulders:

> What makes you think I love Chekhov? This is just a job, I prefer Dostoevsky.

We thanked them all profusely – their museum was wonderful, understated but with a sense of history and appreciation, and they had brought it to life. As we were leaving a visitor came into the vestibule, looked around, sniffed a bit and then left. His loss, for the small museum had been assembled with care and love over years. It was just a shame so few enjoyed it – in the visitors' book were forty signatures per year. Anya, Olga and Sonia were keeping the flame alive and Chekhov would surely have loved to see them – after all they might have stepped out of one of his plays – the three of them had been born on Sakhalin and none had been to Moscow.

Aleksandrovsk, a few hundred miles to the north, is reached either by roads and tracks or by overnight train. We took the train with Temur, the director of the Chekhov museums on Sakhalin, a bearded bear of a man, full of energy and life, a storyteller, amateur actor, teller of endless jokes and singer of folk songs. We got off the train in the dark at a halt 50 miles from Aleksandrovsk and were driven through the mountains in a Land Cruiser, heavy metal rock blaring out of its speakers, passing villages settled during penal colony days, some with old wooden houses.

Our hotel, The Three Brothers, was set across from the main square, 'The Square of Shackles', on the site of the old prison and on flat land above the river. At one end of the square is the Town Hall, with a statue of Lenin, exhorting us, arm outstretched. At the other end, outside our hotel a bust of Chekhov, watching undemonstrably.

The oldest building on Sakhalin is a single-storey house in the middle of Aleksandrovsk, now used as a nursery. The second oldest is the museum to Chekhov, and the house he dined in on his arrival. It lies in the older town, down the hill and towards the Dukya River and the sea. The tarmac road soon gave way to dirt and was lined with dilapidated wooden houses, some inhabited, some ruined, some both. Half a mile down the track lay three single-storey wooden dacha, so smart in their green paint and dark wood stain that they stand out among the other dilapidated houses and shacks. These are the museum. Across the dirt road, in a small open grassy square stands Chekhov's statue, tall, young and slim, hair falling like a rock god. To his right is a modern general store, and behind an old metalwork yard.

The museum, which occupied the main building, was a small, exquisite gem – six rooms of polished wooden floors with curious glass stands and frames to protect or encase the exhibits.[5] We had never seen such ornamental constructions – part time-warp and part shrine, it was obviously a labour of love, unique and completely charming.

Lydia showed us around. She was in her forties, hair in a bun, tortoiseshell glasses, pink twin set and shawl but above all quietly, deeply passionate about Chekhov and the museum. The first room had a collection of letters from Kleopatra Katyrgina, an elaborate triple screen of photos and letters, a photo of Chekhov behind another screen and in the far corner, behind another screen, a reproduction of Chekhov's rubberized raincoat.

I would like to greet you at this literary and historical museum of Chekhov. It is one of the eight world museums devoted to Chekhov. Forgive me for bragging.

Now to Anton Pavlovich. At this age, 30 years, he arrived at Sakhalin. He was a fine man without any signs of illness on his face, but we know he was deadly ill, and he knew it because he made his own diagnosis. And it is admirable that he did such a heavy journey knowing this. By this time this famous and successful writer had a Pushkin Prize, very rare at this age, or any age. Only two writers have this prize, the other Count Lev Nicholivich Tolstoy. Not Turgenev, nor Dostoevsky.

He had a medical practice as well. From the outside, everything is OK. However, if you scrutinise his letters, one finds there that his feelings and internal state are in contrast to the external situation. 'I don't like my Pushkin prize. I have failed to do anything useful for society in my thirty years. I cannot read even one line of my writings without disgust.' On the crest of popularity, he is in deep depression; it is frequently the case with creative people by the way . . . Creating person are very sensitive.

For Chekhov, it was important to find the right way to serve society and the journey to Sakhalin was his practical way to realise it.

To Lydia's right was a stand about Kleopatra Katyrgina, who helped Chekhov and, she omitted to say, his lover – his only older woman.

When his brother died the troupe of Moscow Theatre tried to put him out of his depression and suggested he went to Odessa with their tour. There he met this wonderful actress. Kleopatra had visited Siberia and Sakhalin long before Chekhov and spent not 3 months and 3 days here, but for about 10 years during the 1870s. After her husband died, she joined the Irkutsk theatre and ended up with them for 10 years. On Sakhalin, she went to Douai and, in a southern outpost, played in the open air for prisoners. She and Chekhov talked through the night, drinking tea in her hotel as she described Sakhalin. She wrote a letter of instruction with all necessary information, for example when to do what and what questions may be asked and what questions can never be asked of a convict. They were friends till his death.

A samovar and some cups dominated the second room. Behind a glass was a small table, and a tea pot, supposedly his.

On 21st April Anton Pavlovich departed from Moscow. From Tomsk, the most difficult part his journey began, the most horrible part. In April, the roads were bad, with a mixture of ice and dirt. At times there was no road just a direction. It was an open carriage and he was ill. On such roads, he coughed blood and nearly had to return, but recovered and went on. We have some of his hotel bills so know what he ate and that he drank some vodka as well, but not too much. He had lunch with a tradesman, who had committed arson, and who gave this silver spoon, which cost a fortune, to the great writer.

When he arrived in his quarters a young woman of 18 served him, whose husband was 54; it was not a marriage based on love. She was not amiable when seeing Chekhov and did not allow him to sit. 'I am not going to walk after you.' He said, 'I just want to rest a while.' She relented and started the samovar and covered the table.

Lydia pointed to photographs of women:

Women were never shaven on the head, never in solitary and never shackled. Women were for giving birth to healthy babies to colonise Sakhalin, so only those under 40 were accepted. When they arrived at Aleksandrovsk, they were selectively put into reliable households and set to do the laundry, sewing and cooking. Only half of all convicts had a lady. When a colonist obtained a woman, he and his neighbours discussed this for days. When she started a samovar, neighbours knew he had a woman in the house. Before that officials would examine the house to see if it was prepared for woman. They had 2–3 days to get acquainted. After that they were a household. No official marriages, many had been married in Russia with church registration, so on Sakhalin they were not married but living together and children born were bastards, but took their father's name.

The third room reproduced a prison cell.

Chekhov mentioned that there were large gates and a guard on duty, but anyone went in and out as they liked . . . Then he understood; they were not the aggressive ones and anyway there was no way to escape from the island.

Among 2000 officially registered prisoners he only found 700. Where were the others? The prison administration granted privileges. Then, in the last third of their sentence, a prisoner could live in a house if they built it themselves. But they were not released from their work, eight hours per day.

The heaviest work was coal-mining, road construction and timber – she showed us a photo of two men harnessed on the front and two on the rear of a timber cart. They were chosen from the strongest and, soon after Chekhov's visit, in the middle of the 1890s, were replaced by horses.

Next, she led us to a room with more letters and photographs, all behind elaborate glass, and some fetters and chains. The last room had a reproduction of a painting of Chekhov, some small wooden toys and, in the middle, a six-sided glass case, a little like the controls of the Tardis. Inside were books opened at important places. To the left, behind a screen was a small desk.

Here is a photo of Chekhov with someone awarded a medal, for cooperation between Russia and Japan.

He got back Moscow in December and the newspapers described his return, but then spent a week describing his mongooses, though one was just a type of cat and hid under the wardrobe, attacking everyone. He also brought 2 suitcases of notes on Sakhalin. His friends and family expected him to publish articles immediately. But he told them he would make it academic and it would take three to five years. He wanted it not as fiction but for his thesis. It was very carefully written and re-written and modified. He tried to remove emotional description and replace it with statistics.

The version we read now he treated as special. When his complete works were prepared for publishing, Chekhov told Adolf Mark to publish it as a single separate volume. The last chapters were written on the desk here!! It was presented by a medical society. Many professors stated that the book was the only work on the ethnography of convicts.

One more fact; he never left any rough copies of his works. When the short stories were published, all rough copies were destroyed. The only rough copy he left was of Sakhalin Island, for future generations. He wanted society to pay attention to the condition of people.

After Sakhalin, it was a transformation of his personality, noted alike by friends and enemies. Chekhov himself divided it himself into two periods; before and after Sakhalin.

After some coffee with Temur, Lydia kindly walked with us beyond the museum down to the sea. We passed a large, ruined building, 'The Chekhov School'. As we walked over a bridge, a small boy peed between its railings to the stream below, watched by proud parents. A pack of dogs wandered by the bitch on heat. As a dog mounted her Alex muttered 'a wedding'. We turned left at a bluff – 50 feet above us was a wooden house with tethered baying dogs. The river meandered to our left below, littered with rusting boats – derelict buildings scattered about the foreshore, with only one, a fish factory, still going. We went down a small hill to a ruined stone building. This, Lydia said, was where they brought the women to be picked over when they arrived. Grey sky, grey sea, cold, raining, it was desolate, utterly miserable and yet fascinating.

One afternoon we piled into an old van and headed across the river up into the hills. Up one steep section the van filled with smoke. Andy asked if this was normal. Apparently not, since we evacuated and, when it did not blow up, had a look. Nothing was found so we got back in the van and carried on, though from then on, every time we went up a hill it smoked. We stopped at the top of the hill, in the forest, at a warning sign by the road and got out. Hounds howled from around the corner. Andy asked what the sign said. 'Radiation. Keep Out'. 'But it's OK', Temur explained, 'we are going around the back'.

We went along a rough path, beyond a flattened area and suddenly below us was the sea and huge views to left towards Douai and to the right, over Aleksandrovsk to the north. We were on top of Cap Jonquière, looking down on the lighthouse and the Three Brothers, at the edge of the steeply falling grassy cliff, Temur turned and said, 'Chekhov stood here'.

Temur told us of the Three Brothers, the rocks below us to the right beyond the headland, just out to sea. To our left, the other side of the headland, were three smaller rocks close to the shore. The local tribe, the Ainu, had a legend.

Women were forbidden from seeing the men's work; fishing, hunting and woodcutting. Their jobs were in the tents and villages alone. They were nomadic and tracked fish up and down the coast, as well as reindeer and other beasts. There were three brothers who had each married from the same family. One day they were cutting up a stranded whale and their wives, illegally, came down to the shore to watch. The gods saw and were so angry they sent down lightning and turned the men to stone; The Three Brothers. Their wives were desperate and said to the gods they could either release their husbands back to them or turn them too to stone, so they were not separated from their men. The gods were kind and turned the women to stone, too. The rocks are known as 'The Three Sisters.' They were close to their men, but could not see them, since they were each side of the headland, which in legend was the remains of the whale.

From the Cape, we drove along the mountain track and after a few miles we went down into a gap between the cliffs – suddenly we were at the sea, driving along a road right next to the beach, the most desolate esplanade in the world, with sea one side and cliffs the other. The track disappeared into a deep valley and we got out. This was Douai, where the first settlers had come looking for coal, where Chekhov had appeared one morning at 5.00 am and where people had lived in a small hall, bunkered together, twenty or more to a room. There was narrow straight valley, at right angles to the shore and running a mile inland, with a small stream. The sides were so steep that the bottom saw little sun, even in summer. A few single-storey wooden houses, many long abandoned, lined the track, with some derelict brick buildings scattered around.

Temur walked us up a track and there, on a flattened piece of land above the beach looking across the Tatar Sea, was the most incongruous bandstand. We sheltered from the rain as he told us about the abandoned mines. One, at the head of Douai valley, was rumoured to have uranium, waiting to be needed.

Back in the van to retrace our steps, we stopped where the track came down to the sea. We walked up the track towards a steep-sided valley covered by trees. In front, it flattened out and was deep in grass and bush, all bending in the wind. This was The Chasm of Sorrow, the site of Voyevodsk Prison, home of the Wheelbarrow Men and where convicts wept as they arrived. There was nothing left, no evidence of habitation, no sign, no plaque, just grass and trees and wind and rain. We walked along the beach for a mile or so from the chasm, under the cliffs to a waterfall. It was bleak, cold and wet but beautiful. Temur told us how in winter the sea froze for 5 km out and 1.5 m deep. But it was impossible to imagine seeing it with fear like the convicts – to us it looked like Devon on an autumn afternoon.

Our adventure in theatre was to capture the spirit of the penal colony, so we felt we should see Sakhalin in winter. Andy, Leo Warner, (from 59 Productions, who made the projection content of the show) and I set off in mid-February. Flying over Siberia as the sun rose we looked down on rivers, hills and valleys, white and still and endless. 'Only birds of passage know where it ends'.

At Yuzhno there was snow everywhere and a temperature around −10°C. Chilly rather than cold, said Alex the translator. Unfortunately, his wife was ill, so he had arranged another translator, Alex 2, to come with us to Aleksandrovsk. We took the night train north again.

At 6.00 am the next morning we left the train at the halt. The train was all steam and shiny metal against the station lights and black night. The coldest place in Sakhalin, Alex 2, shouted, as we got into the van to Aleksandrovsk. We drove on snow all the way, piled four feet deep beside the road, its crisp vertical edges like ghostly home-counties hedges. Alex 2 told us that not everyone did badly in Stalin's time. 'There was a huge pig farm over there, the boss made good money'. He pointed out with some relish Derbinskoye, as we drove through, where the governor's blood had coloured the bread.

At Aleksandrovsk the hotel was full 'with a celebration of some sort', so we were taken to student accommodation, where Temur met us with a big hug for everyone.

As the sun rose we headed out to film. Temur drove us over the river and down the far side of the estuary to the beach and the Three Brothers. As far as we could see the sea was frozen – close to the shore it rose into strange, mangled shapes twenty feet high or more – waves turned to ice had been lifted by further waves behind, wintery tectonic plates. There was no shoreline, nor sound – just mesmerizing white and blue. Leo and Andy filmed – only later did we realize that snow on frozen sea has no scale and no focal point, it seduced us but was flat on film.

Once back in Aleksandrovsk we filmed Lydia in the museum. That night Temur entertained us in the museum, with huge amounts of fish, potato, salad and brandy. He and Alex 2 took turns on a guitar. Temur sang a Russian folk song with passion and tenderness, Alex 2 a melancholy version of 'Yesterday'.

Next day, high on Cap Jonquière we looked down onto the Three Brothers and out over the frozen Tatar Straight. The stiff wind took it to −20°C, though Temur seemed not to notice. Then onwards to the Chasm of Sorrow and Douai. Leo and Andy filmed the frozen coastline and Douai valley, derelict buildings under piles of snow. A famous photo from Chekhov's book shows prisoners walking from Voyevodsk prison to Douai along the beach. We photographed the shoreline from the same place for the finish of the theatrical piece.

Back at the museum we gave short interviews for a local TV crew. Andy told of the genesis of the theatre piece and what brought us to Aleksandrovsk, in February of all months. I said what a jewel the museum was, how helpful Temur and Lydia had been and how useful it had all been in understanding Chekhov's visit.

A local historian had asked to see us. His office, in one of the few modern buildings, was high on a hill, looking out over the old town, to the estuary, the Three Brothers and the frozen sea. He had prepared well.

Most people on the island, he told us, had not read *Sakhalin Island*. Then he detailed Chekhov's mistakes.

Though he had done hard work before coming, he still misrepresented much and was too honest in his criticism. He did not give enough credit to the people who made an effort in Sakhalin. It was a heroic feat to develop the regions; at least as good as anything done in the USA over the last 300 years. Chekhov the number 1 playwright in the world, with rich but succinct language and he himself was bright. So why was his account so gloomy?

Chekhov had limitations as a correspondent. The intelligentsia were interested in degradation . . . but he was not Dostoevsky or Gorky.

He removed all the good personalities, so people in Aleksandrovsk were very surprised by the book. The officials were unhappy but despite being told not to, the people showed him everything. Aleksandrovsk people were not impressed and sued him for misrepresentation.

Olga, the guide at the museum in Yuzhno, had suggested the opposite – that he had covered some of the worst parts up, including the varieties of punishments and the executioners' names. Gregory continued:

Was it so bad on Sakhalin? Only 17 people were hanged in 40 years; capital punishment was abolished. Convicts in Australia, you could write a bad book about them too. And not all convicts were bad. One wept at the abdication of Tsar Nicholas II, 'this will be the end of Russia.' One adored grandfather spent 2 years carving the tsarist gate for the church. He could not be bad, surely? 'Sonya, [the notorious murderess known as The Golden Hand] did leave Sakhalin but she volunteered to come back. On the mainland, she was persecuted and had her windows broken in, so after a year she applied to come back.

It was safer here in Sakhalin; no one spat behind her back. Two years later she died of the common cold.

The modern capitalist Lansberg (a successful businessman on Sakhalin) made a remarkable career. He arrived with nothing, married on the island and everything good was down to him; the tunnel, port, jetty, telegraph, and the salt mines. Unfortunately, his family was decimated by diphtheria. He apparently said that, 'Penal servitude was not a real punishment for my crime, the death of my children was the real punishment. That was God's punishment.'

One son of a female convict was actually decorated by the British; a dog handler on Robert Scott's Antarctic Expedition, he found Scott's body in the tent . . . the huskies were from Sakhalin. A descendent from Sakhalin was a virologist in Australia with an international reputation for vaccines research, whilst another's great, great grandson was working as an architect. It was not all bad.

He continued that Chekhov's description of the camps was partial and to suggest that the island was a prison was misleading, since it was just as bad on the mainland. There, settlers could not live in Moscow or any big city either. And a lot of 'criminal romantics' made up stories too. 'An invisible cage is over people; you need to know that you are nothing. There was no big difference between here and the mainland'.

He explained that he treated Chekhov with respect: after all he was 'a great author entitled to some mistakes', but:

To sum up; the people of Sakhalin were proud to have been a 'creative' part of Chekhov's output, even though it was supposed to be a true account. But we don't remember the gloomy material. Over 6000 are buried in the cemetery; all good people helped and developed the colony. 4000 children died . . .

He detailed famous people and events after Chekhov's visit. A zeppelin had once landed to refuel and a local man, the first black belt at judo, created a new form of martial art for feet alone. Yul Brynner was from Aleksandrovsk. His father, a geologist, had, like his son, enjoyed many affairs. They moved to China where he abandoned Yul with his mother.

Who contributed more? The Sakhalin people to Chekhov, or Chekhov to Sakhalin people?

We thanked him profusely and left. Back in the UK, Donald Rayfield explained that Yul Brynner was not from Sakhalin, though he sometimes claimed to have been for effect. The historian's other points were more thought-provoking. At the time no one seemed to contradict Chekhov. But he himself had only spent three months on the island during which he met over 10,000 people while having to assimilate and observe the conditions they lived under. Remember, too, what Chekhov had written about Sakhalin before his visit, that it was a place of the most unendurable suffering, where millions had been left to rot, with all to blame. So, he did not come with an open mind. Maybe he had not seen those pockets in towns and villages where simple humanity continued and where decency was preserved. It was still difficult, however, to see Chekhov's account as being as 'creative' as Gregory claimed. Times were hard elsewhere too, but Sakhalin seemed worse.

Later we left Alex 2 behind and walked around the town, across the bridge where Good Looking's ferry had been, past the power station and old wooden buildings to the estuary. In the light wind the power station's black smoke drifted over the river to the estuary – fallen soot smudged a line across the snow. Chekhov had described the stranded skeleton of a long dead whale – our beached monsters were the rusting remains of fishing boats. Andy and Leo were drawn to them – fantastical terracotta hulks on white virgin snow. In the distance a line of dots – people fishing through the ice. We went back over the frozen river, hoping it would hold our weight, to old Aleksandrovsk, past the ruined Chekhov School, past rusting cars deep in snow, past his statue and the museum, to our flat before the journey home. Temur arrived, with brandy, to say goodbye and played a few tunes. Alex 2 asked me – for once soto voce – if the translation had been OK – he had forgotten his hearing aid and had been working 'creatively'.

Going back to Sakhalin in mid-winter was enthralling and fascinating. We had stood where Chekhov stood, been to Douai and Voyevodsk and tramped at the edge of the frozen sea. But we were neither cold nor hungry, nor trapped there forever. How could we, warm in modern clothes and half-an-hour from shelter, know anything of their lives? And what troubled me also was the use of image. We had taken video and stills of terrible cold, raw scenes, places of mortal danger for a hungry, poorly-clad convict which looked, to us, achingly beautiful. Seeing was not enough. We had to go beyond that, before oil and gas and electricity had transformed how we see the world, to how Chekhov saw it.

Andrew Dawson's play, *The Russian Doctor/The Chasm of Sorrow* (co-directed with Martin Lloyd-Evans and with Stephanie Fleischmann, dramaturg), built on our reading of the book and our visit to Sakhalin, and particularly to its museums. It premiered in 2014, proceeding through a series of vignettes, acted out by Andy, but mostly spoken by a variety of pre-recorded voices off-stage, taken from the book. We met the wheelbarrow men, were shown the sleeping quarters, the shackles and chains in which they lived, a hanging scene and the murder in the bakery and a rape. He also covered the census and the doffing of caps which Chekhov had experienced on his arrival on the island. In between these vignettes Andy also addressed the audience directly, breaking the fourth wall, as an unnamed narrator. Throughout he would be drinking champagne, and only at the end would explain that this was given to doctors on their deathbed, and had been given to Chekhov, too, in 1904. Our visits to Sakhalin gave all these more veracity. The mood was also set by eerily atmospheric music by Johnny Pilcher. Like Chekhov's visit, ours was to form impressions and background, but also contained elements of adventure. To be shown round the museums was such a privilege, and then to be shown the Three Brothers and the Three Sisters, the Cape, the foreshore in Aleksandrovsk, the Chasm of Sorrow and Douai was as extraordinary as it was bleak and beautiful. Right at the end of the play, there was an old photo thrown up on a flap behind the stage. It was of a bedraggled group of convicts walking from the Chasm along the beach to Douai, Andy and Leo had found the exact place where it had been taken. As the piece ended, the photo very slowly morphed from a sepia still to a colour movie of exactly the same scene, as our battered old van drove past. It was a brilliant coup de theatre with which to end.

Back in Yuzhno, the new museum was on the ground floor of a shiny new building sharing with an art gallery and offices. Outside were life-sized statues of people from Chekhov's short stories 'A Lady with a Lap Dog' for instance. Inside, a first edition of *Sakhalin Island* was now behind glass and the census cards digitized and available for relatives. Gone though were the spinning wheel, the moth-eaten ferryman and the trunk. Tableaux with mannequins showed the prison sleeping quarters, a wheelbarrow man, and a doctor and patient, separated by a small cosmetic wooden grill which would stop no-one – the figures life-size but lifeless. Several middle-aged women acted as guides, Russian equivalents of our National Trust volunteers. There was no sign of Katya or Sonia, though Olga came in at one point without recognizing us. What had been a quirky, idiosyncratic museum has been modernized and homogenized. A group of school children arrived. If the history of the penal colony – their history – is more widely known then the sacrifice of the old place, all musty charm and incongruous relics, was understandable, even though the new place seems slightly sanitized and soulless.[6]

Sakhalin has no monument to the colony or its people – and nothing remains of the prisons. Without the two museums, one to his book in Yushno-Sakhalinsk, and the other to his visit to Aleksandrovsk, the penal colony might be lost from view. Without his book, we would never know of Good Looking or The Singing Idiot, or the appalling conditions for women and children, convicts and settlers, or of how – through neglect and incompetence – such a breakdown in law, order and common humanity emerged. Chekhov wondered if his census might be of some use to future generations. Though it did not lead, despite his best efforts, to radically improved conditions, Chekhov's failed MD thesis has done something he probably could not have imagined – it has become the colony's history.

## Notes

1. The passport guard asked us where in Russia we were headed. When we told her, she was bewildered as if to say 'Why would anyone go to Sakhalin?'

2. The direct quotes are all from transcribed, verbatim accounts by our translator. We cannot vouch for the accuracy of translation, nor for the accuracy of the guides' statements either. But, rather, their importance lies in what the museum guides were saying.

3. Donald Rayfield once suggested to me that Chekhov's reputation was not that high among some of the literary elite of the time.

4. Donald Rayfield contests how active censors were during Chekhov's time. Rayfield (*personal communication*).

5. In Temur's office there were pictures of the president, the governor and the local mayor. The president was highest – apparently there was a law covering where on walls photographs of politicians are placed.

6. We were then taken to a modern museum of Russian history. On one wall was showing extraordinary colour cinefilm of Japanese kamikaze planes attacking Russian ships.

# INDEX

# Index

# Index

# Index